Praise for
Ninety-Nine Fir

"From her journey as a fresh-off-the-boat immigrant speaking only Mandarin Chinese, to her voyages back and forth through different spiritual and social frames of mind, Merrill creates a powerful saga of a personal journey replete with emotionally-charged wellsprings of inheritance, discovery, and change."

—D. Donovan, Senior Reviewer,
Midwest Book Review

"*Ninety-Nine Fire Hoops* is a fascinating, important, and well-developed narrative, told by a sympathetic narrator with much urgency and grace."

—Sue William Silverman, author of
How to Survive Death and Other Inconveniences

"Allison Hong Merrill makes three intertwined journeys—through family, faith, and immigration—each filled with danger, heartbreak, and, ultimately, joy. Watching Allison grow from fearful child and unknowing bride into her own power to love and be loved is meaningful and moving, and discovering her native Taiwan through childhood stories is fascinating. A powerful and inspiring journey from loneliness and fear to love and hope."

—Allison K. Williams, Social Media Editor
at *Brevity Magazine* and author of *Seven Drafts:
Self-Edit Like a Pro from Blank Page to Book*

"What an enthralling story from the beginning to the end! *Ninety-Nine Fire Hoops* is a compelling reflection on the American dream. With deep insight and lyrical writing, Allison Hong Merrill deftly narrates an unforgettable tale of love, courage, and determination. Her resilience is a timeless lesson that there's glory in human struggles. An extraordinary offering!"

—Toni Sorenson,
award-winning author of *Redemption Road*

"*Ninety-Nine Fire Hoops* is a beautiful memoir that will bring you to tears and make you laugh in the same few pages. Allison Hong Merrill rises from the ashes of a neglected and abused childhood to arrive in America, only to face harsh disappointments and broken dreams. Interwoven into the compelling scenes is Allison's resilience that burns deep in her soul, until she can fully grasp how her trials have made her stronger, more sympathetic, and more loving. Her knack for blending her remarkable heritage with poignant insights makes this book one to absorb instead of simply reading."

—Heather B. Moore,
author of *The Paper Daughters of Chinatown*

"*Ninety-Nine Fire Hoops* follows Allison's journey from Taiwan to Utah seeking love and belonging after a difficult childhood, marriage, and divorce. The story is heartfelt, brave, ultimately inspiring, and written in a uniquely charming voice."

—Harrison Candelaria Fletcher,
author of *Presentimiento: A Life in Dreams*

"Russian composer Dmitri Shostavoch said, 'When a man is in despair, it means that he still believes in something.' In the case of young Allison Hong Merrill, her desire *to* believe in something may have saved her from ultimate despair. *Ninety-Nine Fire Hoops* masterfully weaves stories of the author's Chinese family, spanning two decades, intermingled with regional history, culture, and culture shock in America. A fascinating tale of both cruelty and compassion."

—Jodi Orgill Brown, interactions expert, speaker, and award-winning author of *The Sun Still Shines*

"Allison Hong Merrill has a gift for writing a dramatic tale while simultaneously sharing her hard-won wisdom. *Ninety-Nine Fire Hoops* reads like a novel. Merrill's story not only gives a reader a greater understanding of Chinese culture, language, and traditions but also provides insight into the human condition while building a bridge between East and West. A brilliant and beautiful debut!"

—Rev. Camilla Sanderson, author of *The Mini Book of Mindfulness*

"*Ninety-Nine Fire Hoops* is a deeply moving memoir that depicts the story of a Taiwanese immigrant bride abandoned in Texas and how she triumphs over tremendous odds to build her American dream. Allison Hong Merrill's gift of storytelling will take you on an exciting, rewarding, and emotional journey and leave you wanting more."

—Dr. Linda Murphy Marshall, author of *Ivy Lodge: A Memoir*

"*Ninety-Nine Fire Hoops* is a captivating coming-of-age story of lost innocence, cultural divides, and transcendence. Alongside her inspiring tale of overcoming daunting circumstances, the author provides fascinating glimpses into Taiwanese customs and Mormon spiritual beliefs. I learned a lot about the Mormon community, and Hong Merrill's voice is incandescent and irresistible. By the end of the book, I wanted to adopt her."

—Heather Diamond, author of *Rabbit in the Moon: A Memoir*

Publication Credits & Awards for the Manuscript

- Inaugural winner of the 2020 Sandra Carpenter Prize for Creative Nonfiction
- Grand Prize winner of the 2019 MAST People of Earth writing contest
- Honorable Mention in the 2020 Tom Howard/John H. Reid Fiction & Essay Contest
- Shortlisted finalist in the 2019 DL Jordan Prize for Literary Excellence
- Shortlisted finalist in the 2020 Fish Publishing Memoir Award
- Shortlisted finalist in the 2019 Eyelands Book Awards (Athens, Greece)
- Featured interviewee for KSL Mormon Times, March 4, 2011
- Featured interviewee for the Latter-day Saints Channel, May 30, 2020
- The Allison Hong Merrill Exhibit, Our History Our Voices Project, March 10, 2021
- *Cosmonauts Avenue*, July 2020

Ninety-Nine
Fire Hoops

Ninety-Nine Fire Hoops

A Memoir

Allison Hong Merrill

She Writes Press, a BookSparks imprint
A Division of SparkPointStudio, LLC.

Published 2021

Printed in the United States of America

Print ISBN: 978-1-64742-189-2
E-ISBN: 978-1-64742-190-8
Library of Congress Control Number: 2021906357

For information, address:
She Writes Press
1569 Solano Ave #546
Berkeley, CA 94707

She Writes Press is a division of SparkPoint Studio, LLC.

With eternal love and gratitude
to my husband
and our sons:

少凡，語翔，語傑，語邘

For Ah-Gung & Ah-Po:

徐東木 & 李春梅

For my rebirth parents:
Burton D. Bushman & Thelys C. Bushman

PART ONE

Loyalty

1

EDINBURG, TEXAS. NOVEMBER 1996

I discovered that I became a starter wife from a light switch. Not a light bulb, like I had a big idea. A light switch. A light switch in my apartment that I flipped on and off but the living room remained dark, and that darkness caused a pricking, tingling sensation in my hands and feet.

When I left the apartment two hours earlier, the lights worked, the heater ran, and Cameron—my husband of sixteen months—was doing homework on our bed. Lately we kept fighting about investing in the boat his father planned to purchase. I said no, and we had been giving each other the cold shoulder for days. Tired of our never-ending arguments, now I wanted reconciliation. This particular day, around dinnertime, I went to seek marriage advice from my classmate, a fellow Taiwanese student. Before leaving, I stood before Cameron and said good-bye. If he heard me, he acted otherwise. So I wrote *I love you, Cam* on a Post-it note and left it on the inside of the front door. It wasn't there now.

Now I had to feel my way to the bedroom.

Felt the bed.

Felt one pillow.

Felt a chill.

I didn't need to keep feeling anymore. Didn't need to avoid bumping into the desk, or the chairs, or Cameron's bike. They weren't in the dark with me.

In the dark, there was no warmth.

No gas for the heater.

No electricity.

No telephone.

No food.

My heartbeat quickened and thundered in my ears. *What happened? Am I in the wrong apartment? Must be. All the units look the same on the outside.* . . .

I felt my way out of the apartment and double-checked the gold number nailed to the door: 21. My apartment, no mistake. *NO!—no, no, no, no, no! Where's Cameron?*

I tucked my hands under my armpits in the November evening chills. My legs trembled as I paced in a circle in small steps. The windows of other units in the building glowed in golden light. Through my next-door neighbors' blinds, I noticed them sitting around the coffee table, *Seinfeld* playing on TV, the waft of their gumbo dinner in the air. It looked warm and inviting where they were. I stood in the cold, dark night, staring past my door into the abyss. For tonight's dinner I'd planned to make chicken stir-fry. Cameron would've enjoyed it on the couch right there, over there, there, there, there, where it was nothing but emptiness now.

The black of the apartment reminded me of a summer night, three months earlier, when the power had gone out in the entire complex. That night Cameron drove back to his parents' home, in the next town, for an air-conditioned room. I didn't go with him because I would've rather eaten dog food than see my in-laws. To say they were bad people would be telling only half the truth. A big part of the problem was me—I avoided them to avoid speaking English.

I was born and raised in Taiwan and was only confident speaking Mandarin Chinese. On this fateful night, I was a fresh-off-the-boat immigrant—having been in the U.S. for only sixteen months—and heavily dependent on Cameron's Chinese-speaking prowess for almost everything. For example, underwear shopping: he had to tag along to tell the lingerie store clerk I wished to get my size measured in the metric system. America's customary system didn't mean anything to me. Another time, I accidentally cut my finger with a rusty utility knife while opening a package. Cameron had to explain to the emergency room nurse why I needed a tetanus shot. For me to carry on English conversations wasn't just a linguistic challenge or an intellectual evaluation; it was an insurmountable task.

Of course, avoiding my in-laws couldn't possibly be healthy for my marriage. But there were other contributing factors to my shaky relationship with Cameron too. To say it was all my doing would be giving me more credit than I deserve. After all, there are always two people in a relationship; one simply can't start a marital war alone. However, I'll say, my short marriage to Cameron helped shorten the emotional distance between him and his father.

Glad to have helped!

2

Upon discovering the non-working light switch, I realized I needed to overcome my dependence on Cameron as my mouthpiece, as well as the fear that crippled my ability to communicate with English speakers, and go immediately to the apartment office in the next building to talk with the manager.

"Hi, I'm Allison." My voice shocked myself more than it did the manager, Jane—an overweight woman in her late fifties whose eyes at this moment were as huge as tennis balls. She'd never heard me speak. In fact, she'd probably never really looked at me before. I was always behind Cameron, who did all the talking with his proud Texan accent and charismatic humor. But the real surprise was hearing myself say the name that my tenth-grade English teacher had given me the way Americans do, without mixing up the *L* and *R*—one of the English-language learning curves that most Chinese people struggle with. Not *Ayhreesong*. I said *Allison*. The parting of my lips + the tip of my tongue kicking off the back of my upper front teeth + the soft dropping of my tongue + short hissing sss juxtaposed with the nasal ending = Allison. I said that.

Jane took off her reading glasses. "Forgot somethin'?"

I shook my head. "Cam—Cameron gone."

"Well, o'course. So should you. Why you still here?"

I knew what she said but didn't understand what she meant. I blurted out "yes" but immediately felt idiotic and frustrated to be stuck with it. "My house, cold." I pointed in the direction of my apartment and hugged myself. I shivered exaggeratedly and chattered my teeth purposely.

Jane shook her head. "K—ma'am, I'm confused. Why you still here anyway? Weren't Cameron's parents here earlier to move you guys out?"

Weren't Cameron's parents here earlier to move you guys out?

Weren't Cameron's parents here earlier to move you guys out?

Weren't Cameron's parents here earlier to move you guys out?

I—got—moved—out?

"Really?" I exclaimed, not caring about mixing up my *L* and *R*.

Jane pushed her office chair away with her bottom and walked to a wall cabinet behind her seat. She fished out a key from rows of hooks and waved it in the air. "See? Number 21. Your apartment. Cameron turned in the key." She put her other hand on her hip and leaned forward. "Question, ma'am: Why you still here?"

I was still here, in the apartment manager's office, in Edinburg, in Texas, in the U.S.A., and I was mighty lost.

"Sorry," I said, my scalp starting to feel numb. "Please, one week"—I held up my index finger—"I find help. I want stay—myself."

I hoped she would not only understand but also have mercy on me. My cheeks and earlobes were burning. My throat was tight, as though I were dry-swallowing a pill. And my head was so heavy I could only look down at my shoes. At this point, everything about my life shared the same theme of emptiness: empty apartment, empty pockets, empty hands—palms up—asking for empathy.

Maybe Jane detected an unusual sense of urgency in the abandoned foreigner on her premises; maybe she fathomed the depth of my trouble and grasped the serious reality that, at this moment, she was the only one who could make the situation a little more bearable for me. Whatever it was, she slumped into her chair, clicked her tongue, pushed a pile of papers on her desk from one side to another, stroked her temple, and then, with her seemingly softened heart, said, "Ay—you stay."

3

Back at the apartment, I didn't take off my shoes before entering. No need now. It wasn't sacred ground anymore, as Chinese culture had taught me what a home was. I'd convinced Cameron to leave his shoes by the door whenever he came back to this place—*our* place. He probably didn't do it earlier when he and his parents were here deliberately ruining my life. This space was likely soiled now.

From now on, my life would be divided into before and after becoming a starter wife. My steps would chart a seam between two periods on my life's timeline: one ending, one beginning, right here where Cameron left nothing behind.

But that wasn't entirely true. He did leave behind the bed we'd bought together at a yard sale. I lay on it and curled into a ball. The utilities couldn't be reconnected at this late hour. No heat. No light. Through the naked mattress, a biting chill seeped into my kidneys, my lungs, my head. I probably would see my breath if I could see anything, but I couldn't even see my fingers when I waved them in front of me. I didn't see it coming, all of this—Cameron teaming up with his parents for the blindside—and now I was in the dark, not knowing what to do next. It was just me here now. A twenty-three-year-old immigrant with a three-year-old's English vocabulary. A newlywed, dumped.

I could cry.

I could curse.

I could scream.

But whatever I did, I would do it all alone.

I–what a lonely word to be left alone with!

4

Four years prior, in 1992, I was a freshman at Fu-Jen Catholic University in Taipei, Taiwan. One rainy December night I walked down the street with an umbrella, past a bus stop, and heard a panicked cry behind me.

"Stop. Stop. Hey—STOP!"

Two unlucky Caucasian young men were chasing the last bus of the night that rolled away without them. An African man slowly caught up to them, his white cane tapping in puddles. Obviously frustrated, one of the Caucasian guys threw his backpack on the sidewalk by my feet. I was shocked and confused. *Should I pick it up and return it? Remain still? Offer him my umbrella?*

I peeked at him from under the umbrella rim. He was Bruce Willis's doppelgänger with full brown hair. Fit, about five foot ten. A crooked nose. Straight-as-a-wall teeth. Penetrating brown eyes. In that precise moment when I caught him looking into my eyes too, my body caught fire, and I had a distinctive revelation that he would someday be my husband. I can't explain where it came from—a tiny thought that percolated through my mind and instantly caused my face and ears to turn hot. I became so shy I struggled to make eye contact when he spoke to me.

"Excuse me, my friend here"—he pointed at the African man— "is going to the school for the . . . for people with . . . um . . . can't-see eyes. He missed the bus."

I nodded sympathetically.

"Can you call a taxi for him? My Chinese is . . ." He sighed and looked away.

I couldn't look away now if I tried. I couldn't even blink. That handsome face . . . Gosh, I had fallen in love with a stranger! Not madly, yet, but the attraction was undeniable. Even though I suspected the feeling was mutual, I had no way of finding out.

I was a nineteen-year-old Taiwanese Mormon girl who spoke pathetic English; he was a twenty-year-old American Mormon missionary who spoke scattered Chinese. Scattered Chinese prevailed, in our case. But it wasn't even the language barrier that kept me guessing if the attraction was mutual. It was because this guy, Elder Cameron Chastain, was required to abide by the church rule forbidding missionaries from getting involved in a romantic relationship during their two-year service. They were expected to serve the Lord with all their heart, might, mind, and strength.

Following that night at the bus stop, I frequently spotted him and his mission companion—the other Caucasian young man I saw that night—walking on campus, usually outside the Foreign Language building, where my classes were. Maybe they had been there every day and I'd just never noticed. Now that I had seen him talking with people in the courtyard, I could no longer sit in the classroom without glancing out the window, looking for him, wanting to see his face and hear his voice. In my notebook I scribbled his name and sketched images of him and dreamed of replacing anyone who occupied the space next to him, who held his time and attention when I couldn't.

Every Sunday, Cameron, his companion, and a group of students from my school who also belonged to the Church of Jesus Christ of Latter-day Saints (nicknamed The Mormon Church) rode the same bus to church. A bus in Taipei on a Sunday usually carried what seemed like double the number of passengers than its maximum capacity. Those who didn't get a seat wrapped their wrists around the ceiling hoops and stood like a thick jungle of trees, their backpacks and handbags smacking into one another like branches in the wind.

It was a battle parting the sea of bodies to get to the back of the bus, but I had to. Stepping on toes, rubbing chests with strangers, inhaling body odor and garlicky breaths, I had to get to the back so I could daringly stare at Cameron from a distance, through the cracks of silhouettes. While he talked to people, I studied the movement of his mouth and imagined the words he said. His slant-lipped smile made me swoon. If the sea of passengers between us was the string that connected two plastic cups—Cameron's mouth pressed into one; my ear to the other—would I hear "I love you" too?

Yeah, I would do anything to be near him, but being too close to him made my heart jumpy and my mind foggy and I broke out in a hot sweat even on a wintery day. It happened whenever we attended the same event or were simply in the same room for single young adult activities at church, Sunday school class, and scripture study in my dorm lounge. The worst was when I asked him to help me with my English homework one day. I couldn't stay away from him like I did on a bus, obviously. I sat next to him at a cafeteria table, his companion across from us, memorizing Chinese words from flashcards.

Cameron carried a pen in his shirt pocket. He used it to write down new Chinese vocabulary he learned in a pocket-size spiral notebook. Watching his fingers wrap around the pen, firmly and tight, I wished I were that pen—that lucky little thing—to be touched by him that way. To be tucked in his shirt pocket, close to his heart. To go home with him, live with him. To be the one thing he couldn't leave the house without. And I fantasized about him writing in his diary that I was his wildest dream.

After editing my paper for my English class, Cameron taught me a Bible message: *To everything there is a season, and a time to every purpose under the heaven . . . A time to love, and a time to hate. . . .*

This *time to love and to hate* concept was fitting and pertinent in our relationship. In that moment, I only felt love. Never had I thought there would be a time when he would walk out of our marriage, leaving me homeless, penniless, and voiceless in a foreign land. No, I couldn't fathom a time when he would make such a hateful choice.

5

After serving six months in my college town, Cameron completed his mission and returned home to Texas. On his departure day, I lay in a dry bathtub in the dorm and counted. *One more hour before he boards the plane. One more minute. His flight is taking off. He's been away from Taiwan for a minute now. An hour. Two. Three. He's gone. . . .* And every second he flew farther away, I ached more in the head, in the eyes, in the nose, the ears, the mouth, the heart, the stomach, the arms, the legs, and I didn't know how to go on with life. All I knew was to fill the bathtub with tears and snot and dangling saliva from my mouth that repeatedly wailed, "Cameron . . . Cam. . . ."

PART TWO

Faith

6

My mama was the first one in her clan who married an outsider and moved out of the farming village. My baba was an honorably released Frogman–the equivalent of a U.S. Navy SEAL–from a poverty-stricken, gang-infested, brothel-rampant fishing village. After his two-year male citizen's obligatory military service, Baba worked as an electrical engineer. He didn't speak Hakkanese, the dialect spoken in Mama's village. But because everyone in Mama's clan was a polyglot, fluent in Chinese, Japanese, Hokkien, and Hakkanese, communication with Baba wasn't a problem. When my parents got married, my maternal grandfather, Ah-Gung, gave them a Japanese garden house as a wedding gift.

Ah-Gung was born in 1922, during Japanese colonialism in Taiwan. At the time, the Japanese government wanted Taiwanese children to learn trade skills such as farming, fishing, and welding, to become laborers. I imagine Ah-Gung's parents made tremendous sacrifices and handsome offerings to government officials for him to go to school with Japanese children, to learn math, science, social studies. Having grown up during the global economic downturn, Ah-Gung lived by the rule of extreme frugality. Instead of throwing out fermented tofu, he used it to make soy custard. He patched holes in his yellow cotton undershirts that he had worn for decades. They used to be white, my grandmother, Ah-Po, said.

Ah-Gung was the director in the Tax Commission Department, possibly one of the highest governmental positions a non-Japanese citizen could achieve at the time. Through a lifetime of scrimping and saving, he became a wealthy man, owning residential land, farmland, mountain land, and commercial districts all over my hometown, Hualien. He funded his relatives' children's education, leased out farmlands to landless farmers, hired unemployed neighbors to raise bees, to work in his rice fields, and to tend to his gardens and orchards, growing vegetables, herbs, bananas, persimmons, and wax apples.

In the Hakka village where Ah-Gung was a highly respected patriarch, he kept the clan tightly united by opening up his compound to his two brothers' families.

Born in 1947, my mama grew up in an environment where her uncles, aunts, and their families all lived under the same roof and took care of one another. There was no difference between cousins and siblings. Everyone was a brother or a sister. Everyone fought through life's challenges together. Generation after generation, the clan stayed strong as one big tribe. One unbreakable chain of love.

Mama's highest academic achievement was sixth grade. According to my grandmother, Ah-Po, it was right after World War II, when kids needed to help rebuild. "Your ma was the oldest child. She had to help me around the house and take care of her little brothers and sisters too." Mama's was the typical story many Taiwanese people in her generation—the baby boomers, as they are called in America—would tell. Victims of history, sacrificed in the name of war.

Mama had a barrel-shaped body, compass-drawn round face, willow-tree-leaf-shaped brows, round eyes with double crease eyelids, full lips that smiled into a heart shape, black mushroom-shaped hairdo.

When I was four, one day I pointed at her chunky arm—dotted

with four round textured vaccine scars—and asked, "Ma, why are your arms like elephant's legs?"

"Thanks to you," she said, "my pre-pregnancy figure took a walk and got lost forever."

That answer was as confusing as why the animal in the backyard and the meat in the stir-fry dish were both called *chicken*. But I had no reason to doubt her words, no matter how perplexing they were. Everything she said, I believed.

7

M ama told me to tell people I was five years old when I was really only four. She didn't teach me to lie. The Chinese have two methods for calculating their ages. One is how everyone else does it—counting the days, months, and years of a person's life starting from his birthdate. The other way is to add a year to a person's actual age, making it his *nominal age*. Because a person's life started before his birth—when he grew and developed as a fetus—the Chinese round up the full-term gestation to a year and declare this time to be so significant and monumental, it shouldn't be forgotten or discounted. Hence, when I was four, my nominal age was five.

However, Mama didn't tell me I was born. She claimed to have witnessed the baby me popping out of a boulder and decided to take me home. It sounded as if I had been a stray puppy on a street and she just happened to be in the mood for a pet that day. But she refused to tell me how I got into a boulder or why I didn't look like a boulder if I came out of one.

I was four—okay, five—when I started wondering about my life's purpose. My parents weren't spiritual, so my understanding of religion came solely from TV shows, which centered around the Buddhist teachings of:

1. Life is a sea of suffering.
2. My suffering in this life is to pay for the debts I owed in my previous life.

3. If I do evil, I'll reincarnate into an animal in the next life, to be abused by humans. More intense suffering.

By age seven (and eight) I desired to find answers to my questions:

1. How did I acquire any debts before birth?
2. Who was my creditor, and how would I know where to find him/her in a world of billions of people?
3. How much did I owe? How will I know when I pay it off?
4. If I pay off all my premortal debts, will my life be suffering-free?
5. Is life after life supposed to be a continuum of suffering? If so, am I supposed to believe that every human being signed up for endless, joyless, meaningless mortal experiences? What's the point, then?
6. Why does the word *happiness* even exist in human languages and expressions if life is all about suffering? Who organized this bewildering, depressing plan anyway?

I asked Baba and he said, "Stop asking. You're too stupid to understand."

I asked Mama and she said, "Can you trade your words for rice? No? Questions like that don't feed an empty stomach, do they now? Think about practical things!"

Yep! It felt as though I were talking to two water buffalos.

I convinced myself that the answers to my questions would naturally come later because some knowledge and skills came with age. I believed that was how Baba knew how to ride a motorcycle and Mama knew how to cook on a gas stove. I would know my life's purpose in time. I just had to wait.

8

Baba was an electrical engineer who frequently went on week-long business trips. Mama was a stay-at-home mom who hardly stayed home. Before I started kindergarten, most days my sister, Dee, and I were left home alone without toys, books, or food.

Dee is twenty-three months younger than I am. At the time we weren't toilet trained and often wore the same pants that we had wet the night before. She followed me around in the yard and on the street, and I led her to our next-door neighbor when I was hungry. A middle-aged woman in that house fed us lunch, taught us how to use the toilet, and let us play with her dog. At night when Mama came home, a yelling match commenced through the fence.

"Your kids stunk up my place. I washed their soiled clothes and fed them too. What have you been doing? They're like orphans!"

Mama chucked potted flowers toward the neighbor's voice and screamed, telling her to go to hell. "Mind your own business! Nobody asks you to take them in!" she roared with such rage that her face turned red, sweaty, and distorted.

The next morning, I held Dee's hand and maneuvered through the household trash the neighbor had thrown over into our yard, then wandered off to the street.

Whenever Mama finished a fight with Baba, she yelled at me.

"I should've suffocated you when you were a baby! If it weren't for you, I wouldn't have to stay in this crappy marriage!"

At age four, I couldn't read, couldn't count past one hundred, couldn't ride a bike, but I sure as heck could tell people with a firm conviction: "My mama is angry because I'm alive."

9

Sometimes Mama left Dee and me with our grandparents, Ah-Gung and Ah-Po, three miles away, then woke us up at night to take us home. When I started school, Mama didn't know what grade I was in. Oblivious, I thought all mothers were physically and emotionally unavailable, until one day I went to a classmate's house to play and saw her mom hugging her.

Hugging!

How shocking!

Mama had never touched me that way, no. Never patted my head and said, "I'm proud of you!" when I continuously won first place in schoolwide writing, drawing, and calligraphy competitions. Never patted my back and praised, "You're amazing!" when I received the Model Student Award year after year. The only time she made physical contact with me was a slap across my face when I, at seven, asked her to teach me how to zip up my uniform jacket.

I don't remember being born, of course. Mama would be the one to remember it for me. But what's the point of remembering someone else's life events for her, if not to share the memories with her?

On the first day of second grade, my teacher sent home a survey for homework—a sheaf of stapled double-sided pages with Chinese characters and checkboxes. I could read the first two questions: *What's your name? When's your birthday?* I studied the two characters that made up the word *birthday*, dissecting them to find the meaning of each character: *birth, day*. I was stuck on *birth*, so I went to the backyard to find help.

Colorful butterflies danced on jasmine shrubs that climbed over the fence. An autumn breeze spread its fragrance across the yard. Groves of phoenix trees swayed gently, as if drunk in the perfumed air. Mama squatted on a concrete pad in front of a garden faucet, hand washing an avalanche of dirty laundry in a tin tub.

"Ma, what's *birthday*?"

She didn't answer, didn't even look up at me. She scrubbed a shirt vigorously with a plastic brush, then kneaded it. Bubbles formed under her hands. She flipped the shirt inside out and scrubbed it again. Her head bobbed with each of her hand movements.

I repeated my question. She still didn't respond. So I asked again, "Ma, what's—"

"Stop!" she growled. "You missed the New Year by a day!" She splashed foamy water at me and barked, "You're a loser from the beginning. Go away!"

I dashed back into the house, all the while wondering if, by "the New Year," she meant January 1 or Chinese New Year. Also, if I missed it by a day, did she mean December 31 or January 2? But what I really missed was her point. If she wanted to tell me when my birthday was, she would have. I wouldn't have to decipher her words. What she made clear was that I was a loser from birth. That was the one thing she remembered for me—her memory of me on the day I was born.

I couldn't read the rest of the survey questions, so I asked Baba for help that night. When he said, "Okay, question number five. Who do you trust the most?" I asked what *trust* meant. He used the example of a person I'd feel safe watching over my snack while I went to the bathroom. Then he asked, "Baba or Mama?" I could see that there were four checkboxes for question number five, but I didn't question him. I looked at my fingers and whispered, "Mama." I wondered if he checked the correct box on the survey form.

In retrospect, I see that I trusted Mama the same way a dog is loyal to its owner. Dogs don't run a background check on their owners to decide whether or not to love them. They don't care about their owners' gender, race, age, marital status, financial standing, or criminal history. They're nonjudgmental, faithful, and true.

Indeed, I was like a stray puppy Mama had brought home.

10

When I was twelve, Baba met two missionaries from the Church of Jesus Christ of Latter-day Saints in Taichung Park, two hundred miles away from home. It took a year for Baba's contact information to be forwarded to the missionaries in our hometown, Hualien. On December 4, 1986, two Caucasian young men knocked on our door. Baba was so stunned he could've fainted. He explained that he had completely forgotten about the encounter. But how could he ever forget having met two foreigners, especially when they were practically the only white people we saw outside of American TV shows and movies? Nevertheless, he forgot, was dumb-struck when they showed up, but politely invited them in.

Taiwanese people believe that as long as a houseguest is in sight, his well-being is the host's responsibility. From the moment the guest is welcomed into the home, the host makes sure the room temperature is right, the couch cushion is comfortable, the treat tray is stocked, and steamy water or tea is served. The host will entertain till the end of the visit. Then he'll stand by the front door and watch, making sure his guest is safe, till he is out of sight. Only then is he released from the hosting duty—the kind of duty that originates from the cultural understanding of respect and courtesy.

My parents were rarely in the same room unless they intended to start a fight. Naturally, this night, Baba called me and Dee, instead of Mama, to the living room to meet the missionaries. He expected us to take Mama's place as the hostess, I knew. I also knew the drill. Without him asking, within a minute, we sisters set up the coffee table with caramel candy, roasted peanuts, shelled sunflower seeds, and boiling water in ceramic mugs.

Both missionaries were taller than the door frame. Probably having learned from painful experience, they ducked, reflexively, while walking through the door.

How interesting! I thought. *These are the first people who unknowingly bow to Baba as they enter his house.*

One of them, blond twenty-year-old Elder York, was from Utah. The other, brown-haired freckle-faced Elder Copinga, was from Idaho.

"Ni hao," they said.

I didn't know how to respond.

Taiwanese people didn't greet one another with "ni hao." Instead, they asked, "Have you eaten?" Other people's well-being was the most important thing they cared about. They were practical and wanted to know if they could take care of others by feeding them, clothing them, making them comfortable.

The missionaries stretched out their hands—bigger than my face—and we girls shook them with uncontrollable giggles. Taiwanese people didn't shake hands. We knew how to do it only because we watched *MacGyver*, *The Cosby Show*, and *The A-Team* on Saturdays after school.

Dee pointed at the black name tags on our guests' shirt pockets. "Why do you both have the same name, 'Elder'?"

"Oh, it's not our name," Copinga said in Chinese with wrong tones for most of the words. "It's a title we use in the church. Like, I call your baba Mr. Hong. Mister is a title."

"But why 'Elder'? You aren't even old," I said.

They smiled, showing perfectly straight teeth. "It's a church position, an office in the organization we belong to. In Chinese, *mister* is what? First born? Born first? What? Why?" York put his hands up in the air with an *I wonder so hard* facial expression.

"Oh, I know!" I said. *"Mister* in Chinese means 'first born.' Because men came first, before women. Right, Ba?" I looked to Baba for validation, but he didn't acknowledge my answer. Instead, he cracked sunflower seed shells with his gapped teeth and chewed the seeds so hard his pulsating temples looked as if an artery was about to burst. His eyes were on the Travel Channel on TV, and I knew it was his way of telling the Elders they weren't welcome. But, of course, the missionaries didn't get the message. They stayed and told us about Adam and Eve in the Garden.

"God created Adam before he created Eve, so it's basically the same story as the Chinese mister thing, right? Yeah!" Copinga put his right palm in the air, and I promptly high-fived it—I had seen Kirk Cameron do it in the TV show *Growing Pains.*

It was fascinating, Christians' version of the Creation. From Chinese folktales I learned that a creature—a snake with a woman's face—made humans with clay, but I'd never heard of anyone worship this goddess. Instead, we made offerings to our progenitors. In fact, the focal point of our living room was a floor-to-ceiling mahogany ancestral altar. Delicate carvings of dragon and phoenix framed panels of our forefathers' names and places of origin, handwritten in calligraphy, standing neatly in display. Traditionally, the adult firstborn son carried the responsibility of keeping the altar in his home and worshipping the ancestors. He was expected to follow the daily ritual of burning incense and, with ascending smoke, sending prayers to the ancestors. In return, the forebears would bless him and his household with prosperity, in Baba's case—posterity.

Baba wasn't the firstborn son. Hosting a duplicate of the ancestral altar in our home was either his way of challenging his brother's birthright or his last measure of hope for a son. Mama gave him no son. No one to carry the surname for him. No one to worship him after he died. It was Baba's verbal weapon whenever my parents fought: Mama, a disgraceful curse.

To me, the belief of son-carries-name-and-worships-ancestors was dark and heavy. Because, really, who was I to Baba and the ancestors? Where did I stand on our pedigree chart? I wished men who discounted, disrespected, and disregarded women's worth could help me understand this: Without women, where do sons even come from?

11

A week later the Elders returned with a movie–slides neatly arranged like dominos in a circular projector tray shaped like a Bundt pan. Before we started the movie, the missionaries asked where Mama was.

"She's washing dirty clothes," Dee said.

"Please, you invite her to watch the movie with us?" York said.

"Don't bother!" Baba shouted. "She stays unseen."

The missionaries passed each other a look, then York said, "Um–okay. But should we at least ask her if she wants to stay unseen?"

"I'll go." Dee leapt out of the couch and bolted to the back of the house. In a minute she skipped back with Mama trailing behind. Both Elders stood. They nodded at Mama and stretched out their hands.

"You shake, like this." Dee took Copinga's hand and swung it forcefully from side to side. Everyone laughed except my parents. They were cold-hearted. Although I don't think they were unhappy with the missionaries. The real problem was themselves. They were unhappy to be in the same room. But Mama sat down to watch the movie with us anyway.

The Elders turned our living room wall into a screen for the projected images. York played a cassette in a tape recorder that was the narration of the movie. At the end of each scene there was a beeping signal, and Copinga would manually change the slide so the image and the sound would synch.

We watched the story of Joseph Smith. The narrator had a fruity voice, and the plot was captivating. But at some point, while the narrator continued to tell the story, the image on the wall not only remained the same, but slowly moved upward, and eventually stopped at the ceiling, distorted by the chandelier like shattered glass. When the cassette ended and Baba turned the chandelier back on, we crumpled into hysterical laughter.

Both Elders had fallen asleep!

Our laughs woke them into a state of embarrassment. For a second they looked disoriented, scanning the room and studying our faces, as if trying to remember where they were.

"Oh, oh, oh—sorry," they said, bowing to Baba. But Baba's silence was clearly a loud declaration: he wasn't interested in Joseph Smith, wasn't interested in the Book of Mormon, wasn't interested in learning how to have an eternal family. He didn't want to be married to Mama forever, he said. "I hate her. I hate daughters!"

He'd said that all my life, ho-hum. But the Elders froze in speechless astonishment; their only moving body part was their eyeballs, which slowly turned away from Baba's direction. Mama didn't utter a sound, but maybe she was crying inside. It's deafening sorrow when someone cries without any sound. Maybe she wanted to run away from the pain and humiliation as she had done countless times before, whenever she and Baba finished a fight. No matter how fast she ran, though, the shadow of the fact that Dee and I needed a mother would always keep up—on her right or on her left, before her or behind her—and she always came back. But maybe it wasn't Dee and I who pulled her back. Maybe the shadow that followed her was the fact that even though her marriage was toxic, deep down, Mama always loved Baba and wanted him to love her back. Now I see that the only way for Mama to get rid of the shadow—to *understand* the profound meaning of staying—was to *stand under* the overhead sun, bright as God's love.

Through the missionaries' message I learned that love is a divine quality, a shared attribute between God and us. Everything God does is out of His infinite love for us, and we have the ability to do likewise, to love our neighbors as ourselves. That knowledge brought me peace, joy, and hope that perhaps Baba would soften his heart and love me the way God does. And if he did, he would willingly give me the ultimate gift a father could ever give—loving my mother.

I asked for nothing more than having that simple wish come true.

12

Unless Baba summoned us, Dee and I had to stay upstairs to do homework whenever houseguests were over. A month after the Elders' first visit, on the night of January 13, 1987, Baba took an unexpectedly long time to talk with the missionaries in the living room before calling for us. Dee turned off her desk lamp, I turned off the radio, and we giggled our way down the stairs.

"Big-Noses here have something to tell you," Baba said, one hand pointing at the Elders, one hand tossing his motorcycle key into the air and catching it. "I'm going for a ride."

Dee and I brought out treats and water, then sat together on the couch, across the coffee table from the missionaries. "What will you teach us today, Elders?" I asked.

Both of them burst out crying. Copinga's face was so red, his freckles were invisible now. York wiped his nose with his sleeve and said, "Sorry, your baba—" He choked on the word *baba*, then went back to crying.

"Did he yell at you?" I asked. "That's okay. He yells at me all the time."

"Because you're fat," Dee said.

"YOU are!" I slapped her on the shoulder.

"Sisters, please!" York said. "Please remember to love one another."

Copinga inhaled deeply and exhaled slowly. "Your baba—uh—your parents are . . . divorced."

Dee and I looked at each other and shrugged.

"We're so sorry," York said.

"Why?" Dee rested her chin on the heel of her hand. "Why are you sad?"

"Because your family is torn apart now." York started bawling again. Copinga followed. "We're so sorry for your pain. Sorry . . ."

Wow! I thought. *The outsiders feel compassionate and empathetic toward Dee and me for the pain we might feel. They're crying for us!*

I had never seen any grown men cry before. The Elders, tall as oak trees, sobbed like small children, their high-pitched cry a sewing machine running at full speed. Were their tears speech? Should I speak with weeping too? I didn't know what to say. No adults had ever taught me how to respond to wailing men. In fact, there weren't any adults in the house right now when I needed guidance. I didn't know where my parents were. Then it dawned on me that it had always been like this: Dee and I left home alone, practically raising ourselves and figuring life out on our own. Now I was the hostess. How could I let my guests be sad in my house? And all this crying! Why was this house filled with endless sorrow?

I got tissues for the Elders and patted them on the back. "It's okay. Don't cry."

The Elders didn't know this event was a long time coming. In my fourteen-year-old mind, I believed Mama was finally released from emotional prison, no longer having to fear Baba chasing her out of the house, into the alleyway, with a butcher's knife, cursing in a drunken rage. The divorce was practically the best thing that could ever happen to her. Then, again, I knew nothing about marriage. How foolish of me to assume Mama was excited to cut ties with Baba!

That morning when I was in school, Baba had forced Mama, at knifepoint, to sign the divorce papers with the agreement that he had full custody while she had no visitation. After Mama moved out, Baba took a step further and forbade us sisters to contact or visit Mama or her side of the relatives, threatening to break our legs if we did. No one told me the rationale behind the arrangement that sounded more like a punishment to Mama, leaving her with absolutely nothing after nineteen years of marriage. But maybe she wanted it that way. She wasn't the nurturing type; this might be liberating to her. Baba wasn't the fatherly type either, though. So did it really matter who had full custody? Dee and I would continue to be neglected anyway. However, I never would've guessed that in merely nine years, I would follow Mama's path to the crushing grief of a divorcée. Except, she took her broken heart to her mama; I took mine to Mama's funeral.

This night while Dee and I were doing homework, Baba told the missionaries to never come back. Funny how my life was turned upside down within hours. Earlier that day I could hardly sit still in class, imagining the fun visit my family would have with the Elders that evening. I went home, and three people in my life—Mama and the missionaries—would never be in the same house, discussing and learning about God, ever again. The same living room where the gospel teachings nurtured my spirit would soon be turned into a battlefield.

And all I could say to the Elders was, "It's okay, don't cry. . . ."

13

A few months after the divorce, Baba married his mistress, whom he had been seeing for five years. As soon as the wedding reception was over, the newlyweds went on their honeymoon, leaving Dee and me home alone. My survival instinct had me call Mama for help, who promptly redirected me to her mama, Ah-Po, for daily meals.

Two weeks later, one day, a white Toyota Camry made its way down our narrow alleyway—cluttered with the neighbors' mopeds, bicycles, outdoor wood furnaces, firewood piles on both sides—and arrived at our house at the end of the road. I rushed out the gate when I heard the honking. The stepmother emerged from the car, looking around and wrinkling her flat nose. "What? We'll live in this dump?" she shrieked in a raucous voice, so rough that it could claw the air into shards.

This woman stood four foot ten. Square-faced. Thin-line eyes. Black rotten teeth. An orc with rice-noodle hair, really. Behind her was a seven-year-old girl, a younger version of the stepmother. While my father was collecting candy wrappers, soda cans, and sucker sticks scattered in the car, she yelled, "Baba, show me my room. Now!"

I wanted to push her into the gutter by our gate for her brazen demand. But strangely, Cinderella's story came to mind, as if out of all the fairy tales I'd heard, I'd tucked this one away in a corner of my brain specifically for this moment. Looking at this girl, seven years my junior, I knew which character each of us played in the Cinderella story. My baba, her baba. My house, her house. But her mama would never be mine.

Little did I know that Baba's new wife would make Cinderella's stepmother look like a saint!

Baba's choice to marry her boggled my mind. She didn't have the looks, nor virtuous qualities. Decades later, Baba's best friend—his only non-drinking friend—Uncle Liu, revealed the truth to me: Baba had owed this woman's wealthy father so much money that the only way out of debt was to be her lover while her husband was in prison, and eventually marry her. Uncle Liu said Baba didn't have a choice.

Didn't he, though?

After the stepmother moved in, Dee's and my only daily meal was school lunch. At night the aroma of steam bun, popcorn chicken, tempura shrimp, and various street food drifted out of the master bedroom. Behind the locked door, Baba, the stepmother, and her daughter laughed at something on a TV game show while Dee and I haunted the dark hall like hungry ghosts.

Baba didn't have a choice? Of course he did: having an affair, divorcing Mama, marrying his mistress. Choice, choice, choice. Dee and I were the ones who didn't. As powerless children, we had no choice but to suffer the consequences of Baba's choices. Did he consider us before doing anything?

I don't know.

All I know is that he was a father who told his girls, "I hate daughters!"

14

During the first fourteen years of my life when Mama lived with us, we didn't interact much. Not until after the divorce and she moved into a two-story house a block away did she initiate secret contact with me.

Through Uncle Liu, Mama found out what class I was in. Having no visitation, she could get in trouble for school visits. Knowing that, she never checked in at the front office. Her first attempt to see me was sneaking onto campus through the side gate at the end of the last period, when all students were doing the daily schoolwide classroom cleanup. It must've taken her tremendous effort to find me among two thousand black-haired middle-school girls with the same haircut, wearing the same uniforms, working like a colony of ants. I was sweeping the concrete corridor when she tiptoed close and whispered in my ear that she would take me to dinner at a noodle shop. Startled, I almost screamed, but then was moved to tears by the surprise.

A few days later she came during the first period when we were taking the morning English quiz. She crouched in the corridor, tapping on the classroom window and asking to speak with me.

"I bought this pink sweater from a Japanese import boutique today," she said, cracking a bag open and showing it to me. "You can have it if you tell me where your ba and that bitch went on their honeymoon. Do they share a bedroom at home?"

When Mama heard that Baba and the stepmother indeed

shared a bedroom, she yelled curses at me, her face red, her eyes watery. The scrutinizing glares of my teacher and classmates burned me with shame and embarrassment.

Being a glutton for punishment, Mama came back to me time and again, asking for the same kind of information she knew would only tear her apart. She must've died inside every time I reported back to her. Somehow she regenerated the courage and strength—or was it stubbornness and foolishness?—to be mentally reborn, each time tougher than ever. But why did she want to be reminded that Baba had cheated on her for years? Why did she want to reexperience the excruciating pain of betrayal? Did the sorrow help her feel alive?

Mama's frequent school visits became my new normal. I didn't much care about the adult world, especially not their love-hate relationships, but I accepted Mama's prying as my duty. I kept a journal of things to report to her. I would tell her anything she wanted to know, anything at all, as long as I was fed and had new outfits to wear.

Yep, my teenage loyalty was only to myself.

15

My youngest sister, May, was born with cerebral palsy. At two, she was sent to live in an institution in town called Bethesda, run by a Christian church for disabled girls. One weekend she came home to visit while Baba was on a business trip. That evening we three sisters huddled on the couch watching TV while the stepmother and her daughter ate dinner in her room. Sometime later the stepmother came toward us; her presence filled the air with a thick alcohol stench. She turned off the TV and scanned us with bloodshot eyes, as if challenging us to a fight. Instantly, a tingling sensation ran down my spine. I looked to Dee and May; both looked terrified.

The stepmother twitched her eyes, making them look like two squirming tadpoles. Then she sucked her saliva loudly, making slurred sounds that were obviously a mocking imitation of May when she spoke. "Oh, l-l-loooook, here—comes M-m-m-ayyyyy."

Amused by her own cruel humor, the stepmother slapped her thigh, laughing. Then she limped across the living room, back hunched, knuckles dragging on the floor. I had never seen anyone so drunk that she looked possessed. Instinctively I assumed the responsibility of protecting the twelve-year-old Dee and the seven-year-old May, except I didn't know how. Who could I ask for help? The ancestors?

Six years earlier when Baba moved us into this house, he hired a carpenter to build the ancestral altar. "This will invite the ancestors' spirits to live here. It's their duty to watch over us," he said. I didn't have the heart to remind him that would actually make our new home a haunted house.

Nothing Baba promised was realized.

This night we sisters were left in the haunted madhouse with a thirty-five-year-old child abuser, but our progenitors didn't rush to surround us in a circle of fire to fend off the stepmother. This house was no sanctuary, no shelter, no haven. I looked around the room and realized the only help we had was ourselves, warrior sisters.

"Hey, you lowlife!" The stepmother pointed her chin at May, who started hiccup-weeping as if her stutter got carried over to crying. I put my arm around her shoulder. Dee did the same.

"Still think your ba will take care of you, huh?" the stepmother snarled. "Well, he's taking care of me and my girl now. But we won't mind if you contribute to our family finances. How about we sell your uterus and ovaries in the black market, huh? It's a lot of money." She rubbed her thumb, index, and middle fingers together, the way Taiwanese people sign money. "I've talked to someone. He's waiting for you!"

She pounced on May with an outstretched hand, her fingers glinting with meat grease. May started screaming and shaking. I hugged her tightly and yelled, "Back off or I'll call the police!"

"Go ahead, I dare you!" The stepmother widened her eyes and stared into mine; flames of war gleamed. Her breath was a mixture of garlic sausage and beer, but her entire being emitted a stink of hate that no one should ever have to inhale.

I thought I could be brave, but I was so scared I looked away and swallowed hard, silently begging no one in particular to stop her. The stepmother leaned forward, pinching my hands and prying my fingers apart. That's when Dee slapped her across the face, hard.

"Whatever you do to May, I'll do it to your daughter too," she growled. Hot pepper Dee.

The stepmother tumbled to the floor but immediately bounced back up. With a high-pitched shrill she charged Dee, grasped her by the hair, dragged her to a concrete wall, and banged her head against it.

Dee howled. Her arms waved wildly in the air and found the stepmother's neck. She choked her. Cussing and cursing. A fierce fight. Gasping for air. A wounded cry. Watching Dee's face distort as she grimaced in pain, I was horrified. I wanted to protect my younger sisters, but it was Dee who defended us. All I did was break out in hives, tremble, and bawl for all the injustice and abandonment that had been forced upon us sisters. I was afraid in my own house, scared for Dee and May.

When I screamed for Dee to stop fighting, she let go of the stepmother and kicked her in the shin. The stepmother screeched and spat on the floor, damning us to the eighteenth level of hell. Interesting that her understanding of hell was so different. I thought child abusers went there.

Dee thrust her fist in front of the stepmother's face and sent her running away. I lunged over to the phone and dialed for Uncle Liu with a trembling finger. As soon as I heard his voice, I wanted to be where he was speaking from, a safe home.

"Come—please, Uncle Liuuuuu—the stepmother's attacking! Please take us to your house. Please! We have no help. . . ." My eyes swelled as I spoke, slowly closing and narrowing my vision. The random notes Baba had scribbled on the whiteboard above the telephone now looked blurry, fading before me like the phone numbers he'd erased: Mama's side of the relatives.

I was in the middle of telling Uncle Liu what had happened when Dee screamed behind me. The stepmother had snuck up on her, pinned her down, and repeatedly socked her in the head with a remote control.

Yeah, a remote control, no big deal. But, when used as an assault weapon, it fractured Dee's skull.

"Call the police. She's killing Dee!" I yelled into the phone receiver before hanging up and leaping over to pull the stepmother away from Dee. By the time Uncle Liu arrived at our house, the stepmother had already escaped with her daughter.

A few days later, the doctor who tended to Dee's wound wrote a notarized statement for her legal guardian—Baba—to use in court, if he planned to take legal action against the assaulter. But Baba wouldn't do it. It would make him lose face, he said. No one should make him lose face.

With the stepmother, Baba destroyed two marriages. Then, like a military strategist regrouping teams of soldiers, he tried to merge two broken families into one, expecting everyone to get along and make him a happy captain.

He miscalculated.

When the stepmother gave me hell, I turned to the Church of Jesus Christ of Latter-day Saints for heaven.

I found it.

16

O n their first visit, the Elders told my family the address to
the church meetinghouse and invited us to attend Sunday
meetings. We never did. But on Sunday, October 9, 1988, I had a
strong impression—a persistent thought—that nudged me to go. I
invited Dee along. We hopped on our bikes; rode two miles past
rice fields, breakfast shops, schools; and arrived at the three-story
building in the heart of Hualien City. Mopeds and bicycles cluttered the veranda. A sign hung across the balcony: *The Church of
Jesus Christ of Latter-day Saints.* No cross.

I leaned my bike against an electric pole and approached an
Asian lady in a dark dress suit by the front door. She looked to be in
her late twenties. About four foot ten. High cheekbones. Thick lips.

"Hi, are Elders Copinga and York here?" I asked.

"No, they went home to America. Can I help you?"

What? How can this be? The sky is falling on me!

With the Elders gone, so was my hope for happiness. Where
would I find the love and peace I'd felt while they taught us the
gospel? My eyes started to sting as they welled up. I told the lady
I wasn't sure how she could possibly help me.

She grinned and asked if I was there to learn about the gospel.
I nodded.

Reaching under her blazer, she pulled her white blouse forward
to show me a black name tag. *Sister Lin,* it read. Astounded, I pointed
at her chest. I didn't know women could be missionaries too.

"I'm a missionary," she said. "I'd love to share the gospel with you."

My heart started to drum. There was hope for happiness after all. "Thanks! Oh, and my sister too. . . ." I turned and called out to Dee, who was shooing away a stray dog on the street.

"Wonderful!" Sister Lin clapped. "Come! I'll introduce you to my companion and church members."

That day I met the kind of people I didn't know existed; people who wrapped their arms around Dee and me like old friends. I also witnessed what I didn't know could be real: fathers and mothers smiling at each other, touching their children's cheeks, finger-combing their hair. I wondered why those kids were so lucky.

I'd always imagined caring parents were like water on earth; there was a constant number of them. A flood in Japan meant a drought in Korea; nurturing parents in other households meant negligent ones in mine. By observing the church members, I realized that caring parents had nothing to do with balance in nature but everything to do with personal choice. Even though I wasn't privileged to grow up in a loving home, I had a choice to become a future mother who gives that blessing to her children. A devoted parent is self-made.

What moved me more than anything else that day was listening to kids, ages three to twelve in the children's Sunday school class, effortlessly talk about the purpose of life. They said that before we were born, we'd lived in Heaven with God, who created our spirits. He's our Heavenly Father who loves us and has provided the Plan of Happiness for us to come to the earth to obtain a physical body, to gain mortal experiences, to learn and to grow. He gives us freedom, known as agency, to choose for ourselves. If we choose to emulate Jesus's examples to keep God's commandments, to love and serve others, then after we die, we'll have a chance to return to God and live with our family forever.

The answers to my questions about life are within this simple truth: I'm a child of God, who loves me so much that He prepared a plan for my eternal happiness. Happiness—I have the power to choose it!

The poet Rumi's words fittingly describe my truth: for years I had a thirsty fish in me that longed to find the fountain of knowledge, to find my life's purpose. That thirst "drove me down to the water, where I drank the moon's reflection." With the newfound knowledge of God and His plan, I started to see that, inside me, I had not only the full moon but the entire universe of God's love.

For over a month Dee and I met with sister missionaries, studying gospel principles and learning to pray. I prayed to know if the church, the Book of Mormon, and the gospel were true. I didn't see a nodding heavenly messenger, but the answers to my prayers were manifested in my thriving desire to be Christ-like, having faith, hope, and charity.

Baba was angry that I spent after-school hours at church every day. He wanted me to always be studying instead. But my grades were great; I didn't mind expanding my learning to spiritual subjects.

Two years after York and Copinga had brought the gospel to us, on November 20, 1988, every church member in Hualien, about forty people, came to support me at my baptism. Reverent and quiet, they stood around the rooftop baptismal font that was essentially a mini swimming pool filled with warm water. Sister Lin prepared a white jumpsuit, a bath towel, and a new dress for me. An Elder baptized me by immersion. After I dried up and changed into the dress, everyone walked downstairs to the chapel, where a priesthood-bearing man placed his hands on my head, confirmed me a member of the church, and gave me the gift of the Holy Ghost with the promise that, if I lived my life in harmony with Christ's teachings, I would have the constant companionship of the Holy Ghost to guide, protect, and teach me.

In the church I learned that "Save a girl, save generations." I realized the prompting I'd felt that Sunday to return to church was God's saving grace, His tender mercy, leading me to the Light and Truth, so that generations of my descendants could live in His love.

After my baptism I went home to find Baba waiting in the living room, his jaw clenched, his eyes narrowed. With alcohol breath, he snarled, "If you dare go to that white devils' church again, I'll break your legs!"

"But I go to church to learn to be a better person. How about you get mad if I join a street gang or go to jail?"

For years, Baba continued to threaten. I continued to rebel to be good. In the church I found my worth; I simply couldn't go back to the old life of depression and cynicism. It was like, if I had a smartphone, why would I go back to a rotary phone?

17

When I was sixteen, one Sunday, a couple senior missionaries showed up at church and introduced themselves as Brother and Sister Bushman from Utah. Brother Bushman was in his seventies. A retired construction company owner. At six foot two, he towered over Taiwanese people like an ostrich among chickens. Every child in the church pointed at him, calling, "Reagan, Reagan!"

He looked like President Ronald Reagan's twin, with full, wavy white hair and broad shoulders.

Sister Bushman had snow-white, short, curly hair. Black-frame glasses. About five foot ten. Fit and healthy.

Like all missionaries, the Bushmans' choice of volunteering required them to fund themselves for their eighteen-month service. Before arriving in Taiwan, they'd spent two months learning Chinese at the Missionary Training Center in Utah. I heard that Chinese is one of the most difficult languages to learn as a foreign language, but the Bushmans made it look easy. They rented an apartment in Hualien, paid bills, and went grocery shopping all on their own. Almost effortlessly, they converted those they conversed with on the street.

The Bushmans opened a free English class for interested people of all ages to meet weekly in the church meetinghouse. In their class I learned to compliment others with "Good job!" "You're amazing!" and "I appreciate you." They also taught us how to write cursive letters, so we could write thank-you notes to other hard-working missionaries.

They invited Dee and me to their apartment and taught us how to bake banana bread in a rice cooker so we could take it to our neighbor, a single mother. They often hosted parties so we could invite our classmates who also wandered up and down the street after school, roaming in and out of dark alleyways as we used to. These were teenage girls who carried cigarette burn scars on the backs of their hands from their smoking fathers, had cut wounds on their arms that their uniforms couldn't cover, and were missing teeth from heavy, violent blows that stole their smiles. Together, we stray children from the street gathered around the Bushmans' dining table of glowing candles and fresh flowers and feasted on a homemade meal.

The Bushmans' kindness brought out the pure happiness hidden deeply within me. They made me feel like royalty, and I had no doubt that's how God Himself would treat each of us. Seeing my classmates laugh for the first time made me want to weep weep weep for joy. I never knew my heart was capable of caring about others so profoundly, not until the Bushmans showed me how.

Never once did the Bushmans mention the word "service," but I learned through their examples what that word truly meant. They personified the saying "Be a lamp, a lifeboat, a ladder. Help someone's soul heal. Walk out of your house like a shepherd."

I grew so close to them that they became my Mom and Dad Bushman. When they finished their mission and returned to Utah in 1990, we stayed in touch through letters—in English cursive letters.

18

The Chinese lived under the heavy influence of the thousand-year-old Imperial Examination System that promised academically successful individuals a comfortable post-college life with respected, high-paying careers—which, in turn, brought honor to their parents and ancestors.

In the early 1990s, the Annual University Entrance Exam in Taiwan admitted only the top twenty percent of high school graduates nationwide into college. My classmates studied like crazy, taking college-prep classes at cram schools every day after regular school hours, English and math classes on weekends. I attended seminary, sang in the choir, participated in church service projects, built cardboard shelters for the homeless, read to nursing home residents, studied, then passed the Entrance Exam. The Education Department matched my score with the schools and majors on my wish list and assigned me to the prestigious Fu-Jen Catholic University in Taipei, three hours north of my hometown. I majored in German.

At twenty-one, in my junior year, I chose to serve a full-time mission. My decision required me to defer my education to preach the gospel—on the street or in the homes of interested people—twelve hours daily for eighteen months without pay. When the semester ended, on Chinese New Year's Eve (February 9, 1994), I went home to tell Baba about my choice to serve a mission. A glassy film glazed over his eyes. His cheek muscles contracted. "You–WHAT? Are you retarded?"

His reaction was fully understandable. I'd expected it. My decision probably sounded as outrageous as accepting a dare, on my life, to turn the Great Wall of China into the world's longest water slide. But instead of worrying about my life, he was concerned about suffering the humiliation of losing his university-child bragging rights.

That's right.

Baba never told me he was proud of me for being the first in our family to attend university. But whenever I went home for holidays, he dragged me with him to visit his drinking buddies.

"Oh, I came straight from the train station. This dog is home from the university." He pointed a thumb at me and chuckled dryly. "Yeah, isn't that something? I have a kid in university!" He smacked his lips and savored those words after he said them, enjoying the glorious moment when they elevated his ego. The ensuing admiring glares from the men traveled between Baba and me, but all the praises went to Baba for raising a successful daughter.

However, he never told his friends that the only things he ever said to me were razor-sharp criticisms:

"Out of you sisters you're the stupidest!"

"Fat! Lazy! Rotten!"

"I hate you!"

He hated me, he said. Now he had one more reason to feel that way because I no longer walked on the charted path of a perfect Chinese child: earn a bachelor's degree at twenty-two; a master's degree at twenty-four; a doctoral degree before thirty, preferably from a U.S. Ivy League school.

So, on this Chinese New Year's Eve when everyone returned home to celebrate with family over the reunion dinner and parents gave children red envelopes stuffed with gift money, I stood in Baba's undecorated living room: no red couplets with New Year wishes and greetings on the front door. No calligraphy character of *Blessings* on red rhombus paper glued upside down on windows, walls, or cabinets. No festive song of *Congratulations on Your Good Fortune* blaring on every TV channel. No chatty voice from Dee, who now spent most of her time at the home of her boyfriend's parents. No high-pitched shrills from the stepmother, who had divorced Baba earlier that year and moved out with her daughter. Baba's house was dead.

I assured him I would finish my degree after my service. But he continued to pace the living room in a circle, red-faced, veins bulging on his forehead. "What a retard!" he huffed. "Disgrace! People will hear what an idiot you are, and I'll lose face because of it!"

"Lose face? Really? I'm going to proselytize, not to prostitute—"

Abruptly, Baba picked up my backpack and threw it across the courtyard, then he kicked my suitcase out of the front door and shoved me out to the porch.

"Go! Go serve your stupid god and don't ever come back!" He slammed the door in my face. I supposed that saved his face. It's better to have a daughter who was dead to him than have a daughter who disgraced him.

Suddenly I was a girl child without Baba's blessings. Perpetually.

Not for my mission.

Not for my emigration.

Not for my wedding celebration.

19

I n the church culture—where children as young as three years old are taught to prepare for their future missions by staying physically, mentally, emotionally, spiritually, financially, and socially fit and healthy—I, a convert without family support or a head start on planning, was in dire need of a missionary fund when I chose to serve. As soon as the Bushmans heard about it, they donated $5,000 USD to sponsor me. During my service in the Taiwan Taichung Mission, they wrote to me regularly—never missing a week—with encouragement and additional financial assistance.

Rebirth parents, the Chinese term that perfectly describes who they were to me. To me, the Bushmans became a verb, like love, like support, like uplift, like nurture, like what every parent should do for his or her child.

PART THREE

Filial Piety

20

While serving my mission in Qishan—a tiny town in southern Taiwan—one day in February 1995, I received a phone call from a hospital in Hualien.

For weeks, Mama had been in the hospital for her type 2 diabetes. There were pending treatments on the condition that her medical bills were paid in full. I talked with my mission president, who wisely counseled me to remember that I could work hard and bring numerous souls unto Christ, but the most important of the Lord's work I could ever do was within the walls of my home. "Go to your mother," he said. "She's your calling now."

That following Sunday I was honorably released from my service, and promptly boarded a train home. With the leftover missionary fund the Bushmans had so generously given me, I paid off Mama's medical bills.

Caring for Mama was a difficult transition in our relationship. Difficult, because we had no relationship. She was like a female adult who lived in the same house with me for the first fourteen years of my life. It could've been anyone else: a bank teller, a grocery store clerk, a fruit stand owner. But now I needed to be her daughter, the kind of human who was expected to have loved her from the moment I opened my newborn-baby eyes. It would've been easier for me to learn to solve a calculus problem, in German.

But I tried.

Ninety-Nine Fire Hoops

I spent two months in the hospital bedside armchair in Mama's ward. When she rested, I studied the scriptures, wrote in my journal, and wrote to Cameron. I'd exchanged mailing addresses with him before he returned home to Texas two years earlier. When Mama was awake, I told her stories from the Book of Mormon. She was soft with me, didn't reject anything I offered. But, as the Chinese say, "A cow taken to Beijing will still be a cow." I was wrong to have thought that my intrusion in her life at this time would motivate her to transform into the mother I'd always wanted.

21

Diabetes slowly took away Mama's vision and shut down her kidneys. She couldn't go to the bathroom, so all her bodily wastes were retained inside, making her swell like a balloon. She couldn't lie down to sleep at night because her heart would be "immersed in water," she said. "I fear I might drown."

Several times I watched in horror as her blood sugar dropped and she started to shake in pouring sweat. And every time, as soon as I pushed the emergency button, a nurse rushed to Mama's side with a slice of birthday cake she'd borrowed from the newborn unit, as if she had gone through an intense drill every day to be able to promptly respond to this situation. I stepped back to make room for the nurse to save Mama's life, all the while silently praying for God to reach down His mighty hands and lay them on her head, to bless her, to pronounce her whole. I prayed for a miracle. But I didn't have sufficient faith for it to happen. Deep down, I didn't believe she would be whole. She didn't obey the doctor's order to eliminate her sugar intake. Nor was she willing to establish a habit of regular exercise. No. No one told her what to do.

Every day she commanded me to forge the doctor's signature and write a fake release note to the nurses. "Get me out of here. I want to go to the market for mochi ice cream, fruit tart, lychee boba drinks. Oh, and taro cake."

I stared at her in awe. Didn't she barely escape death? Didn't she learn anything from it? Didn't she know that forging someone else's signature was wrong?

Furious at me for not complying, she called Ah-Po to complain. After Mama's whining plea for sweets, Ah-Po sent her cousin to the hospital with her choice of comfort food hidden in an oversize shopping tote. My responsibility was to stand watch when she sneak-snacked.

Mama made satisfied grunts while wolfing down the desserts. "Mmm–mmm–my mama, the best!" Watching her indulge in her mama's love, I wondered where and when it happened–what went wrong?

Twenty-two years earlier, Mama's body knew it was time to prepare itself to carry me as a fetus, to deliver me as a newborn, to nurse me as an infant. Her body knew it was becoming my mother, but her mind didn't share the same knowing. Mama's mind tore her body and spirit away, so her soul couldn't touch mine.

Ah-Po loved her daughter; her daughter loved her back. But the same daughter, who became my mother, didn't share that same affection with me–although, skipping Mama, Ah-Po and I loved each other. The chain of love was broken, then unbroken again, leaving a disconnection in the middle. A weak link. That day in the hospital, I thought Mama was it. I thought she'd let go of the link and lost emotional connection with me. Now, I can finally see that the real weak link in the chain was us. Both Mama and me.

22

Two months after I returned home from my mission, Mama was discharged from the hospital. I moved into her house because I had nowhere else to live.

Moss covered the cinderblock exterior wall of Mama's house. The rusty metal front door squeaked. The polycarbonate roofing panels over the foyer were moldy and falling apart. It was a miracle that past typhoons hadn't ripped them all off. Thick layers of black dust caked the screen windows; it was impossible to get a clear view out of them. To enter the house, I had to part the sea of old newspapers, junk mail, calendars, receipts, and bills in the living room. The kitchen walls were covered with soot. The marble floor had lost its shine and was sticky, slippery with years' worth of grease. The toilet was in such a horrific condition; I considered going to the bathroom in a street gutter. Mountains of Mama's shoes, dresses, and purses were all over her upstairs bedroom. It looked like a post-hurricane scene.

Only months earlier, I'd biked with other missionaries in a raging typhoon for an hour to clean a disabled couple's home, ruined in a mud slide. I could clean Mama's place too. She deserved to live in a better environment. But as soon as I offered to help, she accused me of being condescending. She didn't need anyone to tell her how to live her life, she said. Obviously, after having been her daughter for twenty-two years, I was just starting to get to know her.

Despite the disagreement, she did allow me to clear out just enough space in the living room—no more, no less—to set up a lawn chair as her bed, so she wouldn't have to climb the stairs to her bedroom on the second floor. It grieved me to watch her sit in the chair at night, groaning and moaning from pain. This near-stranger was my mother. This misery was her life. How did she arrive here? Had she ever wanted to change? Had she given up on life?

23

During my mission from 1994 to 1995, Cameron wrote to me weekly, telling me about his transition back to student life, about his breakups with different girlfriends, and about the feelings he'd kept secret during his service as a missionary. *I fell in love with a girl. . . . It's you.*

All my life, no one had ever used the word *love* on me. I read his letter over and over until I memorized his confession of attraction, and I could see his cursive *I love you* with my eyes closed. It was surreal to have the confirming knowledge that the deep affection I felt for him was mutual. I refused to think I was likely a rebound from his most recent breakup. Instead, I imagined I was the reason for the breakup. I convinced myself what mattered was he loved me now.

A month after I moved into Mama's house, in May 1995, Cameron called to say that the semester had ended and he was flying to Taiwan to visit me. I'd never told Mama about my social life. Who should I tell her Cameron was? Friend? Crush? How did other people do it, telling their parents they had fallen in love? How did Cameron tell his parents?

Mama and Cameron, how would they receive each other? I was almost certain Cameron wouldn't like Mama. But should I worry—should I care?—if she didn't approve of him? How would that stop me from wanting to be with him?

After numerous practices—coming up with an introduction

line and editing it and discarding it and coming up with something else—I finally told Mama my American boyfriend would be
visiting and we should take him to an air-conditioned restaurant
for a seafood feast. "You only have one chance to meet him for the
first time. Let's take him to a nice place, eat nice food. He's coming all the way from America, so far away. It's the least we can do."

I imagined Mama in her flowery cotton dress and Cameron
using his proper manners and the meeting going pleasantly. But I
forgot that no one could tell her what to do.

24

The night before Cameron's arrival, I stayed up, going through the combinations of seven blouses, five skirts, three dresses, and the only pair of heels I owned, staring into a mirror to decide which outfit best showed off my physique.

Funny how I thought I needed to impress him. It wasn't like we met on a dating website and this was our first meeting. He had seen me after a school volleyball game—unkempt hair, beads of sweat on my nose and above my upper lip, dirty cotton T-shirt stuck to my chest. Yeah, he had seen the disheveled side of me before, but on this night my heart insisted that after two years of being apart, our reunion now would be life changing for both of us, and I needed to look my best for this historical event.

In a turquoise cotton dress and white heels, I showed up at the Chiang Kai-Shek International Airport two hours before his scheduled landing. I picked a corner seat in the waiting area, facing the gigantic overhead screens of arrival flights. The artery in my neck thumped almost audibly. The *tap-tap-tap* of my foot on the marble floor intensified my anxiety, but I couldn't stop. I fanned my face with the newspaper I'd found on a chair. My hands trembled mildly, my palms clammy. I stood, paced around, sat down, wrote in my diary, doodled, and practiced what to say when I saw him.

When Cameron emerged from the glass sliding door separating the customs and the lobby in a gray T-shirt and cargo shorts, I couldn't decide whether to laugh or cry. That same face still made my heart race: clean-shaven, his trademark smile that pushed the right cheek higher than the left, and the white patch of birthmark above his right ear. I stood by the glass railing that lined the walkway into the main hall, looking at him looking for me. A warm current circulated through my body. Never had I felt wanted like this before. Nervously, I inched forward to expose myself to his full vision. Before I knew it, he ran up and gave me a python-like hug, his face in my hair. Through his shirt I felt his quickened heartbeats and smelled his soapy deodorant. This familiar scent triggered a special memory from the night of my twentieth birthday. Cameron bought a slice of cake from a bakery and brought it to my dorm. When I told him that was the first birthday cake I'd ever had in my life, something moved in his eyes. He put his arm around my shoulder and sang "Happy Birthday." I inhaled deeply and memorized that same scent of his skin.

"I missed you so much," he said in Chinese. "I've been waiting for this far too long."

His voice made me dizzy. How could this all be possible, this joy? My mouth was in his armpit; my words came out muffled. "Me too."

He produced a diamond ring from his shorts pocket. No kneeling. No proposing. He slid it onto my finger. Then, cupping my face in his hands, he gave me a passionate, tongue-tangling kiss.

Taiwanese people didn't kiss.

In fact, back in the 1980s and the early 1990s, kissing was such a rare emotional expression among the Taiwanese that when there was a kissing scene in a TV show, it made the newspaper headline in the entertainment section.

All this—the embrace, the kiss, the engagement that composed a monumental life event—took me by surprise. Sure, I'd dreamed of it. But never in the form of a tsunami wave of happiness, coming at me strong, powerful, and all at once. It made me feel as though I had been favored by God. Cameron was His gift to me—the first man who celebrated my birthday; the first man who noticed me among millions of Chinese faces; the first man who told me he loved me.

Around us, children giggled. A girl pointed at us and said, "Mama, take a picture of them!"

Cameron and I laughed and kissed, waving and posing. I wondered how we looked together as a couple. I wondered if any camera could truly capture the meaning of this blissful moment: me, Cameron's fiancée.

25

Cameron and I left the airport around dinnertime and rode in a taxicab, in the rain, to the train station. Outside the droplet-sprawled window, countless strangers were on the same street at the same time, heading toward different destinations. Moped riders and bikers maneuvered between tight rows of cars. Everyone seemed to be in a hurry to get somewhere—home to their loved ones, perhaps? That must've been the reason why people braved the cold, damp, rainy season to be stuck in the chaotic, standstill Taipei traffic.

Pointing at them, I said, "Look at those people, Cam."

Cameron scooted closer to me and looked past my finger to the travelers.

"Everyone you see is a beloved child of God. Each one of them," I said. In that precise moment, I remembered something I'd imagined when I was fifteen: that every human being wears an invisible crown only God can see.

That we don't see the crowns on our heads because we don't fully understand our true divine potential as children of the Most High God.

That until we understand who we really are and realize our powers to become like God, we'll never see our majestic crowns.

That when God looks down from Heaven, He sees our crowns as glowing, moving dots on a dark world map.

That if I work extra hard to be extra good, my deeds will fuel the glow of my crown, making it extra bright, until everyone can see it and know that I'm a precious daughter of God.

All my imagination about the crown made me happy. I smiled at Cameron, who dropped his head into his hands and let out a sigh.

"Aw . . . Allison, you . . . I can't believe this." He lifted up his head and looked into my eyes, his face gentle and tender. "You're so . . . pure!"

For a second, I thought he could see my crown.

26

Mama insisted on hosting Cameron in her house.

I should've been grateful that she cared enough to spend her time and money to entertain, but as a selfish girl, I only cared about how she and her house reflected me. I dreaded every torturing second sitting in her living room next to Cameron on the sticky couch–barely enough space for the two of us, hip to hip, after we'd pushed a shaky pile of calendar pages aside. Wordlessly we ate the seafood dinner Mama had ordered from a restaurant. It was hot in the tropical humidity. A tiny table fan was turned to the highest speed, blowing and scattering bills and receipts around the room. All the while I silently asked, "Why? Why? Why?" I kept hoping Mama would change her mind and say, "Who am I kidding? Why don't we eat out instead?" But that never happened. Cameron's disapproving face as he surveyed the landfill-like surroundings made me feel ashamed. I wondered if Mama could fully fathom the magnitude of my embarrassment–of being me, in this time and space where I didn't want to be. But, of course, I brought the embarrassment upon myself. I chose to live with her. I chose to take Cameron to her place. Perhaps in the premortal life I had even chosen to be her daughter, who knows? For that association with her, and because others' opinions about her felt personal to me, I felt obligated to apologize to those who didn't like her. After all, I was the bone of her bone, flesh of her flesh.

That night, I took Cameron to Mama's brother's home, where he would stay for the rest of his visit. When I apologized to Cameron for Mama's filthy house, he said, "I'm taking you out of that shithole! You don't need to go back. You'll be with me."

My intense desire to please him didn't allow me to be offended by his word choice. In fact, I was overwhelmed by such tremendous gratitude that I confused him for my savior, saving me from my miserable family life. But, in time, I realized that my savior wouldn't take me out of a shithole to put me in hell. Cameron wasn't my savior. I already had one, with a capital *S*. Cameron was merely my bridegroom—a bridge between Taiwan and the U.S.—a heck of a bridge, built with shards of broken glass that I walked across, barefoot, to the destiny of my choosing.

27

esides the engagement ring, Cameron also brought me admission and scholarship applications to the university he was attending. "It's faster and easier to get you to America as a student than as a U.S. citizen's fiancée," he said. This was his vacation, but it wasn't a tourist's pleasure for him at all. We filled out the forms together, requested my transcript from Fu-Jen University, and applied for my passport and student visa. Two weeks later I was accepted by The University of Texas Rio Grande Valley with a scholarship to start in three months, in the fall semester, 1995. Everything developed as Cameron had planned. The next step was for him to fly back to Texas to prepare for my arrival while I stayed in Taiwan to wait for my student visa. He gave me all the Taiwanese dollars in his wallet, more than enough to book myself a one-way trip to Edinburg to unite with him.

I didn't expect our coming-together to be so unusual. We got engaged, got married, and commenced dating, in that order. Though our narrative was unconventional, it developed so smoothly that I was convinced God had approved of it.

But I mistook my wish for God's will.

28

Having watched American TV shows throughout my teenage years, I'd often imagined what it would be like to live in the U.S. Now that I had the acceptance letter from The University of Texas Rio Grande Valley, the student visa that had just arrived in the mail, and the one-way ticket to Edinburg, my imagination was about to become reality.

My departure date was July 4, 1995. Mama had called Uncle Liu and asked him to drive us and Dee and May to the airport. It only took about three and a half hours from Hualien to get to the Chiang Kai-Shek International Airport, but we left a day early to make frequent stops for our carsick mama. That night we made it to Taipei and checked into a hotel. Mama was too weary to go to a night market for dinner, so Uncle Liu went alone and brought back wonton noodle soup, fried chicken drumsticks, shave ice, fresh mangoes, and lychee.

We crammed on the two queen-size beds in the hotel room and devoured the dinner while Uncle Liu stood and watched. When Mama asked him to join us, he said, "It's okay. I can get the food anytime"—he pointed at me and grinned—"but for this young lady going to the greatest nation of the world, it's her last time to enjoy authentic Taiwanese food. Let her eat."

"Great, thanks"—I put down my chopsticks and the soup bowl—"I can't take another bite now that you just made this sound like my last supper."

Dee and May chuckled. Uncle Liu shrugged and said, "Is that some kind of—what? Why is it funny?"

Mama chimed in. "If she's speaking Chinese and you still don't understand her, then it must have something to do with her white god or the scriptures or something Mormon."

Uncle Liu put his hands in the air and excused himself to go to his room. "Someday I might become smart like you. But before then, enjoy your last supper."

Looking back, I see that the last-supper joke was a prophecy. But please don't get me wrong. In no way am I comparing myself to Jesus Christ, no. I'm not worthy. I'm only pointing out the similarity between His last supper and mine: after our meal, a close friend would betray us. In my case, it would be my husband, no less, who would conspire against me.

After eating, I searched for wet towelettes that usually came in the bag with fried chicken drumsticks. But instead of finding a packet in the bag, I found one on the carpet, almost hidden under the bed skirt. Strangely, it wasn't a towelette inside; it was a piece of folded rubber shaped like an uninflated balloon. I lifted it up in the air and examined it, muttering, "How weird, this wet wipe thingy." Unable to figure out what it was, I threw it in the garbage can before going to the bathroom to wash my greasy fingers.

Within seconds, Mama followed me into the bathroom and said, almost in a whisper, "That thing you just threw away—it's called a 'secure sheath.'"

I looked up from the sink at her reflection in the mirror. "Okay?"

"It's best for a husband to use that than for a wife to eat the avoid-pregnancy medicine," Mama said, looking down at her feet. "Avoid-pregnancy medicine is very, very bad. It can turn a woman very, very crazy. Men beat crazy women, don't you know? You must avoid avoid-pregnancy medicine at all costs!"

There was a cautioning spark in her eyes, begging me to

listen. But I shook my head. "Ma, where did this even come from? I don't want to hear this, okay? I'm not planning to get pregnant right away."

But I lied. I hadn't planned anything at all. I didn't know what to plan when it came to my body.

As a little girl, I noticed the differences between my body and Mama's. But she never taught me that, in due time, my body would go through the transformative experience that morphed itself into the shape, the form, and the functions of a woman. Obviously, the problem with not knowing I should be expecting the changes was that, when the process started, I wasn't intellectually or emotionally ready, which created an added measure of discomfort to the growing pains—fear and shame of the body I lived in.

Back in fourth grade, one day during recess, my teacher summoned me to her desk. She pointed at my chest and said I needed to start wearing a training bra. I had no idea what it was or how to get one, but her advice made me self-conscious. Instead of wearing a bra, I slouched.

In that same year, a classmate whispered in my ear—her mouth behind her shielding hand—and told me about intercourse. She'd first learned about it from her older brother and later, by accident, witnessed her parents' nightly bedroom activity. The details she described were unthinkably absurd to me. In one second, I was a naïve child. In the next, I wasn't. When I pushed her away and told her to stop talking, she pinched my butt. "Why do you think men have that extra piece of flesh down there then, huh?"

I was stunned! I'd never thought about it. I had a feeling she'd told the truth, but why was she the one telling me this, a child teaching a child?

In fifth grade I started menstrual bleeding and thought I was dying! One morning, before walking to school, I stuffed layers of toilet paper in my undies and packed a new roll in my book bag. There wasn't any toilet paper in the school bathrooms, and I believed I would need plenty. I couldn't concentrate in class. I was terrified that my blood might overflow and stain not only my uniform skirt but also the classroom chair. At recess I cleaned myself in the bathroom, in confusion, in panic, in terror. On my way back to my classroom, in the corridor, a female teacher I didn't know approached me from behind and asked that I follow her to the teachers' lounge. Convinced I was in trouble, I held back the hot tears welling in my eyes. Turned out, the nightmare of blood stain on my skirt became a reality.

"Does your ma know you're bleeding?" the teacher asked. It felt like being interrogated for a crime I didn't commit. "I'm innocent!" I wanted to shout. "My body is doing its own thing. I can't stop it!" I shook my head and let my tears roll. How should I tell the teacher that my mama didn't know what time I started walking to school every morning because she was still sleeping when I left the house? Or that she didn't know I struggled with reading, math, and science? Or that she didn't know, even if I squinted, I couldn't read the words on the blackboard? I had no reason to believe she would care about my bleeding.

The teacher sighed and gave me a lesson on biology, anatomy, and personal hygiene. This was a monumental moment in my life, learning that my body could bring forth human lives. As an eleven-year-old girl, I finally understood that instead of popping out of a boulder, *I was born.* That second-grade survey question about *birthday* finally made sense! I imagined Mama giving birth to me. And I was overwhelmed by the fact that, in a physical sense, we were once intimately connected. I wept for that sacred knowledge. Why didn't she tell me about this beautiful memory of my birth? Did she love me when the doctor pulled me out of her, cut my cord, and placed me on her chest?

The teacher pulled out a box of feminine pads from a closet, took one out, handed it to me, and put the box back. I stood next to her, my body fevered while a sensation of warm liquid trickled down my legs. I exuded the metallic scent of blood mixed with the stink of nervous, embarrassed sweat, and I desperately wanted to run back home, back to my sleeping Mama, back to her chest, back to her womb, back to a time when she might've loved and cared about me. But her words from the past abruptly ended my thought. "I should've suffocated you when you were a baby!"

As the proverb goes, "It takes a village to raise a child." It's true in my experience. My village was filled with willing people who contributed to the effort of raising me, like the next-door neighbor who fed me lunch and taught me how to use the bathroom; like my classmate and school teachers who gave me the sex education Mama never gave me; like the Bushmans, who showered me with love while Mama was absent, unavailable, and living her own life. She had chosen to miss out on my growth; what could I do? I grew up anyway and traveled far away.

I didn't understand why Mama suddenly decided to talk about birth control hours before I left Taiwan for good. Was this the one and only time she felt the urge to fulfill her parental obligation to deliver a life-lesson type of speech, or was it because my flying away to live on the other side of the Pacific was a rite of passage, and she felt that I was finally ready for adult talks? Whatever it was, I was unwilling to receive it, not then, not from her.

To everything there is a season, and a time to every purpose under the heaven.

There was a time when I needed her to raise me, to teach me, to mother me.

That time had passed.

29

On the flight across the Pacific Ocean heading toward the Beautiful Nation—as America is called in Chinese—I pondered the mysterious way that my life had unfolded up to this point. I was in awe of how I arrived at this moment, in this place, blessed to leave the family drama among my parents and the ex-stepmother.

Ah, the ex-stepmother, the woman who, years earlier while Baba was having eye surgery, stole all the cash for his medical expenses and left him penniless in the hospital with pending treatments.

The woman who, when I was fourteen, commanded Baba to beat me for her viewing pleasure. Which he did.

The woman who brought out suicidal thoughts in me at fifteen.

But without her persecutions, I wouldn't have sought suicide.

Without seeking suicide, I wouldn't have been inspired, instead, to seek God.

Without God, I wouldn't have met Cameron.

Without Cameron, I wouldn't be traveling to America.

Without traveling to America, I would've been like a frog looking up from the bottom of a well, thinking the sky was only a pinhole.

PART FOUR

Humiliation

30

The plane took off from Chiang Kai-Shek International Airport in Taipei on July 4, 1995, crossing longitudes, passing latitudes, and arriving in Los Angeles on the same day. In fact, I arrived earlier than the departure time on my itinerary, as if time stood still—or went backward—while I moved. What do they call this, time and travel? Time travel?

I stepped out of the plane into the new world, eyes wide, palms sweaty, chest bursting. An ocean of people was at immigration and customs: men, women, young, old. A world of beautiful faces: African, Asian, European. A world of cultural apparel: turban, robe, sari. A world of chaotic noises: excited gasp, chatty laughter, exhausted whine. A world of scents: body odor, stale perfume, sour breath. And a world of foreign languages. Signs separated and directed the crowd. No mistake, everyone had a line to stand in. U.S. citizens and permanent residents to the right. Visitors to the left. A uniformed officer looked over the top of his glasses at me, then down at my passport picture. "Welcome to the U.S.A., Miss Hong." He smiled and stamped on page two.

Americans smiled so much, planting a flower in me every time they did.

At my final destination, Edinburg International Airport's baggage claim area, among countless strangers, I recognized a thick-built woman with gold-trim glasses over her blue eyes.

Cameron resembled her. I approached her and asked, "Meees–as Cha–Chassstayyyn?"

She beamed with a motherly glow, her eyes filled with light. "Oh, hi"–she extended her hand for me to shake– "you're here."

I'd imagined her on a two-dimensional blueprint before, the way a doll designer draws a human body on graph paper, adding details one layer at a time. I'd imagined her with a pale, wrinkled face, pointed chin, hook nose, thin lips, broad shoulders, thick torso. Basically, I'd imagined her based on the looks of the German Catholic nuns I had seen every day at Fu-Jen University. Now, standing in front of Mrs. Chastain, I imagined Cameron's and my future children being a quarter of her. One of them might even have her eyes, nose, lips . . .

I was so caught up by the profound complexity of my relationship with her, I didn't pay attention to what she said–although, had I paid attention, I wouldn't have understood her anyway. She talked too fast. Everyone in America did. Once in a while I caught fragments of a sentence she said and remembered the familiar sound of it: home, work, school, dress, flowers, pictures. But I needed to translate those words into Chinese to guess what she meant. By the time I was done translating and ready to continue listening to her, she'd moved on to talking about something else. Or worse, she was waiting for my response.

Cameron had dropped off his mother and gone to park the car. When he returned and found us, his face glowed, his crooked smile fit into his lopsided face. "Hey, my two favorite women in the world!" He enveloped me in a tight embrace. My inside burned with tingling excitement. I wanted to be with him so much I didn't mind being uprooted, giving up a familiar life to live in a place where I didn't understand people around me.

Looking back, part of me wants to warn my younger self to get on the next flight and run away from Cameron. He would become my nemesis. His words would replace mine. His voice would silence mine. And within weeks he would stop saying I was his favorite woman.

But another part of me knows that the hardships I was about to suffer in Texas were the refiner's fire. If I endured well, I would gain more strength and compassion. Historian Jack Weatherford writes: "Those individuals who refuse the option presented by the circumstances of life usually end up broken. Those few who reject what life offers and still find their own paths are rightfully called heroes."

Broken or heroic? Staying with Cameron or running away? It was all up to me. Ultimately, I had the agency to shape the destiny of my own choosing. In the airport that day, when life offered exciting new experiences and promised me the American dream, I chose the joy in the moment.

31

Cameron's parents' house was an 1,800-square-foot rambler built in the 1950s on a two-acre private woodland right off a highway. There was no house number on the curb because there was no sidewalk. There was no sidewalk boarding the property because, I supposed, no one walked on a highway? The only indication of this home's street address was the faded number on the mailbox that required a hawk's eyes to read.

Instead of going through the front door, everyone entered the house through the screened patio door that led into the living room with caramel-colored carpet. The Chastain siblings' senior pictures and wedding photos were in gold frames, neatly arranged on a wood-paneled wall. Cameron's older brother, Christopher, was a law student. His wife, Ginger, had small eyes and a mouthful of oversize crooked teeth. Cameron's two older sisters, Carolyn and Catherine, married two brothers.

A television was tucked in a corner, under a huge picture window. Against the walls were a loveseat and a couch in an L formation. A recliner was a Persian rug's length from the television. Outside the window was the endless, majestic woodland; no neighbors in sight.

Cameron said that his father was a self-made millionaire, successful in his real-estate business. But I didn't understand why a millionaire didn't live in a mansion like that in the movie *Gone with the Wind.* Perhaps, like my grandfather, Ah-Gung, frugality was how Cameron's father became wealthy. Who knows?

About an hour after I started unpacking in the guest bedroom, Cameron's father came home. He wore a dark suit and shiny black shoes. Glasses over his brown eyes. A meticulously trimmed mustache. A power-donut hairdo that looked like a neck pillow hung around the back of his age-spot-dotted bald head.

"Dr. Arthur Chastain," he said in a soft airy tone while stretching out his hand. I shook it. His brows furrowed tightly. The way he pursed his lips made me think the lines around his mouth weren't from smiling.

Cameron pulled out the trundle bed, and we sat on the naked mattress. Dr. Chastain sat at the edge of the top bed, on the soft, freshly laundered comforter, and looked at my open suitcase on the floor, filled with Asian stationery. "What . . . uh . . . your dad. What does he do?"

I looked to Cameron, who promptly interpreted the question into Chinese. I nodded and said, in Chinese, "Electrical engineer."

Cameron interpreted my answer into English. Dr. Chastain made a "huh" sound through his nose, not his throat, then asked, "What car does he drive?"

I heard the word *car* and immediately blurted out, "Fei–ya–te."

Dr. Chastain widened his eyes, pushing his brows high toward what would've been his hairline.

I looked up at him and enunciated each syllable clearly: "Fei–ya–te." The Chinese pronunciation of FIAT.

"Mercedes? Lexus? No?" He glared over the top of his glasses at me. I shook my head. I only understood the last word in that sentence.

"O–kaaayyy." He looked over at Cameron, who shrugged and threw his palms into the air. It looked as if they were trying not to laugh.

"Your folks coming to the wedding? They've got to book a hotel and—" He coughed into his fist. "Y'know, get everything planned out and paid for as soon as possible."

I looked to Cameron for help, who interpreted first, then took over the conversation. Dr. Chastain's brows gradually turned into a tangled mess. He scratched his scalp and said something with a pointing finger before leaving the room.

"He said we need to get married in ten days," Cameron said.

More nervous than excited, I asked, "Why the rush?"

"Well, my parents are going on vacation in ten days. He wants us to already be married when they leave us alone in their house."

"So . . . that's how much he trusts you?" I teased. But my real concern wasn't about Dr. Chastain's trust issue. I'd barely arrived in this foreign land and was emotionally, culturally, linguistically unprepared to be an American wife. Ten days wasn't enough time to fix that problem. My bigger concern, though, was that I was in the same room where the decision concerning my future was made. Why didn't anyone ask for my voice?

32

The day after I arrived in America, Cameron took me to a doctor. "To make sure you're healthy and all."

Struggling with intense jetlag, I got in the car and woke up in the clinic parking lot. Cameron led me into a bright, clean office where a nurse with a clipboard was ready to take me to an examination room. We walked down a hall decorated with posters of pudgy babies, birth announcements, and thank-you notes, then it struck me that I was seeing an OB/GYN.

Wait, what if I don't understand the doctor? Where's Cameron?

I pulled the nurse's sleeve and said, "Cam come." But she shook her head. "He said he'll wait outside."

I wasn't sure if I understood her words correctly, but I knew what the headshake meant. Maybe it was best that Cameron didn't come, I reasoned. He would be uncomfortable interpreting for me and the gynecologist. There would be times like this when I needed to take care of myself, I knew that. I just wished I'd brought my dictionary.

The nurse seated me on an examination bed. She disappeared briefly and returned with an old man in a plaid dress shirt and a pair of khaki pants. In a deep and authoritative voice, he said he was Dr. Williams and that his sons married Cameron's sisters.

"You know Christopher and Ginger? I delivered their child. I love taking care of mothers and babies." Dr. Williams smiled his whole face into a wrinkled ball.

I wanted to tell him I liked him and that I appreciated a great doctor who took pride in what he did, but I didn't have the vocabulary to tell him that in his language, so I gave him a close-lipped smile instead.

This was the first time I had ever seen a gynecologist. I didn't know what to expect. Dr. Williams must've explained to me what he would do before he did anything, but I didn't understand him. He first listened to my heart and lungs. I knew to sit still and breathe deeply. Then he performed the breast exam. I about screamed! No one had ever touched me there before. I looked at the door, wishing Cameron would come in to rescue me. But I also wished he wouldn't come in to see me being handled. To avoid Dr. Williams's eyes, I stared at the wall clock. My embarrassment must've heightened my sense of hearing, the *tick-tock* sounded like blaring honks in rush-hour Taipei traffic. I couldn't stop my fingers from tapping on the bed with the beat. But nothing prepared me for what came next—the pelvic exam. I didn't know anything more humiliating. I felt violated. Why would Cameron order this procedure without fully explaining to me beforehand? Dr. Williams was family, and I liked him, but still . . . he was a stranger, a man! I clenched my fists and bit my lip, wishing Cameron were here to hold my hand or tell me a joke to distract me.

When I got back to the waiting room, Cameron was chatting and laughing with one of the receptionists—a big-haired, square-faced, bushy-browed, cat-eyed young woman. I pulled his sleeve and told him I was ready to leave. But he wasn't. He kept talking and laughing with this girl, and I kept pacing the waiting room like I had when I was little, when Mama had mistaken our visit to the morning market for a gossip session with village housewives. More jetlagged than frustrated, I fell asleep in a chair.

When we finally walked out of the doctor's office, Cameron threw his thumb over his shoulder and said, "That girl back there? Patty. My ex-girlfriend."

"Oh." I nodded.

"Oh what?" Cameron sounded irritated.

"What do you mean *oh what*? What do you want me to say when you tell me that girl is your ex-girlfriend?"

"Be grateful, woman! Patty just stuffed a whole bag with pills for you." Cameron lifted a plastic bag. "For free!"

"What pills? Am I sick?"

Cameron snorted. "You have no idea what pills are, do you?"

His mocking shocked me. When I was twelve, I memorized the English word *pill* as the synonym of *medicine* and thought the former was the informal way of saying the latter, like *kids* and *children*. But even if I didn't know what pills really meant, I didn't deserve to be scorned.

"Cam"—I raised my voice—"if we were in Taiwan and you didn't know what a Chinese word meant, I'd explain it to you in a way you'd understand."

"But we're not in Taiwan, so you don't need to worry about me." He rolled his eyes. "You just need to thank Patty. She gave you pills!"

"But . . . is she a doctor? Why did she think I need pills?"

"No, she's not a doctor, but she makes eight bucks an hour and drives a brand-new Mustang, forgodssake! That's more than what you'll ever make in your whole life!" Cameron shook his head. "Stop questioning her qualifications. I asked her for pills so you won't get pregnant." He pointed a finger at me. "You can't get pregnant. You've got to work to put me through school. Like Patty—if I married her, she would do it without being asked."

I hadn't expected to hear about the pills or Patty or what she would do. I thought for a second, then asked Cameron what would happen after he graduated. I wondered if he meant I would then stop working. Would he want me to get pregnant? I worried I no longer had control over my body or my life.

He waved a hand past his shoulder, as if shooing a fly. "That'll be in, what—six years? Anything can happen in six years. For now, just take your pills every day."

Who would've thought at the time this was a prophecy? Instead of six years, our marriage would only last for sixteen months. And not getting pregnant in this marriage actually turned out to be a tremendous blessing.

Now that I knew what *pills* meant in English, I remembered their horrible side effects Mama had warned me of. But her words didn't stand in the face of Cameron's command. I was going to marry Cameron and planned to live with him for the rest of my life, not with her. Plus, taking pills was nothing; why did she make a big deal about it? Didn't she know it would actually help me keep track of the day in a week? Monday, Tuesday, Wednesday, and every day that I gave up everything back home to live among strangers in a strange land, for the love of Cameron.

33

In Taiwan, traditionally, the groom's family paid for the engagement photoshoot, the clothing rental, the wedding reception, the guests' traveling expenses and hotel stays, the honeymoon, everything. I'd expected Cameron's family to pay for a week-long deluxe wedding photo session on a beach resort with a team of photographers, videographers, bride's secretaries, wardrobe assistants, hair and makeup artists. A reception in a grand hotel that lasted all night, during which Cameron and I changed into a different outfit at the end of each background song. Then, a trip to the Mediterranean Sea as soon as the reception was over.

Instead, we got our one-pose photo taken in the back room of a dank pharmacy. "YOU can't afford a wedding photographer," Cameron said. And that's when I learned that in America the bride paid to carry the groom's name and his children.

What—the—heck?

When we got home from the pharmacy, Mrs. Chastain summoned us to her bedroom. Natural light streamed in through the windows, bathing the bed, dresser, and night stands in a warm glow. Classical music softly played in the background.

"What size are you?" Cameron interpreted her question to me.

American size? How would I know? I shrugged.

From her closet, Mrs. Chastain took out a wedding dress with a beaded top, lace sleeves, and a long train. She pushed the dress against my back. "Hmmm ... right length. Catherine's about your size. This might work. Good. Try it on."

"Catherine's old dress? Brilliant!" Cameron hugged his mother, winked at me, and left the room.

Mrs. Chastain helped me step into the dress. I pulled up my hair, and she pulled up the zipper. Wordlessly. She pulled and tucked the heavily decorated fabric on me, making occasional "uh-huh" sounds that I wasn't sure was her admiration for the dress or her approval of my physique or something else altogether. At this moment, I experienced both excitement and disappointment. This, right here, wasn't my vision. It wasn't exactly my dream.

Sure, I was from humble beginnings, but I'd allowed myself to fantasize this once-in-a-lifetime opportunity of glamour: me on a platform, in a floor-to-ceiling mirrored room of a bridal shop in Taipei. Hand on hip, pin in teeth, measuring-tape necklace, glasses on nose tip, the tailor examined my dress and nodded rhythmically to the beats of Pachelbel's Canon in D. Her assistant took pictures and notes of the dresses I'd tried on and filed them for my decision-making.

Now, as I embraced the reality of becoming a bride, I wanted so much more. But I was also okay with what was happening here, in a quiet small town, in a 1950s dark-paneled bedroom, with a stranger who would soon be my mother-in-law. All things had led me here.

I wanted to tell Mrs. Chastain her son was the prize I'd won for enduring a crappy childhood. I wanted to tell her I wished to show her Taiwan someday. But my throat was empty; no sounds to tell her anything.

She put a bridal veil on my head, led me to a body-length mirror, and nodded. "Perfect," she said. Before the mirror, we silently looked at each other's reflection. We looked like two characters in a framed photograph, like two women of different races coming together in a world-peace poster, cordially smiling. I realized this brief moment with Mrs. Chastain was a blessing I'd long dreamed of—belonging to a family where outward expression of mother-daughter love was attainable. A luxurious wedding wasn't necessary for me to feel special after all.

34

Most of my friends in Taiwan dutifully followed their fathers' faith tradition in Buddhism. Since my baptism, they'd frequently asked about my atypical religious belief. Always, the first thing I clarified was that *Mormon* isn't the correct word to identify myself or those of my faith. We're members of the Church of Jesus Christ of Latter-day Saints. Yes, we call ourselves saints, but by no means do we mean we're perfect. In fact, Nelson Mandela frequently said, "I'm no saint—that is, unless you think a saint is a sinner who keeps on trying." So, we're really latter-day sinners who keep on trying to be like Christ.

Second, the church members keep the Law of Chastity. Specifically, no sexual relations before marriage, and then absolute fidelity in marriage. Old-fashioned, yes, but it's the exact structure and model I needed to feel secure in my future marriage. My baba had never been able to commit to one woman at a time. I wasn't sure if that was his habit or addiction, but I knew it was definitely his choice. The way he simultaneously maintained multiple intimate relationships with different women caused nothing but destructive pain for all those involved, and indirectly gave me hell to grow up in. I simply had no desire to marry a man who chose to live that way.

My friends asked, "That's nice, but does being a Mormon man guarantee he won't cheat?"

Well, of course not. Everyone has God-given agency and

is free to choose for himself. Essentially, the Law of Chastity is an honor system. In the church belief, a marital covenant is between the couple and God. A three-way promise. A triangular commitment: God on top, the couple apart at the bottom. The couple promises to love and cleave unto each other and none else. God promises to bless them with an eternal family relationship as they grow closer together in body, mind, and spirit. A couple committed to each other will have a spiritual result. They move upward toward God and will eventually become one at the top. One in purpose, in righteousness, in all things. And when a couple becomes one, there's no cheating, deceiving, or betraying. They've become like God.

Third, the prophet David O. McKay taught, "No other success can compensate for failure in the home." Because the church emphasizes heavily the importance of family and encourages members to not delay in starting a family, countless church members get married in their early twenties, as Cameron and I were about to do.

My friends asked, "That's nice, but how wise is it to get married so young?"

Well, it's all relative. The concept of *young* is subjective in different eras, regions, and cultures. Back in the 1940s Taiwan, my Ah-Gung and Ah-Po got married when they were nineteen and eighteen. They loved each other and stayed married for the rest of their lives. Marrying young doesn't necessarily constitute an unwise life decision. Breaking marital vows does.

Fourth, to keep the Law of Chastity, most single adults in the church don't cohabit.

My friends argued, "How do you know if you can marry and live with someone if you don't cohabit first?"

Well, my Ah-Gung and Ah-Po got together through a village matchmaker; they'd never met before their wedding. Ah-Po said that *every* marriage requires both spouses to have faith that the relationship will be happy, fulfilling, and successful. Then they need to work intentionally to nurture that belief into reality.

It's the same in all eras, all regions, and all cultures. The ages of a couple and cohabitation don't determine a successful, happy marriage. Faith, sacrifices, and fierce fidelity from both parties do.

It sounds ironic, but despite being deprived of parental love, I'd always wanted to be a mother. Possibly, in my four-year-old subconscious mind, I wished to save myself from abandonment and neglect, but I couldn't. To console myself, I reasoned that I could save my future child instead. It was in the invisible, intangible future generations of my flesh and blood that I had the freedom to imagine the family connections I yearned for.

When I was in first grade, my teacher gave the class the universal writing prompt of *When I grow up, I want to be* . . . Naturally, I wrote *I want to be a wife and a mother.* Then I drew a smiling man next to the adult me cradling a baby in a football-shaped swaddle. My avant-garde, feminist teacher promptly called me to her desk. "You don't need to stay home and raise children. You should be a nurse or a teacher. Think about that!"

I nodded, assuming that was the response she would want. But I didn't understand how she could tell me what I should want. Her suggestion made me think that I didn't plan my future right, hence I wasn't right in the head. She probably tried to persuade me to create my financial independence, which is what most of my Taiwanese girlfriends did, growing up to be career women who didn't stay home to raise children—that was what grandparents and daycare centers were for, they said. With their own money, they went on girls-only trips to New York, Paris, Milan, in designer outfits, with handbags and sunglasses.

But fifteen years after the teacher's counsel, I was still dying to be a wife and a mother. As a wife and a mother, I would also be a nurse and a teacher. I would tend to my baby's needs. Feed him. Help him learn to walk. Teach him to tie his shoes, ride a bike, read a book. Being a stay-at-home mom might not be the most popular thing a modern-day woman pursues, but it felt right to me. I wanted to be a mother who devoted her all to God, her husband, and her children. In a way, that's why the church teachings about eternal family resonated with me when missionaries first taught me the gospel.

I believed Cameron would likewise desire to be the best husband and father he could be, and we would live by the church teachings to create a happy family together. With an understanding of my weaknesses, limitations, and uncertainty of how my future role as a wife in a foreign culture would unfold, I worked with what I had: faith.

35

O n the tenth day after my arrival in America, hours before
Cameron's parents left on vacation, Cameron, his parents,
and I drove seven and a half hours to the Dallas Temple of the
Church of Jesus Christ of Latter-day Saints for our wedding.

The interior of the temple was impeccably clean. White carpet, white curtains, white walls, symbolic of the pure and glorious
nature of God's Kingdom.

Three old men in white suits ushered us into a brightly lit
room for the ceremony. In the center of the room, under a crystal
chandelier, was an altar shaped like a vaulting horse. Cameron
and I knelt on the padded platform that ringed the base of the
altar, facing each other and holding hands across the altar. His
parents sat in the front row of guest seats. Two of the men sat on
either side of the room as witnesses. The third man stood at the
head of the altar and performed the ceremony. Cameron and I
promised God we would stay true. Of course, I didn't understand
everything said during the ceremony, but I didn't doubt for a second that becoming a wife was what I wanted.

After the ceremony, we took pictures on the temple grounds.
Dr. Chastain had a roll of Kodak film, a wedding gift to Cameron
and me. He posed us: where to stand, sit, and hug. After taking
twenty-four shots, he replaced it with a new roll and announced it
was Mrs. Chastain's turn. We stood next to her in front of a bed
of flowers. When the second roll of film ran out, Dr. Chastain

clapped his hands and said, "Okay, we're off to the airport now." Mrs. Chastain kissed Cameron on the cheek, then hugged me good-bye.

Chinese people didn't hug.

Especially not mothers- and daughters-in-law.

Thanks to gender inequality in Chinese culture—a curse that keeps on cursing—unwedded girls were conditioned to fear-hate and tolerate their future mothers-in-law. Traditionally, a daughter-in-law, deemed as marriage property, lived with and served her husband and his parents. She would get up before sunrise and work in rice fields, orchards, and farms. She also needed to cook, clean, and launder the entire family's clothes. Oh yes, she was expected to bear many sons while continuing to work during the pregnancy, till the day of delivery. In the 1960s as the Taiwanese economy surged, she would likely join the rising force of career women and would be harshly criticized for her iconoclastic choice of abandoning her responsibility as a stay-at-home mother. But that's not all. A Chinese wife was to turn a blind eye on her husband's infidelity, drinking problem, or gambling addiction. When a woman was mistreated like that—not only for a day but for her entire married life—she inevitably turned bitter. Her only hope was that, if she survived her marital hell, someday she could take out decades' worth of unjust suffering on her daughter-in-law. In the five-thousand-year Chinese history, there was no tradition of this kind of hostility among fathers- and sons-in-law. So really, who could blame a Chinese mother-in-law? The culture made her mad!

But I had an entire galaxy of shiny stars in my bosom; each one represented my love for my mother-in-law. We were practically still strangers, but I sensed her willingness to welcome me into the family in her shy, quiet way. She hugged me and said she loved me. The power of her simple words left me with overwhelming gratitude for her choice to look beyond our differences to accept me.

I thought I got a mother in her that day.

How naïve of me!

How could I forget that anyone could say "I love you" and not mean it, or change her mind later? In the end she stood by her son, helping him to abandon me. How could I ever forget blood is thicker than water?

The Chinese believed a married daughter was like water thrown out of the window—she couldn't be returned. Disowned by Baba, I was like a baby thrown out with bathwater. Now married, I definitely couldn't return. The Chastains were my new family now, Cameron my first family member by choice. Although, even in the beginning of our life together, Cameron and I didn't share the same experience. In our wedding bliss, Cameron said he was the luckiest man alive to have his two favorite women in each of his arms. Lucky him indeed, starting and ending our marriage with his mom by his side. Me? I wondered how it felt to be hugged and loved by my mama.

Perhaps on the night of the light-switch incident, at the same moment I froze outside of apartment 21 in panic, shock, and disbelief, Mrs. Chastain was hugging Cameron in their heated kitchen, the aroma of pot roast wafting in the air, Beethoven's music, *Wellington's Victory*, playing in the background.

"I love YOU," she probably said.

36

I'd thought I spoke English, at least a little, until I came to America.

A couple days after the wedding, Cameron took me to meet Dr. Chastain's business partner, Dave. In the exact moment when Cameron pulled into Dave's office parking lot and killed the engine, I experienced this almost-tangible feeling, as though my lips were glued together with invisible superglue, then sealed with invisible duct tape. As a result, English—a subject I'd studied from seventh grade through my sophomore year in university—disappeared. The language drained out of me, evaporating like sweat. My English-speaking days came to a full stop the same time Cameron's car stopped. I was suddenly struck mute in English, and fear overcame me. Fear of talking to people. Fear of letting people detect my accent if I tried to speak. Fear of letting people look down on me and judge me for my weaknesses and imperfections. Fear of being a disgrace, of making Cameron lose face.

If a language is a longing for home, then my budding sense of belonging in this new homeland had just mysteriously vanished.

37

C ameron and I got married on a Friday; the following Monday he took me to school to register for classes. What a new concept, choosing my own classes!

At Fu-Jen University, at the beginning of each semester, I received a class schedule from the German Department. If I followed the schedule to a T and didn't fail any class, I would safely graduate in exactly four years with exactly the same classmates who entered the freshman year with me. Now, in a new education system, I surrendered to the new reality that Cameron would replace Fu-Jen University's German Department and be in charge of my academic planning.

He signed me up for Statistics, Linguistics, Medical Sociology, and American Sign Language—all required classes for *his* first year of graduate studies in audiology. "So we can share textbooks. Do you have any idea how much money we'll save?" he said.

Of course I didn't.

On average, a university textbook in Taiwan was around $10 USD, so Cameron's rationale behind take-the-same-class-to-save-on-textbooks was bewildering.

Just for fun, he added a bonus class to my schedule: Physical Education.

In Taiwan I had always done well in school. Never had I thought I would become a struggling student. Now, in class, whenever the teacher, the students, and Cameron laughed together at something and I had no idea what was going on, I looked down at the desk and hoped the bell would ring so I could leave. At home, I didn't know how to tackle homework without first spending four, five hours looking up almost every word in a chapter in the textbook, all the while anxious that I might run out of time in a day and a night to finally understand the same concept that the class already did—while laughing together. If both Cameron and I wanted to be straight-A students, then sharing textbooks to save money was a really dumb idea. I finally asked him to buy me a tape recorder so I could listen to the recording of each class at home, instead of keeping the textbooks to myself all night.

In the school racquetball building, before the P.E. teacher showed up, female students always grouped together to chat and laugh and touch up on their makeup. I squatted in a corner, pulling a blank tape out of my backpack and labeling it *P.E. Racquetball* along with the date. Then I took out the tape I'd used to record a previous class and slid the new one into the recorder.

One day, the P.E. teacher entered the building and stopped in front of me. Staring and pointing at my newly acquired study aid, he looked as if he'd just witnessed a snake do a somersault. "Www—whaaa—the?"

This time I understood exactly why the teacher and the classmates laughed together.

Cameron and I lived in the sunroom-turned-bedroom in the back of his parents' house, next to the laundry room. My spirit withered and shrank in that space, a little bit every day. I often curled up into a ball in bed, crying. All familiar things were an ocean away. My smile was lost. My happiness faded, like the number on the Chastains' mailbox.

38

C ameron and I were both straight-A students—a mighty miracle for me. However, he constantly urged me to drop out of school and work full-time to put him through school. "All my ex-girlfriends would've done it had I married them!"

While others collect rare coins, vintage stamps, or baseball cards, Cameron collected memories of his ex-girlfriends as a badge of honor that he carefully stored in his imaginary hall of fame. His romance history was a cherished validation of his self-worth. His constant reminiscence of those girls turned a part of me hard, like war did to a soldier. But I was no soldier. I was a wife in the Land of the Free and the Home of the Brave; I was free to be anything I wanted. So I chose to be the bravest wife I could be—working among American professionals.

By law, foreign students could only work on campus. I got a job working with Cameron in the international student office, making $4.75 per hour helping process prospective Chinese-speaking students' admission and scholarship applications. When Chinese students called our office from China, Taiwan, Singapore, or various parts of the world to inquire about their admission status, I answered their questions. Although only a student employee, I found gratification and empowerment in this job. The students I helped took me seriously, and I liked to think I had deciding authority over their academic future to change their lives.

On Saturdays, as our side job, Cameron and I mowed lawns

at the apartments Dr. Chastain owned in nearby towns. I rode the lawnmower, he operated the weed eater, and it took us roughly an hour to mow a half-acre lot that paid $40, nearly ten times more than what I made in the office. Cameron wasn't kidding when he said a full-time lawn management business should be my future. "We'd be so rich! Think about it: one hundred percent of the mowing money goes straight into the pocket. No taxes. Better yet, no schooling required. You don't have to suffer through college and deal with recording classes and homework and tests. How frickin' cool is that? None of my ex-girlfriends go to college. They do just fine being hairstylists, nailists, receptionists. Had I married them, they would've put me through school, no question. You should do it too."

I had to really think beyond his words to understand their meaning. I wasn't familiar with Cameron's upbringing. We lived through much of the 1970s, the entire 80s, and two years of the 90s with bicontinental, bilingual, bicultural differences. Besides basic human needs, we shared almost nothing in common. I suspected he wanted one of the two in a spouse:

1. A trophy wife with supermodel looks. All of his beauty-pageant-contestant ex-girlfriends fit in this category.
2. A money-making machine who would put him through school. This seemed to be a common phenomenon in the church, where family is the central element of the doctrine and young single adults are encouraged to marry and start a family without delay. At the time, in the 1990s, many church members met and married in college, and the young wives—out of their free will and choice—commenced the self-sacrifice pattern of a Mrs. degree: dropped out of college, worked full-time, put their husbands through school, birthed babies, and became stay-at-home moms, then cake-baking

grandmas. Some lucky ones, such as Mrs. Chastain, returned to school to finish their degrees when their children were older.

Cameron grew up in that culture and naturally had that expectation for his wife. I admitted that, for me, attending university was a luxurious privilege. Most of my childhood friends, girl cousins, and neighbors didn't. I had been blessed enough. I was almost convinced to drop out—just almost—until one day Cameron said, "Mowing lawns is how you measure up to my ex-girlfriends."

"Since when did I have to measure up to anyone? Don't you understand? Mowing lawns isn't my life's calling!" I roared, even though I had no idea what my calling was.

True, the green grass was endless, the green money was limitless, and I loved the long, distraction-free thinking time I had while mowing. But I just couldn't see myself riding a lawnmower for the rest of my life. That image brought me a deep sense of guilt toward my ancestors.

One unforgettable lesson Baba had taught me happened when I was little and riding on the back of his motorcycle. Whether he planned it or not, wherever we went we always rode past a construction site. Baba would point at the dusty, sweaty workers and say, "If you don't study hard and get a really good education, that's what you'll be doing when you grow up. You want to be a laborer and burn all day like them, or study hard and work in an office?"

Behind Baba, I yelled, "I'll study hard and work in an office!" Even though I couldn't see his face, I imagined he was satisfied with my answer. A grin, even, at my promise.

Receiving a higher education and having an out-of-the-weather career meant glory to the clan and honor to the ancestors. I feared if I dropped out now, I would be stuck with a

Mrs. degree forever. Surely, generations of my progenitors would shake their heads at the lawn-mowing idea. I imagined my great-great-great-grandpa Hong, a silk road merchant, scolding. "Aiya! You sacrificed the hard-earned privilege of a college education to become WHAAAT?"

What exactly was the right thing to do? Was I selfish, unwilling to sacrifice my education so Cameron could continue his? Was his education more important than mine? Why couldn't we have equal opportunity?

39

The missionaries of the Church of Jesus Christ of Latter-day Saints live by a structure that balances the physical, emotional, spiritual, and social aspects of a healthy lifestyle. During my service, I had a fixed daily schedule of doing the same thing at the same time: pray, study the scriptures, work out, proselytize, record mindful reflections in my journal, and so on. Everything I did then was out of my love for and willingness to serve God. In return, God blessed me with immense joy.

In the 1990s, missionaries were only allowed to phone home twice a year, on Mother's Day and Christmas. They were, however, encouraged to write home weekly. During Cameron's two-year service, his then-girlfriend, Thelma Tick, called him from Texas almost every night. The mere fact that I knew about it was proof enough to demonstrate Cameron's unique character. He didn't keep his rule-breaking behavior a secret. Instead, he broadcast it, boasting about a girl waiting faithfully for him at home, and priding himself on being the only one among two hundred missionaries in the Taipei Mission to frequently receive a love call. His choice of action caused other missionaries to shake their heads in disgust. And I was sorely disappointed in his immaturity. Ironically, besides being attracted to Cameron's looks, I was also helplessly attracted to the dark poetry of his brazen badness. He blatantly boasted of winning street fights in his teenage years and how his road rage often turned into a car chase. He was a rebel, no doubt. And that rebellion had a strange gripping power on me. I couldn't escape.

Only five months after being released from my mission, I was now a new wife who desired to continue living the same devoted spiritual life. I thought Cameron and I could start our own Christ-centered family by following the missionary lifestyle we were both familiar with—minus the twelve-hour-a-day proselytizing part, of course. But every morning I prayed alone. During the day I studied the scriptures alone. At bedtime I still prayed alone. Cameron took me to church for the first few Sundays after we got married, then he skipped a few weeks to watch a football game or go fishing or play racquetball. Pretty soon he stopped attending church entirely. One weekend when I suggested we go and worship in the Dallas Temple, he yelled, "You obviously don't know how much that would cost, huh? Seven and a half hours there; seven and a half hours back. You're paying for the gas? The hotel stay too, Mrs. Self-Righteous? And each of us missing fifteen hours of work—how much would that be, huh? All that for what? To make your stupid God happy?"

I didn't need further proof to know that God no longer existed in his heart. I could be wrong, though. Maybe he didn't lose his faith. Maybe he never believed in God to begin with, and deep down he had never been interested in spirituality. Maybe, for him, serving a mission was obligatory. Maybe leaving behind religion and venturing into a new territory of godlessness now was his rite of passage. Whatever it was, we no longer shared the same spiritual belief.

But that's okay! I thought. *I worked with this kind of people every day on my mission. I've got this!*

I loved Cameron and wanted the best for him, even a celestial life. I had the foolish notion to change him, to convert him, to influence him into a saint, to drag him to Heaven. I thought I could. I thought I was the one. I thought that was my calling.

Ninety-Nine Fire Hoops

In high school I learned two rhyming words: *ignorant* and *arrogant*, with assorted letters arranged in different orders before the word *ant*. With their different definitions, I now understand they mean the same thing: me. They mean me with my *Fix Cameron* mentality. I was ignorant and arrogant when, in reality, I was nothing but an ant, so easy to destroy, even by something as insignificant as a catalog image and the ghosts of Cameron's ex-girlfriends—his ex-ghostfriends.

40

O ne day Cameron brought the mail into the kitchen, picked out a rolled-up Victoria's Secret catalog, and went into the bathroom. Sometime later he emerged, pointing at a nearly naked lingerie model kneeling on a bed. She grabbed a handful of her long, unkempt blonde hair to the back of her head; her other hand pulled her bikini down, as if undressing herself. Her bra was too small; her breasts overflowed. She bit her blood-red lower lip and looked seductively into the camera.

"God, Allison! Why can't you look like this?" Cameron groaned.

I looked up from my homework at our bedroom desk, horrified at the catalog image and his words. "You've got to be kidding! Who does that in real life?"

He chucked the catalog in my direction; it landed on the floor. "This girl does important work, forgodssake. She's men's delight. Look at her boobs!"

I wanted to punch him so hard that he wouldn't be able to ever speak again. "Cam, it's female objectification. Glorified pornography!" I said in Chinese, wishing he would understand. But even if he didn't, how could he not know the emotional damage he inflicted on me by saying what he did? Wasn't the hurt universal, no matter the language spoken?

To me, Mother Teresa was "a girl doing important work." And the word *boobs* reminded me of a mother breastfeeding her baby. Cameron misused the sacred nature of a woman's body to imply his lust, and I was supposed to conform to that catalog image to feed his carnal fantasy? He himself didn't even remotely resemble a Calvin Klein male model; how dare he expect me to look like a lingerie model? Maybe this was all too hard for him to comprehend, but if I did look like that Victoria's Secret model, why would I be with him?

Cameron picked up the catalog and flipped through the pages slowly, his finger tracing the outline of the model's silhouette. "You're overreacting," he mumbled without looking up. I watched the same finger he used to touch my hair, my cheek, my hand, now touching another girl vicariously, slowly, carefully, as if playing with fire, and my heart caught a wild fire of jealousy and rage. I was in his sight but not in his heart or mind. Was there even a word for this kind of betrayal?

"Don't forget to wash your hands, Cam," I sneered. "You just left the bathroom!"

41

When did Cameron's pornography addiction start? In his childhood or teenage years? Was he alone or with friends? Did he say, "Just one look," and was never able to look away?

Soon after the Victoria's Secret incident, Cameron found something else in the mailbox that was bathroom-worthy. Out of the bathroom, with a magazine in hand, he came to the desk where I was doing homework and asked, in a hushed voice, if I wanted to buy *it*. He pointed at an advertisement in a tiny classified square on the back of the magazine. Plagued with myopia, I squinted and still couldn't make out the words.

"Just tell me what it is, Cam. I can't read that far."

"This, babe, it's a . . . uh . . . video!" A mysterious grin spread across his face. He winked, pointed a finger gun at me, and looked toward his parents' bedroom, as if checking to see if they could hear him. "For husband and wife." He lowered his voice almost to a whisper. "Sexy stuff!"

"Cam, it's pornography. It corrupts your soul!" I shut my textbook so hard my pen jumped on the desk. "See no evil."

Cameron wiped the smirk off his face and chucked the magazine on the desk. "Shit! Quit being self-righteous! You can't tell me you're not tempted."

The rage from the Victoria's Secret incident returned. Now I really wanted to punch his face—a revolting sight at this moment.

"Look, if you're worried that my mom and dad will find out we order this stuff, don't. It'll come in a blank package with no sender's address. Plus, a married couple should totally watch this together. It enhances love life." He knotted his arms before his chest. One of his eyebrows moved up and down at the word *enhances*.

What brutally crushed my confidence was the unshakeable fact that Cameron had offered porn stars exclusive access to the enclosed space of his head, granting them permanent residence to entertain him in his private, intimate thoughts. I viewed this as him actively having emotional affairs with those strange women. Who was I to him, then? And the lame excuse he used about husband and wife watching porn together? I counter argued, "Why take off your pants to fart? Just fart already!"

"What the—" Cameron laughed so hard he bent at his waist.

"Look! If you want to enhance your love life, then focus your effort to enhance it with your wife. Why involve porn stars?"

Would teaming up with Cameron to be a porn-watching couple really enhance our love life? How about our spiritual life? Would pornography bring us inner peace, inspire us to seek after virtues? From the apostle M. Russell Ballard I learned that each of us is first, foremost, and always a spiritual being. So when we choose to put our carnal nature ahead of our spiritual nature, we are choosing something contrary to our real, organic, authentic spiritual selves. Why would I be untrue to myself?

What saddened me was the way Cameron was positively confident in the knowledge of a discreet package. Did the sender's and the addressee's effort to hide their secretive activity—so no one would make the association of their names with porn—mean that they were embarrassed by, or guilty about, the porn business they were involved in? Did it mean that, deep down, they knew porn was destructive? What happened to Cameron, then, that caused him to lose his ability to discern right from wrong? How would it be if, instead of colorblind, he were pornblind?

Never able to see porn.

Never had the chance to say, "Just one look."

42

Cameron left our bedroom in the middle of the night, same time every night, without even needing to set the alarm clock. I'd never imagined this would be part of my life, but one winter night after he left, I snuck out from the back door, barefoot, walked around the house to the patio, and crouched beneath the living room picture window to stalk him in the bone-chilling darkness. I knew he was in the living room because the television was on. Somehow I also knew that if I peeked at the television screen to see what he watched in the middle of the night every night, my heart would crack in half.

I peeked anyway.

A naked man and a naked woman sported in bed.

The cold of the patio bricks penetrated my soles, shooting up my legs, my torso, my chest. My body tensed and my muscles quivered. My pulse sped and my heart pounded at the sight of Cameron sinking deeply into the recliner, his eyes fixed on the screen, his fist to his teeth. I wanted to get a hammer from the shed, storm into the living room, whack the TV screen, and yell, "I'm here. I'm all you want. Right here!" But why would I punish him when, in reality, he didn't commit any crimes? He looked so innocent and pure, just watching a late-night television show like a poor insomniac. Then again, why did the image of him at this moment ignite such blazing rage inside me?

This Cameron right here wasn't the same guy in the days of

the past when he kissed me across the wedding altar; when he put a ring on my finger; when he said, at our first meeting, "Hello, I'm Elder Chastain. Nice meeting you." At this moment he felt like a stranger from a distant land that my feet couldn't travel to.

I tiptoed back to our room, unable to calm down and rest. I lay in bed, weeping and shaking. My third-grade science teacher taught that if our feet were cold, our entire body would be cold. My feet were freezing now. I moved into the lotus position and rubbed my soles vigorously together, but the friction didn't create enough heat to warm my body. My science teacher also taught that in extreme cold, body heat from someone else's tight embrace was a great way to restore body temperature. Cameron was my someone else. But he was with his own someone else, his space in our marriage bed an icy vacancy.

I was the insomniac that night.

When Cameron returned to bed, I stayed silently awake beside him through his farting, snoring, and teeth grinding. The next morning when he woke up, I confronted him. He flipped the comforter forcibly to cover my face. "That's what American men do!" he yelled. "Last I checked, it's still a free country. I can do whatever I want!" He stomped into the bathroom and slammed the door, drawing a line between us.

One of the scriptures counsels, "Stand ye in holy places, and be not moved" (Doctrine and Covenants 87:8). The bathroom was Cameron's holy place, his sanctuary, his emotional, spiritual sacred grounds where he retreated to escape my confrontation, to calm down and search for peace. I remained out of it, never to enter. Although alone and lonely, I stood in my own holy place. As Hafiz writes, *This place where you are right now, God circled on a map for you.*

I'd traveled across the globe to Cameron's America, 273 times larger than my homeland Taiwan, so vast, so airy, so spacious, but there was no room for me to stand in his free country. We couldn't stand on the same ground as one unified couple.

Looking back, it's clear that, in my indignation, I forgot Cameron had God-given agency to choose for himself, and I needed to respect his choice. I forgot that, as a porn addict, Cameron was still a precious son of God, after all.

43

One day Cameron received a letter. As soon as he finished reading it, he got on the phone, frantic and upset. All I could gather from his angry tone was the word *video*.

Soon, Cameron hung up and stormed into the bedroom where I was doing homework. I knew to stay quiet. He walked past me to the laundry room next door, opening and slamming the cabinet doors, throwing laundry baskets against the wall, spewing explosive, venomous maledictions, among which were hints to the cause of his fury: overdue, penalty, hundreds of dollars, Thelma.

Thelma Tick and Cameron, high school sweethearts who had been engaged before he was assigned to serve a mission in Taiwan. Per Cameron's request, while he was overseas, Dr. Chastain paid for Thelma's food, contact lenses, gas for the car, phone bills, insurance, clothes, shoes, makeup, and—heaven forbid—shampoo in a twelve-ounce bottle that cost $140. However, during Cameron's two-year absence, despite their rule-breaking behavior of frequent international phone calls, she married someone else and moved away, leaving behind a debt for Cameron to settle with Dr. Chastain. Unbeknown to Cameron, Thelma also rented movies from a local video store in his name. This day Cameron received a letter from a debt collection agency for two years' worth of penalties that Thelma never paid in video rental late fees.

Cameron was now pacing the laundry room, tension building up for the coming tempest. When the phone rang, he raced to it.

"Traitor, you pay!" he yelled. Strangely, a minute later, in a voice that sounded of hidden shame, he said, "She's Taiwanese."

I strung all the clues together to make up a hypothesis that turned out to be one-hundred-percent accurate: Cameron called Thelma's family to pass the late fee news to Thelma, who then called Cameron to assure him she would take care of it. She proceeded to take advantage of the occasion to verify the rumor that his wife was indeed a foreigner.

In a place where almost everyone was born, married, and died in the same small town, Cameron's and my coming-together made a brow-raising, rebellious statement. Cameron worried that others might make the false assumption that no girls in town wanted him, leaving him no choice but to settle with a woman of color from a "middle-class country," so he commanded me not to get fat on him, always wear makeup, and always look sexy in public.

He really should've married a manikin.

But why should a woman of color from any country stay skinny, wear makeup, and look sexy to not fail her husband? What part of her requires an artificial appearance to hide? Her homeland? Her culture? Her accent? Are those her flaws, shame, and imperfections that make her husband lose face?

I continued to wear Cameron's shapeless, formless T-shirts that looked like tunics; continued to tie a belt around my waist to hold up Cameron's baggy jeans, with the hem rolled up; continued to refuse to wear makeup. I offered no apologies for my simple defiance.

He said my disobedience pissed him off.

I said I didn't know what part of my face I needed to make up for.

"Isn't smart the new sexy?" I asked.

"If you believe that, then you're both ugly and stupid!"

"What does that make you then?"

Petty, petty Cameron became speechless.

It didn't require a phone conversation longer than an hour to inform Thelma of the trouble she'd caused, but it did. Then it took even longer—days, weeks—before Cameron finally stopped talking about Thelma's private parts. I never knew any man could be that filthy-minded. But this was a man who worshipped pornography, so there's that. If I could get into Cameron's head, I imagine I would see myself forced to stand next to Thelma in a beauty contest where he was the sole judge. Why else would he click his tongue and shake his head disapprovingly, saying, "Allison, you loser. Thelma's got bigger hair, bigger boobs, and a bigger ass"?

People say everything is bigger in Texas. It's true. Big houses. Big trucks. Big boats. I had been pushed into an acid pool of jealousy, drowning in Cameron's ex-ghostfriends' ghostly shadows. But no one knew to rescue the insignificantly tiny me. After all, the pool was Texas size.

44

A few weeks after the video incident, one sunny Saturday afternoon, I sat in the passenger's seat of the 1982 Volvo Cameron and I had purchased together, as he drove down the one-lane country road lined with lush green trees and vibrant wildflowers. Cloudless blue was above us. Grass scent floated in the air. A soft breeze tousled my hair. Abruptly, Cameron pulled over to make way for a parade of cars with lit headlights. As we idled quietly by the roadside, more cars with lit headlights formed a single file behind us.

"What's going on?" I whispered.

"Funeral procession. We wait. It's how we Texans show respect."

This was new to me. Not that Texans' gentlemanly ways surprised me, no. Rather, it was the gracious way they responded to a funeral procession. Where and when I grew up, funeral processions weren't conducted in such a reverent manner. In fact, they could sometimes turn into a riotous social, cultural, religious disarray that made the living wish to die.

Back home, when someone passed away, a vinyl tent deep and wide enough to block traffic in an alleyway would be set up in front of the home of the dead. It served as an outdoor chapel for viewing, dirge singing, and ritual performing. Yes, the neighbors would have to take a detour home for seven to ten days while the tent was up. Oh yes, they would have to endure the Buddhist or Daoist monks' chanting over a microphone day in and day out. And yes, they would also have to tolerate the earsplitting cacophony of a band: the shrill of trumpets, the hollow clanking of cymbals, the hammering of a gong, and the professional mourner howling over a loudspeaker. It was as if these people just showed up at the tent for a week of free play, never rehearsed, never harmonized.

Death ritual in Taiwan was a wailing plea to the heavens, a roaring petition to the earth, for the return of a departed spirit. But who could complain? I mean—gosh!—one only dies once; let him have a festive farewell. Everyone will get a turn.

Then, there was the Taiwanese parade to the cemetery:

A pickup truck about the size of a Toyota Tacoma was the hearse. The casket was loaded onto the open bed. The band members were seated on both sides of the bed and played all the way to the graveyard. Following the truck were other vehicles carrying the family of the dead. No one on the street would pull over and wait in single file with their headlights on to show respect. Nope. People would do whatever they could to quickly pass the funeral parade on the narrow road. Some might even avert their eyes to avoid catching the ill fortune of death, as death was considered something of a plague. That was why neighbors of the dead pasted a strip of red paper on their front door, akin to the Hebrew Passover in Moses's time, when the blood of sheep was brushed on their door posts so the Destruction Angel—death—would pass them over.

Death ritual in Texas was honoring the dead by reverently stopping a clock, for the loving memory of a finished life.

As I waited quietly with Cameron for the river of cars to pass, as I pondered the cultural differences in death ritual, I sensed that our marriage, in fact, was slowly dying. It was as though we dragged our injured relationship toward its grave, a step a day, the way a wounded animal goes into the woods to die.

45

After the funeral procession passed, Cameron drove us to a deserted field. Nothing was in sight except two trailer homes next to each other on a dirt patch. A middle-aged man sat on a stepstool with tools spread out on the ground, a brown dog sleeping by his feet.

"Hey, Tom!" Cameron waved.

The man looked up with a huge yellow crooked-toothed smile. He stood up to shake Cameron's hand and pointed at me. "Your lady?"

Cameron dog-collared the scruff of my neck with his hand. "Yep! Goes by Allison."

I wanted to kick him in the groin.

Immediately after we got married, Cameron started dog-collaring me, only in public. No one had ever done it to me, and I had never seen anyone do it to another human being. I believed this gesture reflected his desire to control me, to grab my nape and dictate to me where to go and when to stop. I always resented it but never had the guts to stop him.

"You did good!" The man patted Cameron on the shoulder and nodded. He took off his baseball cap and extended his greasy hand to me. "Tom. Howdy!"

I shook it.

"There's a funeral today," Cameron said, looking behind him into the vast field.

"Yeah, that's Bob. You know Bob? LeBlanc? Time to go, I guess." Tom put his baseball cap back on. "Soon it'll be Pop." He sighed. There was a brief silence before Tom cleared his throat and said, "You here for Pop?"

"Yes, sir." Cameron nodded. "He awake?"

Tom shrugged and pointed at one of the trailers behind him.

Cameron threw me the car key. "Wait in the car." Then he headed toward the trailer.

As I was walking away, Tom called, "Ma'am!"

I thought he was calling me, but how could he possibly think to call me *ma'am*? Wasn't that title for an old lady or a woman of high class?

"Ma'am," Tom called again. "Allison!"

"Yes, sir." I turned to him.

He scratched his baseball cap; his raised brows squeezed the wrinkles on his forehead into deeper creases. "I just wanna . . . uh . . . thank you. You let Cam come. He's a . . . uh . . . good guy. You know that."

I nodded. I didn't know why he was awkward. It made me want to be awkward too.

"Well, Cam's, uh . . ." He paused and looked down. "He's lucky to have you. Thelma's a goddamn bitch! She don't deserve him."

Thelma?

Wait!

Did he mean the *Thelma I've heard too much about?*

It dawned on me that this man was Thelma's father. I didn't have to pretend to be awkward now. How in the world did I end up here, struggling to know what to do or say?

We stood there, Thelma's father and I, staring at each other and most likely thinking very different thoughts. I never, in a million years, imagined I would be stuck in such an odd situation, having this white man apologize to me, calling his daughter a bitch while doing it. I could only imagine how much courage and humility it required from him. And for this, for what Tom said to me, should I feel any differently about Thelma now? If so, I simply didn't know how.

On the way home, Cameron told me Tom's dying father, Pop, had been trying out a pair of new hearing aids that he had gotten for him. Cameron regularly checked on Pop, making sure the hearing aids worked properly. Maybe that's what Tom meant when he said Cameron was a good guy. In that case, yes, Cameron was good. But Tom never lived with Cameron as his wife, did he now?

Here's the thing: my baba's drinking buddies told me how lucky I was to have a loving, caring father. I never knew how Baba deceived them. Undoubtedly, he treated friends differently than he treated family. I believe most people do. Would Baba brag about beating his wife? Would Cameron brag about his pornography addiction? I snorted at the similarity between Baba and Cameron. My fate, having lived with two praiseworthy men.

I was lucky, they said.

46

A few days after visiting Pop, Cameron received–I would later learn–Pop's death news. That following Saturday morning Cameron got up early, showered, shaved, polished his shoes, and dusted off his Sunday best. Desperately wanting to know where he was going, I contemplated acting like a little girl who whine-begged her older brother to let her tag along on an adventure. But I had a feeling Cameron couldn't see or hear me at that moment. His mind was occupied by those he dressed up for. He left wordlessly, leaving me behind in our room filled with the strong, fresh, mixed scent of his aftershave, hairspray, cologne, and a world of questions. Was I the only one who didn't know what dressing up on a Saturday morning meant? When strangers saw Cameron in his dashing attire, would they know why he acted so grim instead? When would I finally understand the meaning behind the things Cameron did?

In his hometown I would always be an outsider. In the face of his family members, friends, and neighbors, there would always be an introduction for me. I would always be the one learning about their shared memories and inside jokes, the one outside of their social circle, unable to make sense of the life they knew, much like a history student who memorizes details of the Independence War but never fully understands the significant impact of it because she never lived through it.

Me, an outsider, left alone to wonder. What would I be doing if I were in Taiwan right now with my people?

I would be a university senior, getting ready to *emerge into society*—as the Chinese say—to become a real adult with real responsibilities: career, home ownership, marriage, and parenthood. Most likely I would stay in Taipei. Possibly I would teach school. Perhaps I would write for a magazine. Conceivably I would be an interpreter or a translator for the German Institute, or an immigration officer at the American Institute. Maybe I would be a bilingual secretary for an international trading company before becoming a wife and a mother. Whatever career path or life goal I pursued in Taiwan, I wouldn't return home to the poverty, to the gang-infested neighborhood, to the brothel district in Hualien.

I went to the university to never return to that fishing village.

As a child, I never could foresee myself becoming a wife before earning a university diploma, or fighting Thelma, Patty, Victoria's Secret models, and porn stars for my husband's attention. And yet, here I was, living all the unforeseeable circumstances and dying for the day when I could return to Taiwan with Cameron, far away from his ex-ghostfriends. I was reminded of how Mama lived with bitter jealousy and malicious envy toward Baba and the ex-stepmother, much the same way I lived with Cameron's memories of his ex-ghostfriends. The chilling tragedy was that I never learned to forgive; Mama never learned to forget.

47

The Chinese characters for *bird* and *crow* are only one stroke different. Remove the stroke representing eyes in the character for *bird*, and it becomes the character for *crow*. Essentially, crows are birds with such black feathers that it's hard to see their black eyes. Eyes are the window to the soul. Invisible eyes mean invisible soul. Absent soul. Soulless. In Chinese, crows carry a negative connotation, so goes the saying, "If you truly love someone, you'll love the crows on his roof too."

Now I would gladly retreat to the fishing village, as long as I was far away from Cameron's ex-ghostfriends, the crows on his roof.

Cameron came home that night and said he had been asked to be one of the pallbearers at Pop's funeral. He visited with Thelma and all of her friends who used to be Cameron's girlfriends too. This was what they did in a town with only thirty students in a high school graduating class. Then he concluded, "All those girls hate you for being my wife." It felt almost like flattery.

The crows on Cameron's roof were increasing in number, threatening to cave in our home. Me, the outsider, had been invited into Cameron's room, turning his ex-ghostfriends into the new outsiders. Of course they hated me, lady of the house. Could I return their hate for love, though? Could I love Cameron's group of crows?

Well, interesting! I heard that, in English, a group of crows is called a murder. . . .

48

Some changes happen stealthily: autumn leaves, graying hair, growing babies, my hormone levels and mood swings. At first, I cried over little things like Hallmark commercials, the Disney movie *Pocahontas*, or when a random stranger smiled at me at school. Then I developed this uncontrollable, extreme hatred toward all young women Cameron interacted with: classmates, coworkers, waitresses. They all looked fake and evil to me, with eyes of starving lions, hungry for my husband's love, plotting to seduce Cameron. Their lashes were too long, too thick, too curly. Their lips were too red, too plump, too pouty. Their makeup was too excessive, too dramatic, too flirty. I couldn't look at any of them without wishing they would die a million different tortured deaths. My ears shot up whenever Cameron began talking. It didn't matter what he was talking about—fishing, country music, or Cannondale bikes; I listened for female names and the pronoun *she*. When he rounded his mouth to form the *she* sound instead of peeling his lips to either side of the face to say *he*, my blood boiled. I suspected the women he talked about were his mistresses. Naturally, when he left me home alone on the weekends to go fishing, he left me alone to paranoia.

The leaves in the backyard were changing colors, two acres of yellow, orange, red trees swaying in the autumn chill, sifting sunlight. The most glorious time of a leaf's life is right before its death.

One evening Dr. Chastain came home around dinnertime and asked me to rake leaves into giant black garbage bags. "I told Cam's mom to do it, but she's been in bed all day." He sighed. "She sleeps so much, she should be a mattress tester."

I never asked why Mrs. Chastain slept on average fifteen hours a day. She was originally from Utah. Maybe, like me, she was friendless and homesick.

As a child, I learned that napping was a praiseworthy practice—nearly sacred, even. "It provides renewed energy to fuel your body, mind, and spirit," my grandfather, Ah-Gung, said when I fought his house rule of taking a midday nap. After lunch my grandmother, Ah-Po, helped me brush my teeth and wash my face, then she lay down with me on the tatami straw mats in her room that were both the floor and the mattress. I always awoke to snacks as a reward.

The thirty-minute post-lunch nap was a strictly observed part of the school schedule in Taiwan. Back in the 1980s and 1990s, some government buildings and stores were closed from noon to 1:00 p.m. Nap time.

Naturally, whenever Cameron left me home alone, I wrote in my journal and napped. What better thing could I do to practice self-care? I dreamed about watching the sunrise and the sunset from the flat roof of my childhood beach home. The aroma of steamed fish and wonton noodle soup wafted in the salty air. Women gossiped in Chinese and sang in Hokkien. In my dreams there were people I cared about—villagers who worked in rice fields, in orchards, and on fishing boats. I felt safe among them.

God put me to sleep so He could erase the hurt in me, one tiny ounce at a time. In my dreams all my thoughts were somehow corrected to the perfect center on the scale of balanced emotions. I felt as though I'd found the antidote to my obscure cynicism. I felt whole.

One afternoon, Cameron told me to sit on the living room couch and wait. A minute later he returned with his parents. All of them sat around me, tight-lipped, mean-eyed, and unnaturally tense.

"Allison," Dr. Chastain began with a hoarse voice, as if he had just woken up from a nap. "We've noticed that you've been sleeping a lot."

I looked to Cameron, whose blank facial expression made it impossible to know how I should respond. I asked in Chinese, "Why is he saying this to me?"

Instead of answering my question, Cameron pointed at his father. "Look at him when he's talking to you."

That dropped the flame of anger on the arid field of my heart. I wanted to get up and leave but didn't have the guts to.

Dr. Chastain continued, "We're very concerned. You must understand, normal people don't sleep that much. You're sick."

My ears hummed. My body burned. But I didn't say anything to defend myself. I'd always believed what the Irish politician George Bernard Shaw said was true: "Silence is the most perfect expression of scorn."

Cameron weighed in. "Allison, you're not sick as in having a cold or flu. You're sick in the head. Like, you know how people with depression sleep and cry a lot?"

I snapped. "Are you accusing me of being crazy?" As soon as the word *crazy* escaped my lips, I remembered Mama's warning about pills turning women crazy.

Crap! Mama was right!

I wish I'd humbly listened to her, even if I didn't understand the seriousness of the subject matter when she mentioned it. I wished I'd had the courage to fight Cameron when he demanded that I take the pills. But I didn't, because all I wanted was a peaceful, blissful life with the man I loved. I never once thought that a part of my American dream would be ruined by insignificant-looking avoid-pregnancy medicine.

But I denied it. "I'm *not* crazy!"

"See, that just proves you are." Cameron leaned forward and rested his elbows on his knees, his fingers laced, as if he were suddenly a psychiatrist. "First thing a crazy person does is deny—"

"Listen! I sleep because it helps me see Taiwan!" My voice cracked and my eyes welled up. "Don't you understand? I can hear and smell Taiwan in my dreams!"

"What did she say?" Mrs. Chastain asked Cameron, her eyebrows furrowed, pillow mark fresh on her left cheek.

"Said she ain't crazy, ma'am."

"Well, that's not what we see, Allison." Mrs. Chastain shook her bedhead and then pushed her glasses up her nose. "You're suffering from severe depression. . . ."

"Tell her to speak for herself, Cam." I straightened my spine. "She sleeps more than anyone I know. Is she depressed or crazy? Should we talk about her instead?"

"What did she say?" Mrs. Chastain looked to Cameron.

Flush-faced, clench-jawed, Cameron said, "You don't want to know, ma'am."

Mrs. Chastain looked at her husband, then back at me. Finally, she threw her hands in the air and said, "You know what? Forget it! Cam, tell her she needs help." She got up from the loveseat, walked back to her bedroom, and probably crawled right into her bed.

Dr. Chastain said something, his voice no longer calm. Crossing my arms in front of my chest, I no longer listened. At last he yelled, "Fix her!" and walked away.

Cameron erupted into a volcanic rage, pulling me into our bedroom and binding my wrists behind me with cable ties that he found in a messy pile of his stuff on the floor.

"You've got guts to dis my mom!" he yelled, forcibly throwing me like a dodge ball against one wall and pushing me against another wall. Then he shoved me out into the wooded backyard.

In that gray autumn afternoon, the silhouette of bald, interlocking tree branches painted the scene of a haunted forest. Cameron kicked the back of my knee; I knelt. A carpet of fallen leaves were damp under me. I closed my eyes. The wind brushed over my ears, whispering the familiar sound of Mama's words:

Avoid-pregnancy medicine is very, very bad.

It can turn a woman very, very crazy.

Men beat crazy women, don't you know?

No.

I didn't know I would actually become crazy.

Didn't know my craziness gave this man permission to use his fists in anger.

Didn't know there was a world that allowed it, and I'd married into that world.

Crazy!

49

I don't remember when I started to plan it. Maybe it wasn't a plan. Maybe it was an idea I'd always had, buried deeply, surfacing slowly, and I was just beginning to notice it. The longer I lingered on the idea, the more solid of a choice it became.

With my eyes closed I could see the layout of the neighborhood: the path leading to the woods, the bridge where boys gathered with a bucket and a fishing pole, the winding gravel road cutting through a wide-open field to a park with a power plant in the far corner. I could get to any of those places on foot.

The Saturday after the crazy-sick talk, Dr. Chastain went fishing with his business partners; Cameron went fishing with Patty, the pills dealer. I put on Cameron's jacket and tucked a knife in my knee-high sock under the jeans, the one Cameron used to gut the fish he caught. I opened the backyard chain-link gate and started the walk to my death.

The one-lane road bordering the Chastain property was straight and lonely. It seemed to reflect a human yearning—a desire to intersect with another road, to have a contact, a connection. When it finally merged into another road with a stop sign in the corner, I didn't stop to watch for travelers from other directions. There weren't any. I was alone under a gray sky, in a dense forestland. As I walked, I ran over a list of questions in my head:

What's today? November 11, 1995.

Who's the U.S. President? Bill Clinton.

What's the currency exchange rate between the U.S. Dollar and the New Taiwanese Dollar? 1:27.

I rounded the bend of the park corner and walked deep into the tall grass to the power plant. I found a quiet, secluded spot, out of sight of the park, and checked to make sure no one was around.

What are some famous cities in the U.S.? New York, Los Angeles, San Francisco.

What are some popular movies of the year? Apollo 13, Braveheart, Toy Story.

At that, I remembered how much I'd always admired Americans for the great films they produced, and I marveled at my unlikely American dream to live in the land of talented artists. Me, an ordinary girl, from a God-forsaken slum on a tiny island nation. A nation that had petitioned the Olympics committee for decades to recognize its official name and flag, but was never granted that basic dignity.

Like Taiwan's international status, my life's purpose was equally perplexing. There was no explanation for my existence. Where did I stand in the grand scheme of life? Not in my birth family. Not in the Chastain family. Not in Taiwan. Not in America. From the beginning to the end of my life, I'd never belonged.

The end of my life. Now.

I would cut my wrist open. I'd heard that it ended endless miseries.

I was sick of the sadness; tired of the tears; had enough of this life.

No grace.

No promise.

No dignity.

I pulled out the knife.

I stared at the knife.

I stared at my wrist.

I put them together.

Just then, a voice rang in my head—a faint yet clear, penetrating, authoritative voice. "Stop. Don't do it. Stop."

I ignored it.

I didn't know if there was a correct way to slit my wrist. I could see pale blue veins and assumed those were what I should be cutting. But should I cut them horizontally or vertically? Should I pull out the veins and squeeze them for an explosive blood bath? When would I know if I had done enough cutting and it was time to stop? Should I keep sawing my wrist until it was detached from my arm, or until my last breath, whichever came first? How was I supposed to do this?

I stared at the power tower in front of me and waited for inspiration, for answers. But all that came was the voice. "Stop. Don't do it. Stop."

I decided to cut vertically, along the outline of one vein. Blood appeared, which meant I'd done this right. I cut harder.

Then again, that voice. . .

When I started to pay attention, *really* listened to it, I discovered it was more than a voice. It was a thought and a feeling, existing in both my mind and my heart at the same time. But who was calling me back in this moment? Who cared about me that deeply and thought my life was worth saving?

My life was so ironic it was almost a joke: growing up on the beach but never allowed to get in the water, never learned to swim. Some neighbor kids had drowned while swimming in the ocean. "Water kills," the adults warned. Then I was taught to wear a helmet while riding a moped, to refrain from alcohol, drugs, and smoking. Always, I stayed safe and healthy. For twenty-two years I'd followed all precautions to stay alive, just so I could die at my own hands? Was this what all my life experiences prepared me for?

Instead of looking into the future for a hopeful reason to live,

I reflected upon my past in this moment of lonely despair because I simply didn't believe I had a future. I was trapped in a forever-locked space with Cameron and all his crows I couldn't love.

That voice lingered, turning my focus to my deep-rooted Chinese belief that every traveling child should return home at the end of his sojourn, like a falling leaf returning to its roots. If my life ended here, would my spirit wander this unmarked field, unable to reunite with my clan far away in the ancestral land, and become—as the Chinese believe—a lost, lonely, wild ghost? Forgotten forever, haunting and hunting for living victims?

I started to wonder about this—this cutting. My wrist was bleeding. Not gushing, just trickling. It dripped down my elbow and stained the sleeve. This was what I came here to do, what I believed was the only way to release me, to set me free. But it felt wrong. My entire being felt it.

Suddenly a chilling sensation sprawled over my foot. A snake slowly coiled itself into a pie on my left sandal, and horror overcame me! I didn't dare move a muscle, didn't dare breathe hard. My scalp went numb, my hands too. I'd lost feeling in my wrist, or maybe more accurately, I had forgotten about my wrist. In this moment, all I could feel was the weight and the cold of the snake on my foot. Its forked tongue was flicking the air. I wished I'd remembered how to distinguish venomous snakes—I'd read it in a wilderness survival manual before. I feared the snake might be bloodthirsty. I pinched the slit on my wrist, scared that the snake might pick up the scent of my blood and decide to taste it. I realized that I couldn't end my own life. My despair was weaker than my innate desire to stay alive.

When I looked down again, the snake was no longer there. I didn't know when it vanished or whether I'd imagined it all along. I didn't waste any time guessing about the snake. I had a feeling I wouldn't see it again. I stabbed the knife into the ground by my foot. It looked like a marked spot for treasures. But the longer I stared at it, the more I believed it looked like a marked spot for my dead suicide attempt.

I pulled up my collar, tucked my wrist in the jacket pocket. In the gathering dusk I walked back the same way I had come, not looking back. Every traveling child should return home at the end of his sojourn, a falling leaf returning to its roots. My home was where Cameron was.

When I got back, Mrs. Chastain was still sleeping, my journal was still in the nightstand drawer, the clock was still ticking, as it had always been. This was just another ordinary day. So ordinary, nothing unusual was expected to happen—like a suicide in a field.

PART FIVE

Peace

50

Cameron's parents planned to visit their parents in Utah during Christmas break of 1995. Dr. Chastain had so many skymiles that he let Cameron and me tag along.

As soon as I stepped out of the Salt Lake City International Airport, I stepped into an enchanted world of soft-falling snow-flakes. All my life I had seen palm trees swaying in tropical breezes, endless indigo from the ocean to the sky, grassy hills, and lush rice fields. Tank tops, shorts, sandals. Fishermen sat under hundred-year-old banyan trees playing Chinese chess in the amber sunset. Winter scenes in Utah were what I had only seen in magazines and postcards: frosty windows, festive decorations, glowing shops, hot cocoa in a mug, horse-drawn carriages outside Temple Square. Coats, gloves, scarves, boots, and smiling people's breaths clouding the biting cold.

We stayed at Dr. Chastain's parents' home in a dwindling mining town seventeen miles southwest of Salt Lake City, where pre-Depression-era cottages nestled at the base of Bingham Canyon and housed a population of seven hundred people. Roads were deserted. Neighborhood shops had boarded windows.

Cameron's grandparents lived in a 1920s brick bungalow with a broad front porch and a cold, dark basement. Throughout the house the wood floor squeaked. The pipes behind the walls made dripping sounds. Except for the bedrooms, the rest of the basement ceiling was open, exposing old pipes, electric wires, and gauzy cobwebs.

After a few days, this winter wonderland that looked tranquil on the first day looked dreary. The gray sky, the achingly lifeless garden, and everything else hidden under the thick blanket of snow turned the world into a languid wasteland. I wondered how Utahans got out of bed every bitter wintry morning.

Cameron's grandfather was a school janitor who married a school cook. When Dr. Chastain was little, he and his three siblings needed more than their parents could afford. The constant lacking motivated Dr. Chastain to study hard, to earn a doctorate degree, to become a successful businessman and an avid world traveler. It's a universal truth that education empowers people to get out of some undesirable circumstances.

Cameron said his grandpa's health had been going downhill so rapidly that this trip could possibly be the last time Dr. Chastain saw him. Which was confusing, because the father-son duo were only in the same room at mealtime and post-dinner TV time. Even then, they didn't hide their disinterest in interacting with each other.

Also, I would never have guessed Grandpa Chastain grappled with any health problems. This was a thickly built seventy-seven-year-old man who walked upright with steady steps, a baseball cap on his bald head, a glass eye behind his eyeglasses, padded plaid button-down shirt under a pair of stained denim overalls, muddy snow boots on his feet. He resembled a wrinkled boy ready to go ice fishing. But instead of ice fishing, he spent most of his time alone in the tool shed—the little shack that looked as if it could collapse anytime under the weight of snow. Each day he sawed and trimmed wood, cut and banged metal, working loudly on his various tinkering projects. He could be building an ark in the workshop for all I knew. But if he really was so ill, I wondered what he did when he was healthy.

Grandma Chastain, in her midseventies, had a withered, weathered, and weary face that portrayed the story of a hard life, of living through wars and the Great Depression. But she managed to embellish her sunken cheeks with a sparkly denture smile and bless others with freshly baked bread, assorted delicious desserts, and hot homemade meals. While I was afraid of speaking English, I felt less intimidated around her. She invited me to help her prepare meals, clean the kitchen, and fold clean laundry. From her I learned new words such as *apricot*, *potluck*, and *swamp cooler*. Every evening after dinner, Grandma Chastain, Mrs. Chastain, and I crowded over the kitchen trough sink to do dishes. They talked, I listened, and we laughed.

While I shared the bonding time with the women, the men watched the nightly news in the living room. Three Mr. Chastains, three generations, three distinctive life experiences, tied together by blood. Immediately I was shocked by the realization of what this meant, as I saw Grandma Chastain, Mrs. Chastain, and me unintentionally stand in a line, the way we would appear on the pedigree chart—each had her appointed place in the timeline. Three Mrs. Chastains, three generations, three distinctive life experiences, brought together by a choice powered by the love we had for our husbands. I didn't know these people very well, but they were my family—not metaphorically, but in the real sense that we all had a part in creating descendants with shared DNA traits.

Even though no one said it, I had a feeling that Grandma Chastain had been the peacemaker in the home, the Bridge of Peace between her husband and her son. And in the Chastain family—I would later learn—it was required of the wife and the mother to be that bridge. Grandma Chastain and Mrs. Chastain had both answered that calling. I wouldn't have believed it then if anyone told me that the way I would fulfill my calling to bring Cameron and his father together would be to provide the opportunity for them to conspire, blindside, and expel me from their family.

51

The Bushmans were my rebirth parents. Naturally, on my first trip to Utah I wanted to visit them. Unfortunately, the twenty-three-year-old Cameron and the twenty-two-year-old me were too young to rent a car in Utah, where the minimal car-rental age was twenty-five. Fortunately, Dr. Chastain agreed to take us. Mrs. Chastain decided to tag along for the fifty-minute drive "to meet Allison's folks."

As we turned into the seemingly affluent Riverbottoms community in Provo, Dr. Chastain pointed at the European castle homes with private horse pastures and announced, "Allison's got rich parents, y'all."

Pulling in front of a Bavarian Tudor with a wrought-iron gate and a three-tier fountain at the center of the garden, Dr. Chastain announced, "This is it!" He parked on the street and, for the first and only time, walked behind me. I led everyone past the gate and the fountain to the heavy double wood doors. I imagined this was probably what introducing a boyfriend to parents felt like. Bursting with joyful anticipation and wild nervousness, I earnestly hoped the Bushmans and the Chastains would like one another. If they got along, it would be like my rebirth parents' nodding approval of my choice to be with Cameron.

Dr. Chastain scratched his head. Mrs. Chastain stared into a pocket-size mirror and brushed mascara clumps off her cheeks. Cameron surveyed the neighborhood and said, "Check out these freakin' Utah Mormon morons and their vans!" He dipped his chin at me. "Lucky you! I don't give you a van full of shitting babies."

"Cam, don't badmouth Uta—" Mrs. Chastain was in midsentence when the door flew open. Dad Bushman jumped through it to tackle-hug me with a gleeful laugh. My face was squished against his warm wool coat, and through his solid chest I heard his deep voice: "Aw, that's my Allison."

I laughed and gently pulled away from his embrace and saw Mom Bushman standing behind him with a blossoming smile. "Oh, Allison!" She reached past Dad Bushman and pulled me in for a tight hug. A faint scent of lotion floated around her. "It's so wonderful to see you," she said in Chinese. "It's been so long."

The Bushmans shook everyone's hand and invited us in. Stepping into the foyer, I was overjoyed to see scrolls of Chinese calligraphy and brush paintings on the walls. On the left side of the foyer was a long staircase. We followed the Bushmans across the floor of patterned tile that made up colorful interconnected loops and swirls, and entered the grand room where floor-to-ceiling sheer curtains covered the entire windowed wall that looked out to the garden. I'd never stood on any Persian wool rug so thickly cushioned until now. We sat in deep-seated couches, the Bushmans seated in elegant armchairs. I couldn't resist staring past them, into the far end of the room, at a mirrored wall that reflected a regal space, where a crystal chandelier hung over a dining set with twelve high-back velvet chairs. In this sprawling, elegant two-story home, the Bushmans raised seven adopted children and had taken in countless needy, homeless people. Their vast wealth was never theirs alone.

It had been six years since I last saw them. Amidst introduction of family members, there were hearty laughter and happy tears. Dad Bushman had purchased tickets for everyone to the Chinese terracotta army exhibit at Brigham Young University art museum that evening. He also made a dinner reservation at a steakhouse so we could continue visiting afterward.

How thoughtful and generous! I thought. *If I ever had disposable income like them, I'd do the same for others.*

At the exhibit entrance we picked up earphones for the self-guided tour, then walked through different stations of artifacts the recording instructed us to see. I'd learned about the terracotta army in elementary school history class but had never seen an exhibit before. I pressed my nose against the display glass to read the Chinese characters on the text panels, studying attentively each soldier's face while listening to the recording in Chinese. But in my peripheral vision I noticed Cameron banging his head on the display glass. His sigh of boredom was audible even when I had my earphones on. He slowly separated himself from the group and eventually found a corner to sit on the shiny travertine floor.

Checking the exhibit pamphlet, I realized we weren't even halfway through yet. Cameron's silent protest was loud and clear, and I was furious to know this was as far as we would go.

How can he ruin this for me? Why can't he be patient and considerate and cultured? Doesn't he know how much I want to spend time with my rebirth parents?

The Bushmans identified the problem and promptly approached Cameron, who, in an annoyed tone, said that the exhibit was ridiculously boring. "Get me out of here!"

The Bushmans looked stunned. Inevitably, awkward silence ensued. I'd never expected to be in this dilemma, witnessing my husband publicly humiliate my rebirth parents. What should I do? When Cameron first met Mama, I apologized to him for her. Now, should I apologize to the Bushmans for him? Gosh, was there an end to this? I was relieved when Cameron's parents joined us. Surely they would coax him into more mature behaviors.

But I assumed too much.

Piggybacking on Cameron's temper tantrum, Dr. Chastain

announced—as if he'd planned this ahead of time—that he and Mrs. Chastain were leaving for a date. "We'll pick you up at the Bushmans at ten o'clock."

I resisted the temptation to yell at these men, my family. What they did meant they didn't much care about me or my folks. I suspected that Dr. Chastain avoided going to dinner with the Bushmans because he didn't like being a guest, who wouldn't have as much power and control as the host. Maybe he felt intimidated or threatened by the Bushmans' immense wealth, who knows? His choice to leave infuriated me. When he returned his headphones, the self-guided tour recording was still playing, and he scurried away with Mrs. Chastain without saying good-bye.

I hoped he choked on his dinner. Bone in throat!

52

The dinner reservation wasn't until two hours later. Per Cameron's demand, Dad Bushman drove us back to his house to wait. I wondered if Cameron was ashamed of his remorseless attitude. I certainly was.

As soon as we arrived at the Bushmans', Cameron rushed straight into the kitchen and opened the refrigerator door for a thorough scan. He found leftover steak, mashed potatoes, corn, and asparagus. He microwaved them, took them to the grand room, slumped into a recliner, propped up his feet, and devoured the food. Had there been a TV in the room, he probably would've searched—greasy fingers on the remote control—for ESPN.

I watched in horror how he took the saying "Make yourself at home" literally. Selfishly, I wished Cameron would be a trophy husband with proper and courteous behavior, which would reflect my excellent choice of a spouse and, in turn, effortlessly elevate me. All of these expectations were to glorify me, me, me, a shallow wife.

I apologized to the Bushmans on Cameron's behalf. They assured me it was completely fine, and encouraged me to make myself at home too. Because Cameron didn't want to wait for two hours to go to the restaurant, Dad Bushman canceled the reservation. "It's better this way. We get to visit in the comfort of our home." Dad Bushman's wink hushed my embarrassment, lifted my guilt, and redirected my focus to this moment of being with the people I loved and admired. However, the last-minute change of plan pinned Mom Bushman in a corner. She now needed to quickly brainstorm a dinner idea. With the leftovers now in Cameron's digestive system, she had to go from scanning the fridge to eyeing the garage freezer to searching the pantry. She grabbed something out of the fridge, considered it, put it back. She picked something out of the freezer, studied it, put it back. She pulled something down from the pantry shelf, examined it, put it back. She stood quietly in the kitchen for a minute, one hand on her hip, one hand under her chin, then she turned on Christmas music and played it softly in the background. She put on an apron and beamed. "Let's have breakfast for dinner tonight. Wouldn't that be fun?" Her white hair glowed under the kitchen fluorescent lights, but I wondered if it was a halo I saw.

Dad Bushman let out a mighty laugh; his Santa belly wildly jiggled and wiggled. He kissed Mom Bushman's cheek, then put on a matching apron. "May I please help you cook, my lady?"

Of course, I volunteered to help too.

They could still carry on a simple conversation in Chinese. Their effort to communicate with me motivated me to do the same for them. Miraculously I didn't stumble when trying to explain something they didn't know in Chinese. I knew I said lots of wrong words, my grammar was bad, and my accent was terrible, but I also knew they somehow understood me. Perhaps spoken words weren't the only thing that connected us after all.

It took us roughly twenty minutes to produce a meal: pancakes, scrambled eggs, toast, hash browns, sausages, bacon, hot cocoa, fresh orange slices. Then we set the table with a white cloth, fine China, and lit candles. When I went to get Cameron for dinner, he'd fallen asleep. I wished I had known that *hangry* was a thing. Cameron was hungry when we were at the exhibit, and he turned angry. Had I been aware of his needs, I would've been more patient and more understanding. But I was a self-centered girl who only cared about how I looked, and how Cameron made me look.

That night, I had the most enjoyable dinner since my arrival in the U.S. Afterward, we cleared the table to look at the Bushmans' old pictures from Taiwan. Then Mom Bushman pulled out a thousand-piece jigsaw puzzle and invited me to work with her while Dad Bushman read by the fireplace. The house was quiet except the *tick-tock* of a clock, each passing second bringing Dr. Chastain closer. I dreaded going back to Cameron's folks so much that I started to feel nauseated. I couldn't stop wishing Dr. Chastain would get hurt in various ways, or even die, and leave me no choice but to stay with the Bushmans in this celestial moment forever.

When the clock struck 1:00 a.m., Dad Bushman got up from the chair, rubbed his eyes, and suggested we spend the night. I nearly fell off my chair! It was hard to resist the temptation to squeal for joy. I secretly celebrated this miracle and thanked God for His tender mercy. But one person's gain is another's loss. There were a million sorrys I wanted to tell Dad Bushman for Dr. Chastain's broken promise and the consequent inconvenience.

Dad Bushman lugged his exhausted seventy-six-year-old body up the grand stairs, leading Cameron and me to one of the guest bedrooms. He gave us each a good-night hug, then excused himself. Cameron took a quick glance at the room and scoffed. "Your Dad Bushman fed me leftovers and wanted us to sleep in separate beds? How nice!"

"Your dad left us here, Cam." I crawled into one of the two twin beds, separated by a nightstand. "At least we aren't sleeping on the street in the snow."

Cameron murmured something but I wasn't sure what. Soon, the world rested in quietness. Only the clock continued to move time.

Knowing perfectly it was only inevitable, I was still disappointed when Cameron's parents showed up the next day. They made me feel like an undesirable lost-and-found item they'd come to claim. Dr. Chastain didn't explain why he hadn't come the day before, and the Bushmans didn't ask either. In the driveway there were endless hugs, handshakes, and good wishes. There were also endless apologies left unspoken. I quietly sulked in the fact that I had to leave the people who felt like real family to go with the people who were my legal family. I wished I had been the Bushmans' little girl, and this had only been my morning farewell as I headed to school, knowing I would see them again at day's end. If that was too much to ask, I wished I could've at least been the Bushmans' pet puppy, basking in their loving care. If that was still too much to ask, I was willing to be less greedy and keep my wish simple: I wished I could've stored the joy I felt with them in a Ziploc bag and taken it with me, so I could have a portable delight, sealed to last forever.

53

On the way back to Grandma Chastain's, Cameron interrogated his father. "Why did you leave me to suffer through a tough night? That mattress was cheap, man. Jacked up my back."

"What are you, the princess with a pea under her mattress?" Dr. Chastain smirked.

"Shut up, you old fart!" Cameron punched the back of the driver's headrest. "You'd be crying for your mom if you slept on planks all night!"

"Cam, calm—" From the passenger's seat, Mrs. Chastain almost finished saying something, but Dr. Chastain cut her off.

"This is when you're wrong." Dr. Chastain's voice was unusually cold and calm. I sensed that he was warming up for an explosive fight.

I'd witnessed friction between Cameron and his father spark into flames before. It'd happened a few times since I joined the family. There was a hole in the Chastains' dining-room wall where the seventeen-year-old Cameron punched his father in the face and knocked him out. It was self-defense, he told me. "That retard had a bad day at work. Came home and whipped me with his belt. Wouldn't stop." Instead of patching up the hole, they placed a china cabinet there to hide it, maybe to serve as a reminder that violence wasn't the answer.

Now I was forced to watch closely how the father-son duo turned red, veins bulging in their necks, voices erupting through the car roof. Had this fight been a movie scene, the four-letter word flying across the air would have either been bleeped out or made this an R-rated film. I didn't need a dictionary to understand Dr. Chastain's mocking, bullying, and belittling: "Why should I report to you where I was last night? Who are you, my f**king dad? You can't even rent a f**king car! You're a f**king bastard who needs me to drive you around. Want me to wipe your f**king shitty ass too?"

Spoken words are merely combinations of sounds with assigned meanings. If I didn't understand the meanings, then the words wouldn't evoke my emotions when I heard their sounds. But I did understand the meaning of the four-letter word that repeatedly flowed out of Dr. Chastain's and Cameron's angry mouths. Each time it was uttered, I hurt as if there were a nurse poking my arm with a needle, over and over, fishing for a moving vein.

English accepts more curses than any other language or dialect I speak. In fact, there's no equivalent of the word f**k in Hakkanese, the dialect my maternal clan spoke. If I'm wrong, that's because none of my Hakkanese relatives ever spoke it. Which is proof that everyone has the power and freedom to choose clean and kind language.

Dr. Chastain let out a high-pitched baby whine, then shoved his thumb in his mouth and made a loud sucking sound. He wiggled his fingers above his ears and blew raspberries. The scene of this fifty-year-old real-estate tycoon transforming into a demon baby reminded me of the night, eight years earlier, when, in an attempt to dehumanize my sister May, the ex-stepmother acted as if she had cerebral palsy. Evil is the same everywhere, wearing different disguises. That chilling realization left me shaking.

Cameron continuously punched the back of the driver's headrest so hard I thought Dr. Chastain might get a concussion. Dr. Chastain's fury turned into road rage: tailgating, honking at and cutting off other cars, sudden accelerating and braking. This had become a ride to imminent death on the highway to hell. I locked my fingers in a death grip around the ceiling bar and imagined ways I could stop Dr. Chastain, or hurt him.

Sitting directly behind Mrs. Chastain in the backseat, I couldn't see her face or hear her voice. I couldn't imagine how she felt in this situation, a battle between two of her favorite men in the world. She was still, and I wondered if she had fallen asleep or had planned to sleep through this fight. Hiding, avoiding, averting.

Now I saw it clearly: for over two decades Dr. Chastain was the demon that haunted and tormented Cameron. For all the academic degrees he held, he hadn't learned to love his own son. The undistinguishable flame of his abuse continued to engulf Cameron; I could smell a whiff of his charred injury.

Finally I saw tears slipping down Cameron's cheeks.

Something happened inside me the instant I caught Cameron weeping. Something that made me look past all the fights we'd had, and all the pernicious things he had said or done. Something convinced me that there was power in what wounded people could do together—a power that enabled us to break the paternal emotional bondage to build our own happy family. That *something* was best illustrated in writer Jessica Handler's words, "Because so few people have been to the moon, astronauts have found that they can fully connect emotionally only with other astronauts."

Cameron and I had both been to the moon.

54

As soon as we got back to Grandma Chastain's house, Cameron and his father stormed into the shed to continue their fight, their earsplitting yells behind us as I followed Mrs. Chastain down to the basement. It was her husband versus mine in a verbal duel, and I rooted for the one I knew wouldn't win. But then, was the line always so clear for her? Asking her to choose a side was like asking her what she needed more—her palm or the back of her hand.

Red face, wet cheeks, swollen eyes, quivering lips, and shaking head, Mrs. Chastain entered the bedroom Cameron and I shared and sat on the bed. Through hiccup-crying, she told me that when Dr. Chastain was little, his father abused him the same way—physically and emotionally—and that was how he learned to be a father.

I knew tension existed in all families. It's like someone's teeth and tongue live in the same mouth, but sometimes the teeth accidentally bite the tongue. In the Chastains' case, the teeth didn't just bite the tongue, they bit the inside of the cheek too. Suddenly, as if a veil had been lifted from my mind's eye, I gasped at the somber image of Mrs. Chastain crying herself to sleep in her dim bedroom. Her endless naps had meaning and purpose!

This woman was an injured soldier, stuck helplessly and hopelessly in a deep trench of despair. And in the trench there was no one else but me crouching next to her. It was the two of us, wearing the same uniform, carrying the same wound. *The Chastain wives' calling is to be the bridge.*

Grabbing my shoulders and pulling me to her bosom, Mrs. Chastain sobbed bitterly, her quavering voice echoing, "I'msorryI'msorryI'msorry–"

I wrapped my arms around her thick back.

My nose tingled.

My eyes moistened.

My voice cracked.

"I'msorryI'msorryI'msorry–" I cried.

55

With all the money we'd saved from working in the international student office, Cameron and I flew to Taiwan for our first and only anniversary in July 1996. Cameron was studying to become an audiologist and wanted to work in Taiwan after he earned his PhD. For our anniversary trip, we planned to research the audiology market and internship opportunities over there.

Cameron became noticeably happier in Taiwan, perhaps because from the moment we landed in the airport, he was treated like a national hero. Taiwanese people loved Cameron. Some old women were so fascinated by his looks that they boldly touched his hair, face, and arm. When I was growing up, American culture was the leading source that introduced Taiwanese people to the Western world: 80s fashion and hairstyles, rock 'n roll, McDonald's, the NBA. My high school classmates idolized stars such as Brooke Shields, Meg Ryan, and Demi Moore, not for their acting prowess but for their faces. The common belief was that those Caucasian ladies' gorgeous looks were the reason why out of billions of people in the world, they were the select few to enjoy Hollywood fame, wealth, and glamour. Caucasian women embodied the perfect image of a true goddess—white skin; large, deep-set eyes; prominent nose.

I once saw a Taiwanese woman shove her baby into a blonde Caucasian lady's arms, then dash away. About five feet out she turned around and snapped pictures of her baby in the bosom of the aghast foreigner. "YES!" the mother shouted for joy. "Now I can show everyone my daughter has been touched by a white person!"

On my mission I had a few twenty-one-year-old Caucasian companions. It was a common scene to see Taiwanese people circle them at the train station, bus stop, or grocery store. "Wait, don't blink. Let me see your eyes," they demanded. "Oh, I'm so envious! I want your lashes, so long and thick! I wish I had your double crease eyelids too." They ranted about how they would have to spend a fortune on cosmetic surgery to get double crease eyelids like my companions'.

Double crease eyelids are what it sounds like: a crease in the eyelids that make the eyes appear larger. In the Taiwanese beauty culture, bigger eyes are considered more attractive, hence, more desirable. Unfortunately, some Taiwanese people were born with single eyelids. It's no surprise that eyelid surgical centers flourished in Taiwan. But they didn't stop at eyelids. To achieve the Caucasian looks, countless Taiwanese people also went for a nose job, had their jaw bones sawed, dyed their hair blond, wore blue contacts, got skin-bleach injections. I never heard of any skincare product that didn't advertise with the keyword 美白—which literally translates into *beautiful white.* White was the kind of beautiful Taiwanese women wanted.

I'm in no position to judge anyone, no. But considering how much time, money, and energy those people invested to look like Cameron, it seemed that God had favored him. Unavoidably, wherever we went, he garnered countless admiring compliments and stares, friendly greetings and smiles, courteous waves and bows.

Once, three middle-aged men dining at the table next to us in a noodle shop asked Cameron to give them English names. Elbow at the table's edge, Cameron leaned forward and pointed his chopsticks at each man as if dubbing knights. "Okay, you be Black Helmet. You be Monkey's Butt. You be Watery Poop." While two of them struggled with *L* and *R*, Monkey's Butt was the big winner. Nonetheless, they all rejoiced in having established a new identity with a Western name, oblivious of the prank Cameron had played on them.

On the street, high school students often swarmed around Cameron, pointing at his face and shouting, "Bruce Willis, Bruce Willis!" A photo session ensued. Next to Cameron, those kids posed with a tight-lipped smile and Winston Churchill's V sign. Never was I invited to be in the pictures or join the conversations with Cameron and his admirers. I stood aside, invisible, like a Hollywood star's bodyguard. But I was completely okay with it, not jealous of Cameron, not annoyed by his fans. I knew my worth and my place.

Taiwan was possibly the only place Cameron would so effortlessly feel great about himself. If he were smart, he would want to stay on this island forever, where he would never run out of fans. But at the end of each day in Taiwan, he had to return to me. He needed me. His eyes were captivating, sure, but what good were those dreamy eyes if they couldn't understand any Chinese characters? In Taiwan, I was his eyes when it came to reading. When the time came for him to start his own business there, I would read all his schedules, contracts, bills. I would tell him what was on the menu at a business lunch. I would never be a mere invisible bodyguard. I had to be the flashlight in his dark world of illiteracy. This Chinese folktale elucidates my relationship with Cameron:

The god of thunder rides on a dark cloud and travels all over China, looking to punish wasteful people. One rainy evening, he hovers over a small village and sees a woman dumping rice out of a house. In a rage, he strikes her dead. After the rain stops and the sky clears, he's horrified by the mistake he made. The woman didn't throw out rice. She threw out rice bran. The god of all gods—the Jade Emperor—hears about it and decides that the god of thunder should marry the woman, and she should become the goddess of lightning. She'll go before him, lighting the heaven and the earth for her husband when he's working. Today, we see the lightning before hearing the thunder.

I couldn't possibly be invisible.

I was Cameron's lightning.

56

Since we got married, Cameron had been speaking only Chinese with me. In this year-long language immersion, his Chinese verbal communication skill had improved so much that he could travel around Taiwan alone if he wanted to. But that was partly because train stations, freeway exits, and street signs in major cities had English translations. Also, Taiwanese people were forgiving of his tonal errors. Cameron loved Taiwanese food: thousand-year eggs, pig intestines, even chicken feet. He had no problem with the tropical climate: the humidity, the typhoons, even the unbearable summer heat. What's more, his education and training in the U.S. were greatly valued in Taiwan. Each hearing aid company recruiting manager we visited expressed feelings of "being flattered" that Cameron would think of leaving the world's financially strongest nation to dwell on a tiny island, to work for his unworthy firm. They bowed to him and said, "Please accept my deepest gratitude. I'm honored."

Cameron was confident that his career would effortlessly take off in Taiwan. He claimed that an audiology summit on that island couldn't start without him. Many times he wrapped his arm around me and said he could see us living there for the rest of our lives. I considered that a huge sacrifice on his part to condescend to my level, to take a step back to reside in a tiny country that was expelled by the United Nations, excluded by the World

Health Organization, and denied by the International Olympic Committee, because he loved me.

In Taiwan, I had the tourist mentality: *Oh, Cameron and I could be happy here forever.* In that euphoric state of mind, my head was crammed with assurance and conviction that in Taiwan our marital problems would somehow work out, and there would be promising possibilities ahead of us. I became hopeful and bold enough to fantasize about us living in a penthouse in the financial district of Taipei; frequenting every noodle shop, steakhouse, and barbecue vendor in all the night markets; sending our children to the best school on the island; vacationing in Hong Kong, Bali, and Japan; buying a summerhouse on my hometown beach for getaways.

And we would never return to Dr. Chastain's house.

57

Following in Mama's footsteps, her younger brother married a lady outside of the village who didn't speak Hakkanese. A uniformed employee at Far Eastern Airlines, she'd never worked on the farm or in rice fields or orchards. During the first few years of their marriage, Uncle and his wife lived with my grandparents, Ah-Gung and Ah-Po. Later, Ah-Gung purchased an entire block of premium lot in the heart of bustling downtown and built a multipurpose community. One of the buildings in the block was leased out to an English cram school, one to a breakfast shop, one to a 7-Eleven, one to an art supplies store, while another to China Airlines as their branch office, where my sister Dee had been working since graduating from college. As a belated-wedding gift, Ah-Gung gave his firstborn son the most luxurious home in the community, a six-story house with a gated courtyard and a private elevator. His flat roof provided a panoramic city view, orange sunrises and pink sunsets, behind the oceanic azure. A year earlier, Cameron stayed in Uncle's mansion during his visit to propose to me. Now we were staying here again for our anniversary trip.

Of course, a trip back home with a new husband wouldn't be complete without celebratory dinners with my friends who had missed my wedding, festive get-togethers with my classmates, nice-to-meet-you outings with my sisters, and here's-your-American-grandson-in-law meeting with Ah-Gung and Ah-Po.

The Chinese have a tradition for jubilant occasions such as

births, weddings, job promotions, new homes, and Chinese New Year—they give away cash in a red envelope. During our anniversary trip, well-wishing people showered Cameron and me with red envelopes. Ah-Gung pulled me aside and gave me $10,000 USD. A significantly generous gift. Before he disowned me, in 1994, Baba's monthly income was about $1,250 USD, enough to support a family of four, to maintain a country club membership, and to pay for my private-university tuitions.

"For you only," Ah-Gung said. "Put it in a private, safe place. Use it for emergency, but I hope you never have to. I hope you spend it on your education. The best investment you can make is in yourself. No one in our clan has achieved as high as you. You're good at this school thing. . . ."

I was highly honored by Ah-Gung's words of approval. But he was mistaken. I wasn't naturally good at this school thing. I worked hard to get good grades, to get into university, to sit in the same classroom with foreigners, to receive their education, to be far, far away from all the domestic dramas.

Education was my way to get away.

The problem was, though I might've been a tiny bit book-smart, I wasn't smart in life at all. I made a grievous mistake with Ah-Gung's gift money. He was a wise man, no doubt, but he was also the one who taught me that "to please your husband, you must kneel by the door when he comes home from work and change his shoes into house slippers. Give him a hot towel to wash the dirt off his face. Have a hot, delicious homemade dinner ready for him. Then give him a neck massage when he relaxes in front of the television."

Um—no.

Thank you very much, but no.

I thanked Ah-Gung for the money. I thanked, thanked, and thanked, because that was truly how much I appreciated it. But in the time, age, and place I became a wife, I had a different idea about how to be a good one. I wanted an equal partnership. So I told Cameron about Ah-Gung's $10,000.

After the anniversary trip, Cameron and I returned to Texas $15,000 richer and ready to head into the second year of our blissfully blessed marriage. At the time I was on a generous scholarship, Cameron received the Pell grant, and we lived with his parents, rent-free, so Cameron decided to put my gift money in our joint account at the university credit union. With the pay from our on-campus and lawn management jobs, we now had about $20,000 in the bank.

I had never been this rich.

58

For our entire anniversary trip, I struggled with the decision to visit Mama. Knowing how much Cameron loathed and was disgusted by her house, I shied away from it, shunning her. But I'd never once passed it by without feeling that dagger-to-heart pain. Despite being a horrible housekeeper, she was my mother. I couldn't cruise around town pretending to be unrelated to her. Before flying back to America, I wanted to at least have a chance to say good-bye.

Cameron refused to step into her house. He sat on the moped we borrowed from Uncle and waited in the alley. As I entered Mama's foyer, I heard little foot-stomping noises behind me and the neighborhood kids shouting, "American! American! Big-Nose American!"

Everything in the house was still grossly cluttered and unkempt. Mama was in a white cotton slip that barely covered her knees. She wore nothing underneath, so the outline of her frail, thin body was visible through the fabric, her sagging nipples jutting out. She'd lost a great deal of strength; walking and breathing was a challenging undertaking. She wanted to fix lunch for me and Cameron, but I declined the offer. I said I had a flight to catch, no time to stay.

"But it won't take long. I'll . . . uh–" She coughed; her right hand reflexively held her crotch. The more violently she coughed, the harder she pinched her genital area. When a circle of wet spot appeared behind her clenched fist, she was still coughing.

I was enormously shocked by this horrifying, heartrending

sight. Yet, an unequivocal relief washed over me. I was glad Cameron didn't witness her cough-and-leak plight. I feel sick and guilty now, remembering my merciless, heartless attitude toward her in that moment when my head was full of myself.

Mama leaned against the living room wall that had turned black from the aged mixture of dust and humidity, asking repeatedly, "I cook. You eat. Tell me about America." But I had become such a hellish girl child, I couldn't even grant her that simple, little wish. I told her Cameron was waiting outside and I must go. "I don't have time, Ma."

But deep down I knew—

I had always known—

Family was what God gave me time for.

As I walked out of her living room, out of the foyer, out of the metal front door, to Cameron, she called my name behind me in her weak, trembling voice. But I refused to look back. I kept walking, back to my life with my porn-addict husband in a foreign land. I kept walking even though my nose tingled, my lips quivered, and my vision became blurry with tears. I hopped on the moped behind Cameron, but Mama managed to catch up to me. Her body was twisted unnaturally into a pretzel-like shape. She panted and grimaced from pain.

"Ma, go back to the house!" I demanded. I was concerned about how she would embarrass me—practically naked in that thin cotton slip—in front of Cameron and the neighborhood kids. But more than that, it killed me to watch her struggling to stand up straight. She leaned against the mossy cinderblock wall, trying to catch her breath. I patted Cameron on the back and told him I needed to tell Mama something real quick. He slapped the moped handlebars and yelled, "I don't believe this!" Then he buried his head in his hands.

I got off the moped and stood in front of Mama, hands on hips. "I'm leaving, Ma."

She shook her head with great effort, then burst out sobbing. The dagger-to-heart kind of pain returned, and I broke out sobbing alongside her. Cameron called impatiently to me, but I didn't respond. I was crying my heart out, for Mama, for myself, for my toxic relationship with Cameron, for the shaky state our marriage was in, for the uncertainty of whether or not I would ever see Mama again. For all the hurt, the aches, the pain, I howled.

The neighborhood kids dispersed. Cameron turned on the moped and threatened, "Don't make me leave you here in this shithole!"

I gazed at Mama, who said between hiccups, "Why . . . can't you . . . stayyy?"

"Bye, Ma," I said.

She shook her head.

"Say good-bye, Ma." I wiped my cheeks with the back of my hand. "Say it so I can go."

She was dying before my eyes, I knew. I knew she would sit up in the lawn chair that night after I left, exhausted and yet unable to close her eyes. She would continue crying till she ran out of energy and breath. Alone. In the dark.

When I was so little—not even old enough for kindergarten—whenever she left me home alone, I sob-begged her to stay so hard that I got a sore throat and chest pain. I knew that separation anxiety. How could I do this to her now, eighteen years later?

But what choice did I have?

I hopped back on the moped. Cameron took me away.

Her earsplitting plea rang in the air. "Stay . . . Stay . . . Come baaackkkk!"

As we rounded the corner of the alley, Mama's last call was still echoing,

Echoing,

Echoing . . .

59

Cameron and I arrived at the Chiang Kai-Shek International Airport two hours before our departure time, found seats by the boarding gate, and started reading the novels we packed in the carry-on bag.

During the short time I went to the restroom and back, three Taiwanese college-aged girls sat in a row in front of Cameron, joking and laughing. Their shiny long hair was neatly oiled and combed. Their powdered faces, maroon lips, and flowery dresses made them look as if they were flying to a job interview. As I got closer, I wasn't surprised to hear them talking, in Chinese, about Cameron. However, I was shocked that Cameron kept his eyes on the book and pretended he didn't understand them. To eavesdrop on those girls for as long as possible, I bent down to tie my shoes.

One of them said, "Don't look now, but that white guy in front of us totally looks like Bruce Willis."

"I know. He's so handsome. I want to be his girlfriend," the second girl said.

But the third girl pushed her arm and protested, "No! I want to be his girlfriend!"

"He won't like you," the second girl said. "You're too ugly."

"What? YOU are too ugly!" The third girl said.

"Hey, stop it." The first girl pointed her chin at another Caucasian young man walking toward them. This guy looked about six foot two. Dark wavy short hair and clean-shaven. While sitting down next to the girls, he nodded to Cameron with a gentle smile and said, "Hi." Cameron looked up from his book and saluted him with two fingers off his forehead.

The first girl said, "One of you can be *his* girlfriend."

The other two girls laughed heartily. Then the second girl said, somewhat seriously, "He's handsome, but I still want Bruce Willis. I want to marry him."

A tingling sensation trickled down my spine. In my mind I waggled a finger at that girl. "No, you don't. His wife will break you like a toothpick."

Surely Cameron was listening too and understood every word. What was going through his mind?

The third girl pulled the second one's hair lightly. "No, you can't. He's mine."

The second girl slapped her right back in the arm. "Well, how about you go ask him to choose between us, huh? In English, I dare you."

I couldn't listen to any more of this ridiculousness. Maneuvering around the girls' backpacks and handbags on the floor, I forced myself to nod politely to them while sitting back into my seat next to Cameron. In a split second their faces stiffened, and they fell silent. I enjoyed the dramatic effect of my presence. As soon as I sat down, Cameron swept me into his arms and gave me a long, passionate, tongue-tangling kiss. Then, in Chinese, he said, "I love you, sweetie. I'll love you forever. You're the most beautiful girl in the world. I'm so lucky to be married to you!"

The girls gasped. They stared at one another with horror that looked something like, *Oh, crap! Shoot me right now!*

Just when I thought nothing more comical could happen, the Caucasian young man sitting across from us said, in flawless Chinese, "Man! That's just perfect!" He snapped his fingers, then gestured a finger gun at Cameron.

I was so stunned that I dropped my jaw the way the girls did.

That young man stood up, leaning over to Cameron with a huge smile and an extended hand. "Tyler Tanner. They call me Tang. Nice to meet you," he said in English, except when he said "Tang," he said it in Chinese with the long vowel in second tone. It was an ancient Chinese dynasty name, also a surname.

Cameron stood up, cupped Tang's hand in his, and said in English, "Cameron Chastain. Pleasure." He pulled me up from my seat and said, "My wife, Allison."

Tang nodded at me while extending his hand. "Nice meeting you, Allison."

He reminded me of John Kennedy, Jr. Soulful brown eyes under bushy masculine brows. Sculpted jawlines that framed a hint of mystery in his face. I shook his hand and probably stared at his enchanting face a second too long, because Cameron tugged me at the elbow, sending a burning embarrassment down to my stomach. I sat down and looked away, pretending I wasn't eavesdropping on Cameron and Tang, pretending I didn't hear that Tang was on the same flight with us, or that his final destination was Salt Lake City.

But I didn't pretend to be amused when I watched the girls swiftly gather their belongings and frantically scurry away.

PART SIX

Harmony

60

With the generous gift money from Ah-Gung and friends, Cameron and I could finally afford to rent a student apartment.

Eight months had passed since Cameron and his father fought in the car; the tension between them hadn't subsided. Cameron didn't want to give his father any chance to comment on our decision to become independent, so we waited till Dr. Chastain went on a business trip to pack up everything in our bedroom—a desk, two chairs, a computer, a bed, a bike, clothes—and load them onto the truck we'd borrowed from a friend. Mrs. Chastain kept stuffing bags of frozen food into the already-crowded backseat. Her eyes were bloodshot and swollen; her hair stuck out stiffly every which way in the back.

"You can come back and do your laundry if you want." She nodded to me, then she gave Cameron a long hug, as if he were moving to Taiwan, never to return. Tears wet her cheeks. Her lips quivered, her voice soft. "Be good, Cam." She patted him on the back. "Love ya."

Cameron nodded and waved, then we were off, heading to an apartment complex by the university in Edinburg. It felt different this time traveling on the same highway we had been taking for the past year to school. Different, because when I looked at the reflection of Cameron's childhood home in the sideview mirror, gradually becoming more distant and smaller, I knew that at the end of the day I wouldn't go back to that bottomless pit of miseries. I wouldn't have to force myself to believe where I'd been waking up every morning for the past year was my home.

It was the last time I ever saw that house of dread.

I felt free, like a high school graduate on her way to the future she'd dreamed of all her life. Rolling down the truck window and letting the August breeze brush through my hair, I hummed along with the country music on the radio. Warmth, happiness, and harmony were finally starting to fill my life. Finally!

Cameron and I rented a one-bedroom apartment, number 21 in a 1970s complex, with a brown door, brown carpet, brown cabinets, and a rough patch job on the uneven walls. We didn't have designer furniture to dress the space, but apartment 21 was beautiful to me. Here we had a living room, a kitchen, and a new beginning. Instantly apartment 21 became my favorite place.

It was perfect.

It was ours.

61

When Dr. Chastain returned from his trip and heard that we'd moved out, he called Cameron. After hanging up, Cameron asked me, "So, the money from Taiwan . . . A lot of money, huh?"

Right away I sensed something fishy going on if a phone conversation with Dr. Chastain led to the topic of money from Taiwan. "Your dad wants it?"

"Well . . ." Cameron cleared his throat. "He . . . uh . . . wants me to take that money and invest it in a boat he's been thinking about buying."

"No," I said firmly. "We need the money. It's all we have. Your dad already has millions. Why does he need our $15,000?"

Of course Dr. Chastain didn't need our money. He wanted to dry up our financial resources to break us. Penniless, we would be forced to turn to him for help, crawling back to his house, being at his mercy. As Cameron and I were finally able to experiment our independence, this was Dr. Chastain's way of reclaiming his power, being back in control, reinforcing his patriarchal authority.

But Cameron disagreed. He was convinced that by handing over all our money to his father, it would miraculously, permanently erase the hate between them. This was a peace offering to his father, his way of mending the hole in their relationship, rectifying their misunderstandings, creating a bond. Every day Cameron asked for my consent. Every day I asked him to come to his senses. Some days his father took him to lunch to talk about the investment. Some days Cameron went to his parents' house to continue talking about it. Always, I wished he and I could be on the same page. Always, I wished he would stop toying with the idea of the boat investment.

But no.

In apartment 21, where Cameron and I had barely started a new life together, we were promptly whirled back to the old life of loud arguments and fierce fights, except now we not only argued about his constant talk of his ex-ghostfriends, his porn addiction, and why I should or shouldn't be on pills and wear makeup; we also fought about the stupid boat.

Gosh, the boat! The nonexistent boat that sent us to bed every night in a damaging marital rage.

Trying to get Cameron to be on the same page was like trying to drink up the Pacific Ocean with a straw. Every day I lost a little more energy, hope, and the emotional connection I'd developed with him while witnessing his father bully him in the car.

Long ago, I'd heard of a tribal mindset:

Fight father.

With father, fight uncles.

With father and uncles, fight enemy.

In Cameron's case, he fought his father. Then, instead of fighting uncles, he and his father fought me—their common enemy. For almost three months we fought, till one evening I returned to apartment 21 to discover a light switch that didn't work. . . .

62

Cameron took an anatomy class in the winter semester. The final exam was scheduled on a Monday in April 1996. Every day leading to the end of the semester, he spent most of his waking hours studying for the final, highlighting his textbook, making flash cards, drawing illustrations of body parts. The night before the exam he tossed and turned in bed, mumbling about random things as though he were reciting the entire textbook.

I understood his anxiety. I grew up in an academically competitive culture; the entire society was a Tiger Mom club. Almost all Chinese babies were born into a boot camp for scholarly excellence, expected to honor their clan elders and glorify their ancestors with perfect test scores. Some couldn't survive this system, though. I'd heard about Taiwanese high schoolers jumping off tall buildings on a test day. *Can't live with the stress anymore*, their suicide notes read. Seventeen-year-olds, eighteen, kids. Dreaded, defeated, dead.

But Cameron's was a completely different story. He wasn't driven by any obligation to honor or glorify his progenitors. He didn't much care about them. In fact, this is a guy who didn't even know his mother's maiden name. "It's a long German word I can't pronounce. Who cares about what it is? She's a Chastain now." But his goal to maintain a high GPA was, perhaps, motivated by pride. "Got to show my dad he won't be the only Dr. Chastain in the family."

The sleepless night turned drastic. Cameron dashed to the bathroom, and I heard him vomiting, followed by flushing. This was strange. I thought only dogs stuck their heads in a toilet. I only knew people who threw up into a sink. In the remote village I was from, most of the household bathrooms had a squatting toilet, much like an underground hole in a Porta Potty. Retching into it meant getting splashed in the face with standstill human waste.

The next morning Cameron's panic attack woke me.

"Daylight savings?" He threw the alarm clock across the room—textbook, notebook, and flashcards too. "Daylight savings? Really? How about saving my ass?"

It was April 8, 1996, the Monday after Daylight Savings started, the morning of Cameron's final exam. Time had stealthily sprung forward an hour in the night. Head in toilet, Cameron had missed the shift. Missed the final. All those grueling hours of study went down the drain. He stormed into the bathroom, kicked the wall, stuck his head in the toilet again.

His despair was a shocking mystery to me. I'd never heard of Daylight Savings. I couldn't understand how anyone accidentally lost an hour. I could never imagine that somewhere in the world men had determined that time change twice a year.

Taiwan is a tropical island without seasonal daylight changes, no need for Daylight Savings. Also, Taiwan is roughly the size of Maryland, not large enough to acquire multiple time zones. Everyone on that island nation experiences every second together. In my narrow country girl's mind, I could never imagine a division of time—the way Americans live in different zones, Bostonians in morning commute the same time Californians still in slumber.

Time is a peculiar, mystic concept: invisible, intangible, inaudible. How do men decide the beginning and the end? How do men declare to all creatures in the world, "Now we start the day. Then we end the night"? As apostle Neal A. Maxwell so profoundly states, "Time is clearly not our natural dimension. Thus it is that we are never really at home in time. Alternately, we find ourselves wishing to hasten the passage of time or to hold back the dawn. We can do neither, of course, but whereas the fish is at home in water, we are clearly not at home in time—because we belong to eternity."

Taiwan is thirteen hours ahead of Texas in time, or fourteen, depending on America's Daylight Savings. When Mama was pregnant with me and went into labor on New Year's Eve, she was hopeful to win the First Baby of the Year prizes. Unfortunately, the labor slipped past New Year's midnight, and I was "born a loser," as she said. I've always wondered about the perplexity of my birthday. In the early morning of January 2 when I entered the world, the sun was on my side of the earth. I was born to welcome it. There's no loser in a child born into the light. In that exact moment, Cameron was a six-month-old baby sleeping in the New Year's night. While Taiwan had already moved on to tomorrow, Texas remained January 1. The mystery of time manifests in my birth certificate, which shows that I was born a day *later*. A day *after* Cameron's Texas time.

Time and space. Sometimes I don't understand; sometimes I don't belong.

Cameron's mishap made me wonder what it would be like if I could stealthily escape with the missing hour, wherever that sixty minutes disappeared into. What if I magically ended up in a place outside of the Chastains' tiny hometown, never having to deal with Cameron or the crows on his roof ever again? And why did the thought of running away from my husband feel so exuberantly optimistic?

On this day after Daylight Savings, I had a sharp, unmistakable realization that I existed in the wrong space with the wrong person and, as such, couldn't feel fully at home, couldn't experience true joy. I was with the man I'd once loved, but yearned for eternal happiness elsewhere, with other people. It'd become increasingly clear to me that I had two choices: stay with the man who continuously expected me to be someone else, or simply leave.

Leave Cameron,

Leave Texas,

Leave this cancerous relationship that speedily headed toward utter destruction.

I knew what I wanted. Unfortunately, I lacked the courage to choose it.

Maybe this is precisely why Mama had stayed in her miserable marriage for nineteen years, repeating the yo-yo pattern of running away from and returning to the same man she frankly didn't know how to live with or without.

63

One day in August 1996, when Cameron and I sat together at the front desk at work, stuffing and licking envelopes, a man walked in. He was a younger version of Ed Harris in a T-shirt and cargo shorts, sunglasses resting in his sun-bleached brown hair. About six feet tall, tanned, lean, and fit. His deep-set blue eyes turned into new moons when he smiled. His perfectly straight teeth couldn't possibly be real; I would later learn that he was a hockey player.

"Hello, my name is Ethan Leroy," he said, looking from Cameron to me, then back to Cameron.

"Howdy. How can I help you?" Cameron chucked a licked envelope into the outgoing basket.

"Me and my wife"—Ethan looked out the door—"just got here."

"Okay." Cameron leaned forward and crossed his arms on the desk.

"I'm wondering . . . I'm thinking, maybe you can help me."

"Shoot!" Cameron leaned back deep into the swivel office chair, his shoulders pushing back in a rotation movement that made the chair spin from side to side.

"Yeah . . . so, I just drove by. Oh, I'm from Canada, by the way. I've been on the road the whole summer. Just seeing places, meeting people, you know? Anyway, I camped on a beach in

Mexico these past few days. Last night, the whole night I was thinking about how I wanted to do something different with my life. So I got up and started driving and decided to go to the first university I saw on the way north. Uh . . . I didn't even apply . . . but I'm wondering if I can start classes right away. . . ."

"You didn't even apply?" Cameron laughed. "Now, that's interesting. Let me ask the boss."

Cameron did all the talking, I did all the paperwork, Ethan was accepted that afternoon. With one lifted brow, Cameron handed Ethan the new student orientation packet and asked, "So, working on your master's in psychology, eh?"

Ethan smiled his eyes into crescent moons and nodded. Before heading out of the office, he asked if we could help him find an apartment. After work, we walked him over to Jane, our apartment manager. Ethan asked me a few questions on the way. This kind of individual attention from a strange man made my face fevered and my palms sweaty. I glanced over at Cameron for help, and he promptly answered every question for me.

"Oh, she's my wife."

"Oh, she's from Taiwan."

"Oh, I was a missionary over there."

"Oh, yeah, all Asian chicks are shy like that."

I nodded at each of Cameron's answers, except the last one, which was an overly generalized assumption of a huge, specific population. He didn't know *all* Asian chicks. I looked toward Cameron to shake my head at his false statement, only to see Ethan winking at me with a fatherly smile. *Fatherly*, because he was slightly wrinkled. And if the birthdate he put down on the application form was real—which, of course, isn't something people lie about on a university application form—he was turning thirty-six in a few days.

Thirty-six. So old!

Growing up, I was programed to hold the Chinese cultural

expectation of getting a doctorate degree before thirty as life's golden compass. It's different now, but from 1970s to 1990s while I lived in Taiwan, I'd never heard of anyone older than thirty still studying in university. Nope. Never ever heard of it. The decade of the thirties in a Chinese person's life was, according to Confucius's teachings, to be dedicated to establishing a career and starting a family. Naturally, Ethan's decision to return to school at thirty-six made me think it was an inspired birthday resolution. An epiphany, maybe. Whatever motivated Ethan's decision, I admired his courage to act on it.

At the apartment manager's office, Jane told Ethan there was a vacancy coming up in a few days, but not that very same day. Ethan chuckled and put a bundle of American dollars on the counter. "No biggie! I've got a van."

An image of Ethan eating cold canned soup in his vehicle formed in my mind. I squeezed Cameron's hand and asked him, in Chinese, to invite Ethan to stay with us for a few days.

Cameron locked eyes with me. "You sure?"

I nodded.

He clicked his tongue and patted Ethan on the shoulder. "Yo, come stay with us for a few days. We live just right here. Number 21."

"For real?" Ethan's eyes were soft.

"Yeah, man. Just don't touch my babe!"

Heat rose up from my chest and settled in my cheeks. I knew Cameron was only joking, but it gave me a strange sense of self-worth—if only for a split second—that he sounded protective of me, as if I had value.

The two men, two new friends, laughed in their distinctive voices. For some reason I found safety and security in seeing them getting along so well. Walking on the sunset-spilt golden sidewalk back to apartment 21, trailing behind Bruce Willis and Ed Harris look-alikes, I saw this moment as the awakening inspiration of my

American dream. If a thirty-six-year-old foreigner could return to school as an impromptu plan, what couldn't I do?

Ethan effortlessly transformed our almost-barren living room into a summer paradise: a sleeping bag next to a lounge chair and a side table with a built-in beach umbrella, a can of soda, a towel, a novel, a straw hat, and sandals. I kept wondering about his wife, but never gathered enough courage to ask Cameron to ask Ethan about her. Why wasn't she with him? Didn't he say he arrived in Edinburg with a wife? Did she decide to go back to Canada alone? Did he actually say, upon arriving at school, "Me and my *bike* just got here . . ."?

His wife didn't show up by nightfall. Or the next day. Or ever. A few days later an apartment became available, and Ethan moved in. Number 12. The end unit on the second floor, on the side of the complex that bordered Hardee's fast-food restaurant. Sometimes I saw a blonde young woman knock on his door, and I knew a wife would never knock on her husband's door.

Ethan had to be single.

64

One Saturday Ethan went to mow the lawns with Cameron so I could do homework. When they returned, Cameron said, "It's Ethan's birthday. Let's take him hiking."

There were enchanting woods by the apartment complex. We walked under canopies of trees, Cameron in the middle so he could talk to Ethan and me in our own language. I wondered if anyone who saw us thought we were an unlikely trio.

We talked about food. And when Ethan said he liked Tex-Mex tons more than authentic Mexican food, Cameron cracked his trademark slant-lipped smile and gave him a fist bump. "That, my friend, seals our brotherhood!"

Oh, family we were—Ethan, Cameron, and I.

Only a few minutes into the woods, nature called. I was shy and mostly just awkward around Ethan, so I didn't dare tell Cameron I had to go, until walking became difficult. I squeezed Cameron's hand and whispered in his ear. He rolled his eyes, waving at nowhere in particular. "Geez, just go already!"

I bolted away, hid behind a thick grove, and squatted steadily to take care of the human business. When I returned to the men, Ethan stared at me with a combination of bewilderment, disbelief, and—dare I guess?—he was impressed. Pointing at me and tilting his head to look at Cameron, Ethan asked, "Whoa! Did Allison just go to the bathroom, like, behind the bushes?"

A fever spread across my body. I dropped my gaze down at

the ground, curled my toes in my shoes, and kicked small rocks off the trail. I wanted to hook Cameron's elbow and run away. Before Cameron said anything, Ethan continued, "I'd kill someone to have a girlfriend who goes behind a tree. You can take her anywhere: top of a mountain, bottom of an ocean, doesn't matter. She won't whine about a broken nail or smudged mascara. God! I want a girl like that." Ethan narrowed his eyes and pretended to fan out steam from between his lips. "Mama! She's sexy!"

Sexy?

Me?

Well, obviously he didn't know that, as a child, I was nicknamed Fatty for my Michelin tire torso, thunder thighs, dinner-plate-shaped face. There was hardly any tolerance for a round body type in the 1970s–1990s Taiwan. Living in that culture with a full figure like mine was to position myself under daily public scrutiny. It was like being pecked to death by ducks. Also, I was deathly conscious about my crooked, gapped teeth—a grain of uncooked rice could fit snuggly between my front teeth—so much so that I always laughed behind my hand.

But after Ethan's overrated remarks, Cameron reassured me I was fat in all the right places. "And your gapped front teeth? A symbol of sexy, like Madonna," he said with a whistle.

Why did Cameron's and Ethan's comments flatter me to no end? Even though they were essentially having a locker room talk with a shade of sexism, I needed to hear it to feel validated. Never having been accepted in my own culture for my looks, I loved the affirmation that in this rare, brief moment, two men appreciated my appearance, even though I didn't wear any makeup or have a supermodel's physique. Maybe my tanned skin, flat nose, and curvy shape weren't as ugly as everyone said, after all.

65

Three months passed since the birthday hike. Late, really late on the night of the light-switch incident, I knocked on Ethan's door for the first time.

Outside his door I probably appeared miserable. I had been crying in the bed that felt like an ice block, and I couldn't tell if I was shivering from the sobs or the cold. It was all the shivering that turned me to the only person I could think of for help at the time.

Ethan opened the door, bare-chested.

"Hi." I waved.

"Oh, hi, Allison." It looked as if I had woken him up, which I'm sure I had. He squinted and looked behind me, then stuck his head out to the corridor, looking to the right and the left.

"He's not here," I said, pulling up the collar of my oversize button-down shirt. Cameron's shirt.

"Whoa! You speak English?" Ethan's eyes were open wide.

I lifted my right hand and held my thumb and index finger close together. "Just a little." But in that precise moment when I glanced at my own fingers, gesturing how small my vocabulary was, I felt the invisible duct tape peel off my lips, and words came back to me. It felt as if all the words I'd heard Cameron say in the past year since we got married had been neatly organized and stored on library shelves somewhere in my brain, and it wasn't until now that the library was mysteriously unlocked, and words were being checked out row by row, aisle by aisle, forming meaningful sentences as they exited my mouth.

"Crazy! You're here without Cam and you speak English? What's next?"

"I need help, Ethan." Hearing my own voice saying those words, I burst out sobbing.

"Whoa, Allison! What happened? Come here!" He pulled me into his apartment and shut the door behind me. The heated living room brought me instant warmth. He pulled me into his arms for a comforting embrace, rocking me from side to side and letting me cry into his broad, hairy chest.

"Does Cam know where you are?" he whispered.

"Do I know where Cam is?"

Ethan pushed me away from him. "Is he missing?"

"No, sorry. He's not missing. He moved back to his parents' house."

"You guys . . . had a fight?"

I thought for a second. We had been fighting for a while now and never seemed to run out of things to fight about. Usually, after a fight Cameron would go fishing, play racquetball, or shoot a bow in the woods with a friend. He always came back, still angry or not. But not today.

"Yes . . . also, um . . . it's cold in my apartment. Do you have an extra blanket I can borrow?"

"Sure. Is the heater not working in your apartment? Did you tell Jane—"

I shook my head and explained what happened.

"That son of a bitch!" Ethan fell into deep thought, then gave me a serious look. "Did he hurt you?"

Did he hurt me? Cameron?

I'd never had to respond to this question before. How should I give the right answer when it was more than a yes-no question?

Did Cameron hurt me? Sure he did. I was hurting right now.

Whether or not the question was directed toward the physical or emotional hurt, the answer would always be an affirmative yes; the latter always followed the former. Cameron's was the kind of violence that left no visible wound.

I nodded to Ethan's question, and he slumped into the couch, staring blankly ahead. I wished I could read his mind. Was it cluttered with Cameron's false golden-boy images? The young, bilingual, world-traveling, ambitious doctor-to-be. It must've been hard for Ethan to process the news of our sudden breakup, and the consequent reality of him stuck in the middle. It must've been tricky. After all, weren't we a family only three months earlier?

I never could find the courage to ask Ethan for food. I only borrowed his sleeping bag and an extra blanket. He made me promise to let him help with everything else I needed till I could be independent.

But when would that be, being independent in a foreign country . . . ?

66

T he morning after the light-switch incident, I walked over to the credit union right behind the apartment to check the balance on the account. I closely watched the teller's heavily powdered face. Her eyes concentrated on the computer monitor, and her penciled-in brows tied in a knot. Finally, she squeezed out each word slowly. "I'm sorry, ma'am. This account was closed yesterday."

"EXCUSE ME?" I felt an artery pulsing on the side of my head. Immediately I lowered my voice. "What happened?"

"The account was closed yesterday, ma'am."

"Yes, thank you. I heard that. But what happened? Who closed it?" I already knew what happened. I didn't need to hear it from a strange Texan lady, but I wanted to hear it.

"The other account owner–" She threw me a weird look as if testing, or waiting, to see if I could provide the rightful account owner's full name, maybe birthdate and blood type too, to prove I was the other rightful account owner.

"Chastain," I said. "Cameron Liam Chastain. My husband."

Cameron Liam Chastain. My husband.

Why did it hurt so much to say these words right now? These were the exact words I spoke to introduce him to my classmates, my friends, my sisters, Ah-Gung, and Ah-Po. But I couldn't feel any pride and joy in that name now.

I also reported Cameron's birthdate and his social security number without her asking.

"Oh, thank you, ma'am. Looks like Mr. Chastain withdrew all the money in this account and transferred it to another account."

"He has another account?"

The lady instantly put on an uncomfortable facial expression that read something between *Why did I just tell you that?* and *No way am I saying another word!*

I leaned forward, my chest pushing against the counter and forcing more pressure into my already-aching heart. I was tempted to yell at her. But she was innocent, just doing her job, and was maybe confused about the line she was trying not to cross.

"Excuse me—" I searched her name on the desk plaque. "Sandy? Yes—Sandy. I'm a co-owner of this account. I believe I have a right to know where my money went. Please tell me."

She looked down at the counter for a second, seemingly gasping for air, or maybe the courage to tell the truth. Finally, she said, "Right, okay—it was transferred into Dr. Arthur Chastain's account."

Dr. Arthur Chastain?

Of course.

Who else?

If anything, my short marriage to Cameron helped shorten the emotional distance between him and his father.

The loss of $5,000 couldn't make me wince. It was a gift, after all. I didn't work for it. But I couldn't bear the thought of losing Ah-Gung's $10,000 because I knew how hard he must've worked—in the rice field, the orchard, on the farm—to save up that much, then to give it away, to be *stolen* away.

Dr. Arthur Chastain and Cameron Liam Chastain didn't need my Ah-Gung's $10,000. Dr. Chastain wanted to buy a boat for deep sea fishing in the Gulf of Mexico. Cameron wanted to invest my $10,000 in the boat so his father would make him a fishing buddy. But that money could pay the rent of apartment 21 for three years. It could buy our daily meals for over a year. It could get us a nice used car. It could buy Ah-Gung a lifetime supply of bar soaps, so he wouldn't have to save up soap scraps and cake them together to make a new bar. It could pay years of his water bills so he wouldn't have to collect rainwater for dishwashing and garden watering. It could replace the wood stove in Ah-Po's centennial kitchen with a water heater. And Ah-Gung wouldn't have to endure every sweltering, humid, tropical summer day without turning on a fan, to save on electric bills.

Gosh—what had I done to Ah-Gung?

And what was this crushing pain in my head and my neck and my shoulders and elbows and knees and ankles? My lungs were having a seizure! Where did all the air go? Was this how it felt to lose my soul?

I would do anything to get the money back and return it to Ah-Gung. I wasn't worthy of that gift. How could Cameron and Dr. Chastain ever think to do all this? Putting me through the pain and setting me up for new social status: penniless, homeless, family-less, soulless . . .

67

On the third morning after Cameron left, I opened my eyes and waited for my vision to come to a focus on the ceiling fixture.

Am I in Taiwan? Wait—where? Texas?

Crap!

It took me about as long to focus my vision as it did to remember I was still in the fresh, husbandless rut. Looking to where Cameron usually slept in bed—the space he abandoned, I knew that from now on this would be my story: when I woke up, Cameron wouldn't be here to tell me our schedule for the day. I had to be Atlas the Titan of my own life, holding up my own sky.

Yeah, but that was if I could stand up to hold up.

I slept away most of the first two days after the light-switch incident. From my bed I could see Hardee's store sign outside the window. The letters were dancing now. The *H* and *a* and *r* and *d* and both of the *e* and that *s*, even the apostrophe, all of them. And watching the sign made my stomach growl. Hunger took me on a sensory exploration: fatigue, nausea, and light-headedness all together. Between Cameron and me there was one shared wallet, and it always sat in his jeans back pocket. I wished it sat in mine now.

I wondered what day it was. How many meals had I missed? Two? Four? Did I have to be in class right now? I couldn't remember. My eyelids were heavy, my body even heavier. While drifting in and out of sleep, I heard knocking on my door and someone calling my name. As I slowly unzipped the sleeping bag and struggled to swing my legs over the edge of the bed, the knock grew more intense and urgent. I cracked the door open a little and peeked out but didn't see anyone. I opened the door all the way, and in front of me was a strange young man.

"Allison Hong?" he asked, scrunching his bushy unibrow and making it look like a crawling caterpillar. "You Allison or not?"

"Yeah. You here for Cameron?"

"No, but this is for you." He handed me a manila envelope, then left.

Inside the envelope was a sheaf of stapled papers, the words *Restraining Order* printed across the top of the cover page. An attorney's business card was paper-clipped to it.

I wanted to laugh.

One unexpected outcome of separating from Cameron was the opportunity for me to start learning new words, learning to talk with people who had been there all along, those I had seen every day but never needed to talk to: Jane, Ethan, the teller. Yeah, I talked to people on my own now just fine, but what in the world did *Restraining Order* mean?

Humans learn the words they need most. I would soon learn to speak both lawyers' and beggars' words.

I took the papers to apartment 12. Ethan stood in the doorway, flipping through the pages and gasping. "What's going on between you two?"

"What . . . what's restraining order?" Such a hard question to ask, so many *R*s in those words, so little energy in me. I walked into the living room and leaned against a wall.

"Um . . . it means . . . well, it says here that you can't contact Cam in any way. Can't talk to him anymore. Not allowed. You two had a real bad fight, eh?"

"Our fights were never good."

"Well, yeah! He's filed for divorce!"

Divorce?

I'm getting a divorce? Me?

How's this even possible? Isn't divorce for noncommittal people like Baba?

But as soon as I thought of Baba, I remembered there were innocent wives like Mama.

Cameron filed for divorce. In those four words, my world collapsed and I was reduced to an unwanted spouse.

My legs turned into cooked noodles; I struggled to stand. The little strength in me didn't know where to go—to my head to read the divorce papers or to my feet to hold up a crumpling, starving body. Dizzy, I rested on the couch. Ethan sat next to me.

Hands over face, I asked him in a muffled voice, "Mind reading the whole stack of papers for me?"

"Nah." He gently squeezed my knee and went on reading silently.

How could this all happen? One day I came home to an empty apartment, then a closed bank account, then a restraining order, then a divorce. Exactly how did Cameron grow to abhor me so much? Exactly how much hate did he put into all the plotting? Exactly what did he want from all this? The $15,000 gift money from Taiwan? That was it? Between $15,000 and his wife, he chose the money? Where was the Cameron who put a ring on my finger and said I was his true love? What did he truly love?

Everything Cameron had planned leading to the divorce only proved that he deathly feared me.

Of course he did.

Here's how:

There's an ancient Chinese adage: "It's virtuous for women to be talentless." Obviously it originated from one man's insecurity—his fear of womanly power, really. I believe, a long time ago, men understood women's true worth as an embodiment of godliness, holiness, and divinity. They realized that women had infinite potential, boundless abilities, and mighty influences. However, through time, men's respect transformed into fear. They feared that, given the chance, women would embrace their natural matriarchal leadership, be in power, in charge, in control. And some men couldn't swallow it, perhaps for the same reason they had problems asking for directions.

From birth, Chinese girls were shamed into believing they were unwanted, a burden, and, as such, deserved to be punished. It was a mind game men played to blindfold women, so they couldn't see their true powers, potential, and worth. Because, really, how hard is it to see that women are strong and tenacious? Their monthly bleeding doesn't kill them. Their carrying, laboring, and delivering human lives doesn't faze them. Chinese newborn girls were wrapped in newspapers and abandoned on the street. Those girls grew up to birth men, all men. All men are half women. How could men think to protect Mother Earth and not to respect their mother dear? How could they make women cry and not know God counts women's tears?

With the restraining order, Cameron tried to silence me, to make me voiceless, so I couldn't ask him to give back the money he had stolen. However I looked at it, Cameron's doing was merely a manifestation of his fear. Fear of me finding out I could speak for myself. Fear of me knowing I didn't need him to survive in his country. Fear of me remembering I was born a ferocious warrior.

All of this, this restraining order: his petty, petty fear.

68

I begged.

While Ethan read my divorce papers, I asked him for $5.

"Five bucks?" he held out all the fingers on his right hand. I dipped my chin for an embarrassed, awkward nod. I didn't know his financial situation. Was he a poor student too?

Without another word, he pulled his wallet out of his jeans pocket and handed me the money—a piece of light, worn green paper. It delivered warmth from being tucked in his pocket, absorbing his body heat. It delivered renewed power, assuring me my circumstance was temporary and I wouldn't be stuck in this challenge forever, permeating in hurt, absorbing cynicism.

I grabbed my papers from Ethan's hand. "Thanks. Got to go."

"Where?" He leaned back and watched me stuff the papers into the manila envelope.

"Back home, of course. Homework." I hurried to the door. "Thanks for the money."

He followed me. "Wait—what are you doing on Thanksgiving? Next Thursday. You've got plan?"

I shrugged. I hadn't thought that far ahead yet.

"I'll make dinner. You and me. How's that?" There was a sparkle in his eyes when he said, "Come, okay?"

I said *okay*. Then, with the strange energy from out of nowhere, I dashed away like a little child with candy money in hand, heading toward Hardee's. At the turn of the staircase I glanced over my shoulder and saw Ethan leaning on the doorframe, watching me. I almost skipped a step and fell over.

I speed-walked into the cold November afternoon, past a dumpster in the corner of the parking lot to Hardee's, and thought of Cameron.

The morning after we moved into apartment 21, he requested scrambled eggs for breakfast. I pulled out eggs from the fridge and noticed there was no expiration date on the carton.

"Cam, I'm not sure if these eggs are still good. Eating bad eggs gives you gas, you know?"

He laughed. "C'mon, I'll show you how we Americans tell if eggs are bad."

He took the carton and led me to the parking lot. After picking out an egg, he said, "I'll chuck it at the dumpster. If smoke comes out when it cracks, then it's bad. Look for the smoke. Ready?"

I nodded. Cameron threw the egg at the dumpster. Smashed yolk and a string of clear liquid dripped down the dumpster front. No smoke.

"That one was good, Cam!" I clapped.

He chucked another one at the dumpster. No smoke. Then another, and another, till all the eggs in the carton successfully passed the smoke test.

"They were all good!" I looked at the empty carton. "But we don't have any eggs left."

"God, you're frickin' stupid!" With his big hand, Cameron clenched my nape like a dog collar and walked me back to apartment 21.

It's easy to see that he was right: I was stupid. Stupid to be thinking about the smoky-egg trick and missing laughing with him and wanting to see him after he'd served me divorce papers. I was like a human-trafficking victim offering to count the money the criminal made from selling me.

Stupid me indeed.

69

Standing at Hardee's counter, I looked up at the fluorescent backlit menu screens with various meal choices. The aroma of burgers and fries activated a violent churning movement in my stomach. I wanted to eat everything in their kitchen, but I only had five bucks. Five bucks! What healthy, nutritious food should I get?

Not cookies, obviously.

Not shakes, oh shoot!

Not soda, so sad.

Gosh! Why did I have to do mental math and practice self-control while my weak limbs shook with hunger anyway?

The cashier tapped at the counter. "Ready, ma'am?"

I wasn't. But my fingers tapped at the counter the way she did, and I said, in a fake confident voice, "I'll just get a cheeseburger, that's all. Not too hungry."

I walked back to apartment 21 with the warm burger, all my pockets full of mini ketchup packets, and a newfound hope that maybe I could survive in America after all, that I could speak English, that my voice would be heard.

I sat on my freezing bed, the burger a tempting aroma, and suddenly a thought came, like the right-shoulder angel: "Wait, don't chow down the whole burger! This is the only food you have till Thanksgiving dinner next week at Ethan's, remember? Eat responsibly!"

Another thought—the left-shoulder angel—instantaneously arrived. "Oh, c'mon! She's starving, can't you see? This small burger isn't even enough to stuff the gap between her teeth! She can just suck on ketchup later when she gets hungry again."

In the end, the right-shoulder angel won. I took a tiny bite of the burger, stared at it, did the mental and visual calculation of how much I should eat a day so the burger would last me for five days till Thanksgiving dinner at Ethan's. The flavor of grilled meat still lingered on my tongue, crispy bits of lettuce and moistened morsel of bun stuck between my teeth. Half-content, I wrapped the burger back in the paper liner and put it in the fridge that wasn't running.

When I was four, one night I left the house alone. Next thing I knew, I sat on a glass-top desk in an open-plan office, surrounded by five, maybe six, uniformed policemen. Each of them had a question for me, and all of them came at the same time. "What's your name?" "How old are you?" "What were you doing out on the street alone?" "Where's your mama?" "What are your parents' names?" "Where do you live? What's your address?" "What's your phone number?" "How long have you been lost?"

I sat quietly at the desk's edge and swung my legs. I didn't think I was lost. I thought my parents were. My then-two-year-old sister, Dee, and I were home alone. She wouldn't stop crying, so I left the house to look for Baba and Mama. I was standing in the middle of a zebra-stripe crosswalk when a man carried me to the police station.

I'm not lost, I thought.

I didn't know why the policemen wanted to have a conversation with me. In my clan, it was considered rude for little children to bother adult relatives with a conversation. "You kids talk nonsense. We big people don't have time to waste on you," they said. But now, my silence caused the policemen to make wrong hypotheses: "Maybe she's deaf." "She might be mute." "What kid doesn't know her own name? She's probably just dumb."

I'm not dumb.

So I answered all their questions. In fact, I spoke so much, I even talked the policemen into buying me snacks from the corner general store. When my parents came to the police station to report a missing child, I was eating rice crackers on the desktop.

I talked. I got fed. I was found.

Now in Texas, I wasn't merely an immigrant. I was a refugee. But, like my four-year-old self in the police station, I knew I was capable of opening my mouth and finding help. I knew my voice would be heard, even in a foreign language. I would be okay.

I had a begging mouth now.

When the burger's aftertaste was gone, I would beg again.

70

I needed more than an occasional burger, and the only person
I could think of, besides Ethan, who might be willing to help
was the local bishop from the Church of Jesus Christ of Latter-day
Saints—a friend I hadn't met.

I found the number to a local church meetinghouse in a
phonebook and went to Ethan's apartment to use his phone. This
was awkward, asking a complete stranger for monetary assistance. Double awkward, knowing Ethan would be in the same
room and eavesdrop on my begging. But as soon as I picked up
the phone and glanced sheepishly at Ethan, he nodded and left
the apartment.

After I introduced myself, the man on the phone said, "Thanks
for calling, Sister Hong. This is Bishop Webb, and I'll do everything I can to help you."

This was like listening to a radio host's voice and guessing what
he looked like. Judging from his silvery voice, I imagined Bishop
Webb as a slim, tall, balding, middle-aged man with black-rimmed
glasses. That evening I borrowed my Taiwanese classmate's car to
meet with Bishop Webb at the church meetinghouse. He looked
eerily close to my imagination, with an ear-to-ear smile and a firm
handshake.

In his office, there was a huge gold-framed painting on the
wall behind the mahogany desk. In the painting, Jesus Christ is
at the Pool of Bethesda. He extends one hand to lift a makeshift

tent above a sick man and lifts up the man from the ground with his other hand, healing him. I had seen this very image numerous times at church, art museums, and in Christian magazines, but that evening as Bishop Webb placed his hands on my head, at my request, and pronounced blessings and comfort in a modulated voice I imagined Jesus's own would sound like, I knew I was like that man at the Pool of Bethesda.

I knew I would be able to get up and walk.

Bishop Webb used the donated money from church members—designated to help the poor and the needy—to help me with groceries, utilities, and rent until the end of the semester. Because Cameron had taken all the clothes we shared, the bishop also bought me a sweater and a coat.

Receiving help from the bishop was the immediate solution to my crisis, yes. But my pride suddenly kicked in, and I became conscious about being a charity case. When I told the bishop about it, he assured me it was natural to feel that way. "Just know that when you allow others to help you, you allow them an opportunity to receive blessings from Heaven. When you're able, pay it forward."

His words brought me new understanding: Sometimes we give, sometimes we receive. It's through service that we learn and grow to be better people, to develop a love for all humankind.

Human*kind*. We can be both.

71

Two weeks after I received the restraining order, one day I was in the statistics class, the professor had yet to show up. Cameron sat in his usual seat in front of me and was in such high spirits that he started bragging to me, in Chinese, about how quickly he'd moved on and gotten back with Patty, the pills dealer. Then he raved about having gone on dates with another Taiwanese student whose admission application I'd processed, taking her to the same places he had taken me. He would have me know that this girl was taller than I was, wore colorful makeup and her own clothes—delicate, expensive, feminine designer dresses—and brought a lot more money with her from Taiwan than a meager $15,000.

His lips moved. His disgusting voice hummed in my ears. And I had a burning urge to slap him across the face with the one-thousand-page textbook, again and again. I wanted to yell at him, but I wasn't sure if I should. I was afraid the restraining order would get me arrested and sent to jail, so I screamed inside my head instead. I hated how, to him, I was only a target of bullying, mockery, and betrayal. But then it dawned on me that at this point, after he'd brought me to the lowest of low, I had nothing left. If I had nothing left, then I had nothing to lose.

What about yelling at Cameron? Insulting him? Humiliating him? What about getting arrested and sent to jail?

Who's afraid? I have nothing to lose!

Cameron wouldn't stop bragging. The raging fire inside was consuming me, driving me to stand up and push my desk forcibly against his chair.

"Shut up!" I shouted in English. Cameron's face instantly registered a mixture of shock and confusion. Oh, how this invigorated me! This was the most gratifying sight I'd witnessed since he walked out on me. And because I could, I roared my mightiest roar for everyone in the classroom to hear. "You're gonna burn in hell forever!" I pounded my fist on the desk. "Burn forever!"

It immediately became quiet. I scanned the room and saw all eyes on me. If they were judging me, I simply didn't care.

Cameron didn't respond. I wished I had a camera to capture this precious moment of his widened eyes, dropped jaw, and pale face. Surely, he knew he had awakened a sleeping lioness.

"You remember this"—I stuck a finger in his face—"karma! Cameron Liam Chastain, karma will get you. Just you wait!"

I picked up my backpack and stormed out of the room, brushing shoulders with the professor as he entered, and felt a strange bliss bubbling inside.

72

I planned to transfer to Brigham Young University in Utah after the semester was over and needed help to make the transition. I called Dad Bushman, who bought me a one-way ticket to Utah scheduled for the day I finished my finals. He assured me that he and Mom Bushman would do everything they could to help me till I could be on my own. "But don't forget, the Lord anxiously wants to help you. He's the master healer. Let Him heal you."

Ethan once told me "time heals." I knew he meant well, but I could see God healing me, not time.

I knew God; I didn't know time.

I could pray to God; I couldn't pray to time.

The poet Rumi writes, *The wound is the place where the Light enters you.* It's true. Defeated by pain and sorrow, I came to God's feet, pleading for His blessings. He answered my prayers by guiding kind, loving, generous people to sit next to me, listen to me, cry with me, take me in. His light and grace completed my healing.

Anatomy of Ethan's (un)belief:
1. He can't believe in a God he can't see.
2. Because he doesn't believe God exists, he doesn't believe there's punishment or consequences for his actions.
3. Because there's no punishment or consequences for his actions, he can do whatever he wants. Eat, drink, and be merry (but don't be married).

I told him believing in an unseen God was the same as believing in his unseen ancestors. Just because he never saw or met his progenitors doesn't mean they didn't exist. Ancestors exist in all of us, in our blood, in the colors of our eyes and hair, in the entirety of us. But ultimately, I'd rather live my life believing there's a God and die to find out there isn't than live my life believing there isn't a God and die to find out there is.

My goal was clear: I wanted to have a Christ-centered family of my own. I'd thought I could change Cameron into a God-loving man, but I flattered myself and misunderstood my role. I couldn't change anyone. But even with my failed marriage to Cameron, I hadn't lost hope of my dream. In fact, it reinforced my belief and conviction that this starter-wife experience was the training wheels on the vehicle that would take me to the right person, to whom I would be married for time and all eternity through the power of God. Our marriage and our family relationships with our children will last past mortality. The literal, true meaning of *Families are forever.*

I envisioned my future husband and I weeding our single-mother neighbor's garden together, visiting the ninety-five-year-old veteran widower next door, feeding missionaries in our home, and volunteering in the community children and youth programs weekly. We would study the scriptures together, pray together, teach our children together about the God we both loved so deeply.

Ethan said he couldn't live with that kind of imagination. Even though he didn't share my belief, during the last month of my time in Texas he was undoubtedly an answer to my prayers— someone to take away my loneliness. We went to the library to do homework together during the day, cooked dinner together in his apartment at night. We talked about history, cultures, psychology, hockey, and world travel till the sun went down. Almost every night a different girl showed up at Ethan's door, and he excused himself to talk to her in the corridor, never letting her in the apartment when I was there. I peeked out through the open door and saw a blonde in a denim jacket, the next night a brunette in leather pants, then the next night a redhead in high heels. I heard them complain about me being there and robbing them of Ethan. When he came back, he wouldn't allow me to apologize for ruining his social life. "Don't worry about them." He waved away my guilt. "You're here with me. That's all I want."

On the day I was scheduled to fly to Utah, Ethan made a dinner reservation for us before my red-eye flight. He'd planned to take me to the airport afterward. But that morning while he was taking his finals, I asked a Taiwanese classmate to drop me off at Edinburg International Airport.

The airport was packed with travelers, coming and going. It was also packed with feelings and memories, coming and going.

This was the same airport I flew in from Taiwan a year ago, where I started my American dream; where I met Mrs. Chastain; where excitement, anticipation, and anxiety came to me all at once; where my childhood home, the Pacific, and Taiwanese food left me all at once. What would never leave was the memory of how Cameron entered my life. I would never forget how he left either.

I sat alone in the boarding area for the entire day, waiting for my midnight flight. No one knew who I was. No one came to see me off. No one told me, "Good luck with your new life in Utah!" No one cared I had come eight thousand miles across the globe to end up being a charity case, wearing a donated sweater and coat, eating donated canned food, traveling with a donated plane ticket. No one knew that only four months earlier I was in the Chiang Kai-Shek International Airport with Cameron, and he'd swept me into his arms, kissing me passionately, saying, "I love you, sweetie. I'll love you forever. You're the most beautiful girl in the world. I'm so lucky to be married to you!"

A year ago I came to this airport for Cameron. Now I was leaving this airport because of him too. Gladly, I bid farewell to him, to his dysfunctional family, to his frivolous ex-ghostfriends. But I couldn't bring myself to say good-bye to a tender man whose eyes smiled when I talked; whose voice was soft and gentle; who inconvenienced himself with time, money, friendships, and said, "You're here with me. That's all I want."

PART SEVEN

Charity

73

After the initial shock of discovering a non-working light switch, my entire attention was focused on problem-solving. *How am I going to keep a roof over my head? To get the electricity running in the apartment? To stop my hunger? To keep out the cold? To finish school? Here, here, talk to Jane. Okay, okay, talk to Ethan. Right, right, talk to the bishop. Yes, yes, talk to the Bushmans.*

My mind was so occupied by the rushed urge to meet my basic human needs, I didn't let the grief of abandonment completely sink in. I didn't know that it was only after I let anguish, sadness, and vulnerability boil over that I could clear room in my heart for hope, dreams, and ambition. Nor did I know that sorrow could strike in the most unexpected moment.

Mom Bushman led me to the same guest bedroom Cameron and I had stayed in a year earlier, leaving me to unpack and rest. I stood in the middle of the room and scanned the brass light fixture, the floral wallpaper, the mirrored closet, the dresser, the nightstand, the stained-glass lamp, the sheer curtains, the blue carpet, the glowing nightlight, the bed neatly made with white bedding. And—oh my gosh!—why did everything have to look the same as it did a year ago? The only difference was Cameron's absence.

But wait! He was here!

Look! He was tossing and turning in that bed.

Listen! He was complaining about the stiff mattress.

Smell! It was his Suave shampoo. His L.A. Looks styling gel. His Dial bar soap.

And why couldn't I stop crying for missing him? Why was I wondering where he was and who he was with as I wailed like a wounded animal in his memories? Why did sorrow find me when I was barely strong enough to care for myself?

Mom and Dad Bushman only let me grieve in the room for a day, then they invited me to clean up, get dressed, and get on with life. We went to BYU campus to start the transfer process. I quickly became inseparable from them: grocery shopping, visiting neighbors, taking German classes, babysitting grandchildren, going to concerts, plays, and church meetings. They introduced me to everyone as their daughter.

Having felt like an emotional orphan my entire life, this was my first experience feeling loved as a child. They mentioned my name in the family prayer every night, asking God to bless me. One day when I missed Cameron terribly, and all I wanted to do was curl up under layers of blankets and cry all day, they delivered to my room a bowl of hot chicken noodle soup with rice, a slice of banana bread, fresh fruit, and a glass of milk. On the tray was a note: *We love you, Allison. Never forget the worth of your soul is great in the eyes of God.*

If the worth of my soul was great in God's eyes, then I was a heroine, the equivalent of the Greek Nike and the Roman Victoria. So why did I accept defeat at Cameron's hands and whine endlessly in a victim's voice? Why did it take me a month of staying with the Bushmans to finally realize I was in a sacred home, among spiritual giants? Keeping Cameron's memories alive here was like painting graffiti on the walls of a temple where the spirit of God resided. In a way, I'd turned my mind into a bad neighborhood too, trashed with thoughts of Cameron. I had to move out and move on if I really wanted to start a new life, to mingle with good single young adults, to form new relationships. The

Bushmans supported my choice and agreed that it was better for me to intentionally build my social life around people my age.

I leafed through my contact book and considered carefully each name. When I saw Lily's, I had a strong impression to call her.

Lily was of Chinese descent. She and I were roommates for two months when we served together as missionaries. After her mission she returned to Utah and got married. She sounded surprised when I called but said that she and her husband, Jeff, were excited to host me for as long as needed.

The next day they came to take me to their home in Salt Lake City. When their car arrived at the Bushmans' house, I ran out to greet them. But before I had a chance to say anything, a stout woman jumped out of the Nissan Pathfinder, stood in a warrior's stance, and crossed her arms before her chest. "Hold on, stop right there!"

I didn't know what to stop: walking? Waving? Smiling? What? It took me a few more seconds to realize she meant for me to stop the impulse to ask the scrutinizing question she had been asked far too often: "Lily, how in the world did you gain so much weight since I saw you last?"

I wouldn't have recognized her if not for her single-lid eyes, glowing skin, and lip-corner dimples. But she was obviously shocked to see me too. Pointing at me and eyeing me up and down, she yelled, "Whatever happened to you? Anorexic much?"

I looked down at my sweater, the one Bishop Webb bought me, and it dawned on me that I also looked different now. Since my crisis erupted in the Lone Star state, I had gone from 105 pounds to 89 pounds within two months. Instead of a size 2, I was now a size 0.

Lily opened the backseat door and pointed at an infant strapped in a car seat. "Baby Mikey. He's why I'm fat now." Then she pointed at the Asian man in the driver's seat. "Jeff, my husband. Chop, chop. Let's go!"

No nonsense, still the same old Lily.

Since Jeff and Lily both had to immediately get back to work night shift at the post office, they politely declined the invitation to go in the house to visit with the Bushmans. I ran back in to grab my suitcase and to say good-bye. Mom and Dad stopped their scripture study by the fireplace and walked me out to the car, nodding and waving to Jeff and Lily. "Ni hao! Ni hao!" They smiled at my friends and then hugged me. They hugged so freely, I took it for granted. Had I known how meaningful the hugs were at this moment—had I known the Bushmans would spend the next few years serving another mission, then another, and Dad would pass away first, then Mom—I would've appreciated this moment more deeply, held on to them more tightly, taken time to look into their eyes just a little longer, to say thank you more sincerely. Had I known, I wouldn't have run out of these spiritual giants' home so eagerly that I forgot I was running away from holy grounds, into a fallen world.

74

Jeff and Lily owned a 1974 two-story, three-bedroom house in the southwest side of Salt Lake City. They lived in the unfinished basement with Mikey and rented out one of the upstairs bedrooms to Sharon, a Taiwanese girl in her early twenties who came here to learn English.

Lily suggested that I apply to University of Utah, twenty minutes away from her house. If I got accepted, I could continue to stay with her. Knowing I was on a student visa and wasn't allowed to work legally off campus, she agreed that, in exchange for rent and food, I would help out with household chores, run errands, and babysit Mikey.

One day, I went to a grocery store with Sharon, who invited me to a party that night at her friend's house. This was exactly why I moved out of the Bushmans', yes. But I wasn't entirely ready just yet. I told her I was awkward and would probably ruin the party and embarrass her. But she insisted.

"My secret crush will be there. I've invited him to come before, but this is the first time he can finally make it." Sharon shook her head and pounded her fist on the steering wheel. "Oh my gosh! Just thinking about him drives me crazy." She screamed, and I laughed.

"You have to come, Allison. He's one of a kind. I want you to see him."

So I did.

The party was in a haunted-looking house: peeling yellowed wallpaper, brown shaggy carpet, warped vinyl kitchen floor, Formica laminate sheet broken off the kitchen counter. Single-pane aluminum windows shook violently in the howling wind that accompanied the snowstorm, but I doubted anyone would notice even if the roof caved in. The guests were too focused on playing UNO, eating, and laughing.

Sharon introduced everyone to me. "My friends." Her arms spread out widely in a fan shape, as if offering an invisible group hug to the four bone-skinny, giggling Chinese girls crammed on the loveseat. Then she pointed at the five white young men who looked to be in their early twenties, telling me their names and where they had served their Chinese-speaking missions. When she got to the last guy in the group, she winked at me with a cheerful grin, and I knew he was her crush.

"Shuai. He served in the Taiwan Taipei Mission." She pronounced his name in the Chinese fourth tone, turning that name into a deliberate claim of his looks.

I asked reluctantly, "Shuai, as in—"

"Yes, as in *handsome.*" Sharon proudly finished the introduction of her crush. "I gave him that nickname, thank you very much. Look at this guy! Don't you think it's fitting?"

All the girls laughed, and I thought, *Yeah, it's fitting, but stupid. Why can't we just call him by his name, handsome or not?*

Shuai smiled as he walked up to shake my hand. "Nice to meet you, uh . . ."

I told him my name and where I was from. Then Sharon clapped enthusiastically. "Okay, let's play!"

We all sat around the coffee table for the card game UNO. But Sharon spent more time going in and out of the kitchen to dish up our plates with piles of chicken dumplings, rice cakes, and beef noodle soup than she actually sat down to play. About every two minutes she checked and made sure our glasses were full of juice, milk, soda, or water.

Shuai sat next to me on the carpet. I glanced at his profile and wondered why he looked so familiar. Where had I seen him before? I'd only lived in Salt Lake City for a week and hadn't been anywhere except the grocery store. Could that be where I had seen him? Was he the cashier? The bagger? The stocker? Maybe he was neither. Maybe he was on one of those gossip magazine covers in the check-out line.

At some point while Sharon was cooking in the kitchen, Shuai asked me if I was going out with anyone. I wasn't sure if my heart beat erratically because this was the first time a guy asked me such a question and I was trapped in that thrill, or because the person who asked was my friend's crush and I was caught in that guilt. Either way, I reckoned it was only a yes-no question, no big deal. So I shook my head. But then—heaven forbid!—he asked if I had anything planned for later that night.

I had two choices: lose Sharon's friendship or continue sulking in my new divorcée identity. And I had to make that choice fast. I inhaled sharply and methodically shook my head. His lips curled into a warm smile. "Want to come to my house after this?"

I was young, immature, and desperate. Mostly desperate. I envisioned myself in a post-divorce dating race against Cameron and panicked at the knowledge that he'd already had a head start. He was the hare in "The Tortoise and the Hare" story. My pride allowed me only one option: to win. After all that he had done, I couldn't let him keep thinking I was easily defeated. I was no loser. I had to win this imaginary race at all costs. I would say *yes* to any decent-looking, younger returned missionary, knowing perfectly well I would possibly have to repeat the *put the husband through college* process. But I would do it in a heartbeat.

I took a deep breath and nodded slowly at Shuai's invitation, feeling my cheeks burn. I said haltingly, "When the party's over,

I'll wait on the sidewalk. You go tell Sharon you want to give me a ride home."

For the rest of the party I couldn't enjoy the game, couldn't remember details of my life to answer other people's questions, couldn't stop shifting my weight from right to left and back. The food became tasteless; I couldn't eat any, even though my stomach growled. I kept glancing at the wall clock, wanting and not wanting the party to end, wanting and not wanting to go to Shuai's house.

Finally, as other guests got up and shook hands and hugged good night, I crawled out of the living room without speaking to anyone. Then I dashed out to the snowstorm and shivered on the sidewalk. So guilty, so undignified, so dishonorable.

Shuai must be talking to Sharon right now, I thought. *How's she taking this? How will I face her when I get home tonight?*

I contemplated going back to the house and apologizing to Sharon, but I was a coward. I was also freezing, starving, and altogether confused. My fingers and toes were numb from the cold; so was my head. I couldn't tell if I was doing the right thing or not. I didn't know how long I'd paced around the lamppost by the sidewalk, counting the cars parked on the street and reading their license plates. I didn't know if Shuai was leaving the party too, or if I was only making a big fool out of myself.

Snow got in under my shirt through my hoodie, and I ducked my chin into the collar like a tortoise into its shell. I did, in fact, feel like a headless tortoise, not having the decency to stick out my head and say to Shuai, "Sorry, maybe it's best I don't go to your place." Or to Sharon, "Sorry, I can't control who Shuai asks out." But I hid the cold truth and my courage from both friends. I kept my mouth shut, kept my head in my tortoise shell, and headed steadily toward the goal of going on a date, of winning the race by getting married before Cameron did.

I was helplessly young, painfully immature, and mostly desperate. . . .

75

S huai lived with his parents in an affluent neighborhood in East Salt Lake City. I couldn't make out the exterior of their house because the snowstorm killed the visibility. But the grandiose interior was nothing I had ever seen: shiny marble floor, vaulted ceiling with recessed lighting, grand staircase with a Persian rug running down the center of each step. At the top of the staircase was a bridge that overlooked the entire front hall. One end of the front hall was the reading room. Built-in bookshelves lined the walls. In front of a fireplace, recliners sat next to side tables and floor lamps. A stack of books rested on the window seat cushion. Scrolls of Chinese brush paintings hung on the wall.

Shuai took me to the kitchen for snacks. When he saw a woman reading a book and eating a slice of pie at the island, he ran up to hug her from behind. "Ma! You're back!"

The woman turned, cupped Shuai's face in her hands, kissed him on the forehead, and said she missed him. Then she smiled at me with a nod.

"Oh, Ma. This is Allison Hong. We met at Sharon's party tonight. She's from Taiwan."

I waved and said hi to this woman who couldn't possibly have a son in his twenties. She looked as if she was in her twenties herself! She stood about my height of five foot four, so I could see the details of her face clearly: olive skin, hazel eyes, high cheekbones, black silky long hair, equal parts Ashley Judd and Disney's animated Pocahontas. There was ambiguity in her facial features. Perhaps a *mix-blood*, as the Taiwanese call it. She hugged me and said, in Chinese, "Very happy to know you. My name is Lee."

I was stunned—which was ridiculous; anyone could learn to speak Chinese. But Lee sounded like a native, like me. I looked at her, then to Shuai, demanding an explanation. He shrugged. "My ma is half-Chinese," he said, to which she chuckled and corrected, "Half-Taiwanese, actually."

I was never enthusiastic about the perpetual hot debate on where Taiwan stood. I wasn't antipatriotic; I simply lacked interest in politics, that's all.

Lee barely got home from Taiwan. The snowstorm delayed hours of her travel, and she was now exhausted. "Make yourself at home, Allison. Tai will show you around. I hope to see you again, after I get over the jetlag." She politely excused herself and left the kitchen.

"Tai?" I looked at Shuai. "Is that—your name?"

"Yep. Too bad it doesn't mean *handsome*." He grinned, then opened the pantry door and gestured for me to help myself. I grabbed a bag of potato chips. He swept his arm toward the grand stairs. "This way, please."

In Shuai's room, there were clothes on the back of a chair, on the dresser, on the floor. Books were scattered on the bed, on the desk, on the nightstand. I didn't know where to stand or sit. Shuai kicked away some of the clothes on the floor to make way and shoved books to one side of the bed to make room. "Come sit."

I sat on the edge of the bed and noticed that his room was also full of trophies and framed certificates of achievements.

Shuai sat next to me. "When was the last time you went back to Taiwan?"

"Last July," I said.

"No way!" He widened his eyes. "Me too! Last summer."

"Really? What were you doing in Taiwan? Just visiting?"

"Yeah. I went to visit my grandpa. He moved back to Taiwan after my grandma died two years ago."

Then it hit me!

Out of nowhere, it hit me in the head and in the heart. It hit me from all directions, and it hit me so hard that I was immediately awoken from my oblivion. Why didn't I see it this entire time? It was so obvious!

This guy—Shuai, or Tai—was actually Tyler Tanner at the Chiang Kai-Shek International Airport!

I stared at his face, and I was sure of it. That firm conviction made me sick to my stomach. My throat suddenly felt so dry that I repeatedly gulped down my saliva. I squinted to read the name on one of the certificates on the wall, and—oh my gosh! What had I done? To betray Sharon, to steal a date, and to make myself the world's biggest idiot!

Tyler hadn't recognized me for who I was, which was understandable. I looked anorexic, according to Lily. I was also overdue for a haircut but couldn't afford it. And now, I was in a dilemma: *Do I, or do I not, tell Tyler who I am?* If I did, what would he do? If I didn't now, how long would it be before I had to tell him? How would he react if he found out on his own later?

Maybe it was best I told him from the beginning. I was already dishonest with Sharon, and I didn't like how it felt to hide the truth. But I couldn't bring myself to tell Tyler anything. I couldn't. Because, strange as it was, within only a few hours since I saw him at the party, I'd become attracted to him—a devout church member, a returned missionary, a Chinese speaker, physically attractive. And he seemed to like me. He must; he asked me to leave a party to come to his house! Also, his mother seemed to like me too. This could work out, if I just knew when to tell the truth.

I was so focused on resolving the dilemma, I didn't pay any attention to Tyler. When he pushed a photo album in front of me, I didn't know how to respond.

"Look," he pointed at a picture of himself with an old man. I immediately recognized the background to be Chiang Kai-Shek International Airport. It wasn't like I needed any more evidence, but this picture further confirmed his identity.

"My grandpa." Tyler tapped his finger at the old man through the clear plastic sheet of the photo album. "This is last summer when he dropped me off at the airport."

I nodded. There was a flame blazing inside, urging me to take advantage of this precise instant to tell him we'd met before. That urge was so strong, I knew if I ignored it, I would have a harder time telling him the same thing later.

"Tai . . ." I kept my gaze on the picture, afraid to look at him. "This . . . the trip to Taiwan, um—" I ran through a list of random vocabulary in my head, searching for the right one to finish the sentence, but I was lost in words. A tiny thought promptly crept into my mind. *Be smart for once, will you? How often do you meet someone like this, a full package with a bonus? His mom is your people! Tyler is a godsend!*

I started to sweat a little. "It's warm in here."

"Oh, is the heater too strong?" Tyler gestured at a distant wall. "Want me to turn it down?"

I looked up to meet his eyes. I was sweating more profusely by the second. My palms turned slimy. "It's okay." I stroked my long bangs, pushing them to the left side of my hot face. "You left Taiwan, last time . . . in the airport . . ."

"Yeah, I always fly." He winked. "Don't you?"

"Of course." I broke out in a nervous chuckle, then swallowed hard. "Yeah, so, the last time you were in the airport, uh . . . I was there too." The last four words were the dropping of my vocal weight.

"You were? How do you know?"

"I . . . I was there." My armpits were damp now. "With Cam."

"Who's that?"

"Cam? Cameron Chastain. My . . . uh . . ." I suddenly didn't know how to tell people about Cameron. Was he my ex-husband *yet?* We hadn't signed any papers, so did that mean from now till we finalized the divorce we were only *separated?* If so, then Cameron was still, legally, my husband, which made this thing I was doing with Tyler—dared I think?—an affair?

Oh my gosh, the sky's falling on me! How many wrong things can I possibly do in a day?

"Wait!" Tyler stared into my eyes, then there was a long pause. I wished there was a cloud above his head that revealed all his thoughts. This intense silence was unnerving.

"Cameron? The white guy who spoke Chinese? You—with him?"

I didn't nod. I didn't say *yes.* I didn't hum "uh-huh." I said, "Cameron Chastain is my husband. Ex . . . We're getting divo—"

"You that girl?" Tyler pointed at me, his mouth hanging open.

"Not one of the three tofu brains, if that's who you're thinking," I clarified.

"No, no, no." Tyler shook his head. "The hot one with the white guy. Was that really you?"

I almost burst out laughing. Was he questioning if I was the girl with Cameron, or was he questioning my hotness? Unexpectedly, this brief moment of comic relief brought a sense of clarity. A minute ago I felt as if I'd been pushed into the Pacific with a boulder tied to my neck; now the Pacific and the boulder were replaced by strength and courage to tell the truth. It was liberating just *thinking about* choosing honesty. I felt so light I could ninja-hop from roof to roof.

Closing the photo album, I turned to face Tyler, not worried or afraid anymore. "Yes, it's really me. Cam and I are getting divorced, but as for now, I'm still married."

"What?" Tyler's mouth was hanging even wider open now. "How—?"

How? How did I blatantly snatch this new crush from Sharon, just to discover he was the guy who had witnessed me and Cameron kissing passionately as husband and wife? I don't know. But if I could only use one word to summarize this experience, it would be *kismet*.

Tyler fixed his round eyes on my face, utterly stunned. If his eyes could speak, in this moment they were saying, "Wow, totally didn't see that coming!" He covered his lips with his hand, fingers delicately sprawling across the bottom half of his face.

I gently put the photo album back on the bed and stood up. "So nice to see you again, Tai."

Tyler propped himself down on his elbows, looking up at me and shaking his head. "You, the girl in the airport?"

"I'm sorry," I said, not quite sure why I felt apologizing was the next right thing to do. For some strange reason, becoming a divorcée made me feel inferior, as if I were an unpardonable sinner annihilated from God's grace. Unworthy. Ostracized. Marginalized.

Tyler was still saying *wow* as he absent-mindedly grabbed a coat from the back of a chair. When we made our way out to his car, Lee emerged from a room in a scarlet silk nightgown that matched her bloodshot eyes. "Oh, Allison," she called, stretching out her arms to hug me. "Leaving already?"

I nodded.

"Okay, well, come visit again soon." She squeezed out a sweet smile. "I love meeting Taiwanese friends."

She would likely watch me get into Tyler's car and wave till she couldn't see the license plate anymore. I looked out the shotgun window and waved at her till she was out of sight, my breath fogging up the glass, my head stuck in a fog of confusion. I couldn't make sense of my peculiar encounter with Tyler. What was the meaning of our meeting in the airport in a comedic way, then meeting again, six months later, across the globe, in a dramatic way, just to come to this abrupt ending? Why couldn't life be predictable like windshield wipers' mechanical, rhythmical movement? Swish. Silence. Snowflakes on glass. Swish. Silence. Snowflakes gone. If I knew what was coming, I would be better prepared for it.

Tyler and I parted ways wordlessly. A few weeks later he called to tell me he had been diagnosed with brain cancer. That was the last time I heard his voice. . . .

PART EIGHT

Ritual

76

Early morning on February 22, 1997, Lily knocked on my bedroom door. Before I got out of bed, she poked her head in and said, "Phone."

"What time is it?" I asked, my feet feeling for my slippers under the bed.

"Too early. Four?" She tossed the cordless phone toward me and slammed the door.

I spoke "hello" into the receiver and was astonished to hear the repetitive Chinese phone greeting "wei, wei, wei." But more astounding than receiving a call from Taiwan right here—I didn't tell anyone in Taiwan I was staying with Lily—was that I knew exactly who the caller was. I would never forget that voice. Nor would I ever expect this person to call me in a million years.

"What?" I barked.

The ex-stepmother announced, "Your ma DIED!" Her tone was a clear declaration of joy.

Your ma died.
Your ma died.
Your ma died.
Muahahaha~

Just like that, those three little words that took less than two seconds to say changed Mama from present tense to past.

The ensuing moment was contorted into a standstill. A sharp twinge of disbelief came first—swarming, invading, flooding my entire being. Then I was choked up in an uncontrollable rage. For my entire life I'd wondered how this would happen: Which one of my parents would go first? Who would tell me the news? How would the news be delivered? But I'd never imagined when Mama's death news arrived at dawn, I'd wake up to the ex-step-mother's laughing at my grief.

By now, Baba and the ex-stepmother had been divorced for three years. Who was she to tell me my mama had passed away? No matter how hard I tried to understand why she was the messenger, I couldn't find a rational reason. This woman didn't deserve any of my time or any space of my mind, so I stopped thinking about it and hung up. I refused to give her the thrilling gratification of hearing me bawl in my vulnerable state. I screamed into the pillow, screamed and screamed and screamed till I was snotty and the pillow was slobbery, then I fell to my knees by the bed, trembling.

I prayed.

"Heavenly Father, my ma died. I think she died in the middle of the night. I don't know. Is she pain-free now?"

As soon as I uttered the last sentence, I was broken. Broken! I couldn't stop myself from the hideous howl that escaped my mouth. I heard the door squeak open and Lily ask if I was okay. I didn't get up. I didn't look up. I kept my head down and said, for the very first time in my life, "My ma is dead. . . ."

The power of those four words made the mourning official.

Lily wrapped her arm around my shoulder. We knelt together in silence—an almost sacred atmosphere of reverence, a moment our souls communicated in a voice that didn't require words—then she quietly left the room.

I called Baba's home phone, the same number he'd made me memorize the day I was carried to the police station when I was four. I hadn't dialed that number since the day he disowned me three years earlier. When Dee answered "wei," I said, "Dee, it's me." She instantly bawled.

Dee and I, we had the same voice. She physically resembled Baba; I, Mama. She was the beautiful one and all those other things too: skinny, athletic, funny, loved MacGyver. When we were in high school and her countless admirers called her at our home, she'd mercifully let me take over some of the conversations, just to satisfy my flaming curiosity of what it was like to talk to boys. None of the callers ever found out Dee and I switched back and forth, not even when the subject of conversation became bizarrely different every few minutes.

Now, listening to Dee cry, it sounded like my own lamenting voice echoing between two continents, across the deep, dark Pacific. We'd had different life experiences up until now but became motherless at the same time, grieving in the same voice into each other's consolation through the phone lines. We said, "So strange Ma is gone. I saw her just a few months ago." "So strange Ma is gone. She looked okay last week." And we couldn't believe it. Nothing prepared me for the reality that Mama was no more. Nothing prepared me for what Dee said next:

"She died on her birthday, you know that?"

Died on her birthday!

Mama entered and left this world on the same date within fifty years. Ah-Po remembered for her the details of her birth. She told me about it once: Ah-Po was nine months pregnant and still working in rice fields. One day she went into labor, squatted down, and, by water buffalos' hooves, gave birth to her first child. According to Ah-Po's religious belief, this was why Mama's life was hard. "She reincarnated into a woman's body but had to live a water buffalo's hard life. That's why your baba didn't treat her like a human being. He was her creditor in the previous life, see?"

I loved and respected Ah-Po with all my heart, but it's preposterous that she actually believed that nonsense. Mama's life was hard because *everyone's life is hard*! It's called mortal experience. Baba didn't treat her like a human being, true, but it had nothing

to do with him being her premortal creditor. It had everything
to do with his agency—his power, freedom, and ability to choose.
He chose to abuse. No one should excuse his behavior by saying
it was fate. It wasn't. The suck-it-up-because-it's-your-premor-
tal-debt theory victimizes innocent individuals by empowering
abusers. It negates the powerful reality that everyone has agency.
I refuse to believe the universe is so lawless that it functions on
the principle of human debtors reincarnating into animal forms to
be rightfully abused.

Dee remembered the details of Mama's death. I listened
intently as she shared her memory:

A few weeks before her passing, Mama became so ill that a
live-in nurse was required to care for her. She moved back with
Ah-Gung and Ah-Po. In the tight-knit clan village Mama's relatives had been living in for generations, helping take care of
Mama became everyone's job. Each man took a shift in her doctor's appointment carpool schedule and prescription refill/pickup
routine. The aunts and female cousins took turns cooking meals
for Ah-Gung, Ah-Po, and Mama. They did dishes and laundry
and cleaned the house. Mama's cousin—the one who sneaked
snacks into the hospital—volunteered to bathe Mama every night.

This cousin later reported to the clan that on the night of
Mama's fiftieth birthday, after her bath, she put a clean slip on
Mama. When she helped Mama walk to the bedroom, Mama
frantically shooed away some invisible personages.

"No, no, no! Go away!" Mama begged, her knees buckled,
and she fell into the cousin's bosom. "Go away! I'm not ready—
can't go home yet!"

When the cousin asked Mama who she was talking to, Mama
cried, "Men—Can't you see? Coming to take me—"

Her last words.

Mama collapsed.

An ambulance was called.

The cousin hopped on her moped and followed the ambulance to the emergency room.

The traffic was ruthless.

Mama arrived in the emergency room without any vital signs.

The medical team tried to resuscitate her. At the thirty-minute mark they stopped.

The in-house undertaker immediately wrapped Mama's head in a clean diaper to absorb the blood pouring out of her mouth.

"Donor? Is she a donor?" someone on the medical team yelled. "Any family here?"

The cousin stood next to Mama's lifeless body, too shaken to speak. The salesmen from various mortuaries stationed at the ER approached her with business cards anyway.

"What time?" I asked Dee.

"Oh, if the traffic was bad, it was probably still early. Like, ten thirty? Maybe eleven. I got the call before midnight."

What was I doing when Mama passed, February 22, 1997, at 11:00 p.m. Taiwan time? Was I alone? Was I talking to Tyler Tanner when Mama was talking to the invisible men? Why didn't I feel anything—anything at all—at that exact time when she died?

It's said that if we don't remember someone out loud, then that person died twice. I don't wish to erase Mama's memory or her name from my speech. What was the very first thing I said to her when I was a babbling baby? I don't remember. But I'll never forget the last thing I said to her in this life: "Say good-bye so I can go."

She never did.

77

There was an $800 flight between me and Mama's funeral, and I didn't have $800.

Lily suggested that I seek financial assistance from the bishop at the Salt Lake City Chinese Ward. I didn't know the man. But when I called him on the phone, he said, "Sister Hong, I'm sorry for your loss. We all strive to be more like our Savior Jesus Christ. If He were here right now, He would definitely help you get to your mother's funeral. That's what I'll do."

I was in awe of his profound generosity and kindness. But more than that, I was deeply touched by his choice to do good, to uplift, to console, to bless others the way Christ would.

Within an hour of the phone conversation I sat in the bishop's office on the University of Utah campus. Bishop Chen was a middle-aged, gray-haired Asian man in a dark suit. Printed on his silk necktie were the traditional Chinese characters that read: *No Other Success Can Compensate for Failure in a Home.* He shook my hand and handed me an $800 USD check, issued by the Church of Jesus Christ of Latter-day Saints. "Have a safe trip home, Sister Hong. May the Lord comfort you and your family."

I thanked him over and over, knowing I would never see him again, knowing I would never forget him. As I walked out of his office, a small voice rang in my head. "Pay it forward. Pay it forward."

I looked back and saw the bishop waving, his other hand over his heart. Had my spiritual eyes been opened, I believe I would've seen the Lord standing behind him, patting him on the shoulder and saying, "Well done, thou good and faithful servant. . . ."

78

It was only six months earlier when Cameron and I landed in Taipei together. Taiwan, of course, didn't change that much within the half year when my life was upended and I was thrown off the orbit of a newlywed-and-new-immigrant track, losing focus and direction in the circle of my mental, emotional, and social life. Six months: that was all it took to whip me back to the bottom of what Cameron called a shithole.

From Taipei, I took a three-hour train ride back to my hometown, Hualien, lacing through the coastal railroad, in and out of mountain tunnels, bordering the endless beach. I'd traveled this route countless times, but none of those trips felt as heavy, long, and mysteriously uncertain. I wasn't sure if going home this time marked the end of my American dream. In our sixteen-month marriage, Cameron never filed my immigration papers to apply for my green card, which meant I had been staying in the U.S. on a student visa the whole time. When we traveled together between America and Taiwan, we were in different lines to pass customs and immigration. Citizen versus visitor. We never stood on the same ground.

What if my application to BYU and U of U both got rejected and I was no longer a student? What then? I wished I knew where I stood in life. Who was I? Not a daughter. Not a wife. Not a girlfriend. Not a college graduate. Not a career woman. A lost ghost floating among the knowing living.

Dee picked me up at the train station in her China Airlines uniform—a modern design patterned after the traditional Chinese form-fitting, high-slit qipao with choker collar and a line of frog buttons running across the right side of the chest. It brought out the curves of her figure. She wore heavy makeup: bright red lips, bold purple eyeshadows on her single eyelids, thick clumpy mascara coating her lashes. Her pixie hairstyle framed her heart-shaped face. She walked with her chin up; her high heels clicked loudly on Hualien City's trademark marble sidewalks, and the scent of LANCÔME TRÉSOR wafted in the air. She made street folks turn heads. While most girls her age still got around town on small, buzzing mopeds, Dee drove the brand-new 1997 Toyota Camry she purchased with her own money. We went straight to the hospital basement where Mama's body was stored.

The undertaker lived in an under-the-stairs storage room in the hospital basement. He stood up to my chin, wrinkled and bald and boney. His dirty white tank top emitted an unpleasant odor, his breath the alcoholic stench. There were black holes in his mouth where teeth were missing, and the few remaining teeth were caramel-colored. He recognized Dee. But when he saw me, he pointed at my nose and said, in Hokkien, "This one looks just like your ma."

In life and death, Mama's only visible connection with me was the face. Same face, similar fate: dead-end marriage, untrustworthy husband. My life started with her in the hospital, my arrival delayed. Her life ended without me in the hospital, my arrival delayed, once again. Her untimely death made it impossible for me to repent and start a belated mother-daughter relationship. In life, we briefly crossed paths but mostly missed each other like two trains on parallel tracks, heading in opposite directions. We each boarded a different one. When the trains met, then passed each other, we waved through the window. *Hello. Good-bye. Travel safe.*

The undertaker took a set of keys off a nail on the wall and

gestured for us to follow him. We went down a dark hall of concrete walls and marble floor, then he unlocked the double metal
doors to a room full of oversize stainless-steel freezer chests. He
led us through a maze of chests to one against a wall. Under the
sweating glass top of the freezer, Mama laid on a bed of ice. Her
face was swollen. Her eyes didn't close completely. Someone had
dressed her in street clothes I had never seen before. She wore
light makeup, but the lip color wasn't her usual choice of cherry.
She had on a pair of new white walking shoes that looked at least
two sizes larger than how big I remembered her feet were.

"What's with the huge shoes?" I asked the undertaker.

"Oh, the shoes." He nodded. "You know your ma had diabetes, right? Her kidneys failed, couldn't go to the bathroom. All
that waste—trapped in her body, you know? So her legs and feet
swelled. Really big." He did the explosion movement with both
of his hands around his right shin. "Okay, that happened. She
must've been miserable, her last days."

She must've been miserable, her last days.

And I was away, eight thousand miles away, so far away that
on the night she silently turned fifty and quietly died, when someone in the emergency room yelled, "Any family here?" I wasn't
the one to say, "Here! I'm her daughter. I'm right here."

I tasted a little bile in my mouth. Guilt and regret came to me
in the form of water in my eyes.

"No tears!" The undertaker waggled a finger to warn me.
"With even one drop of your tear, you'll make her bleed from the
seven cavities of her head." He looked into my eyes with a little
too much intimidating authority. "I used a diaper"—he hovered
over his groin with both open hands and did a pull-up-the-pants
movement—"to suck the blood off her face. . . ."

His words echoed what my fifth-grade teacher talked about
once: when someone dies without family members by his side,
but moments later his family arrives at the scene, the deceased

person will bleed from the seven cavities of the head—eyes, nostrils, ears, and mouth—as a way to express his lingering love for his family and say the belated good-bye before his spirit heads down to the underworld.

Is there any scientific proof to sustain the bleed-from-seven-cavities theory? Who knows? But the image of Mama bleeding when her spirit left her body haunted me. Fear covered me entirely, like dust. *It happened to Mama; it could happen to me.* But was this about love or fear? I pondered the deeper meaning of this hypothetical yet powerful concept: even in death, people try to use up every last drop of energy to bond with their families. To me, bleeding meant hurt, wounds, injury. Bleeding from seven cavities meant overflowing pain. But could it be that the deceased loved his family so much that he couldn't bear watching them grieve in heartbreak, so he cried on their behalf? All of his tears for all of his loved ones. When he ran out of tears, he cried blood.

Blood is thicker than water.

Perhaps this is why the undertaker said, "Your ma, she cried all her blood tears so you don't have to."

79

After seeing Mama's body in the hospital basement, Dee drove me to Uncle's home. Six months earlier on our anniversary trip, Cameron and I stayed here, in a room with a shiny white marble floor, a built-in mahogany desk and bookshelves, and wall-to-wall, floor-to-ceiling windows that looked out to the green-tunnel road where old trees lined both sides. I was now unpacking the same suitcase in the same room, Cameron out of my life, Mama gone.

The next morning, Dee and I went to the hospital for the funeral.

The Chinese believe that no parents should outlive their children; such occurrence is simply against natural law. Children who put their parents through the heartbreak of burying their offspring are considered to have failed to fulfill their filial piety. In this case, Mama was a bad daughter who owed her parents apologies. I'd heard of this moral theory but had never seen it play out ceremonially until this day. Abiding by the natural law, Ah-Gung and Ah-Po didn't attend Mama's funeral. Uncle became the acting patriarch.

My youngest sister, May, now a high school sophomore, could hardly move without a walker. Uncle excused her from school and sent her to Ah-Gung's house to mourn, sparing her the all-day funeral ritual of kneeling and kowtowing, but also to hide her from the public eye. He said, "Ah-Gung is a prominent figure.

Having a crippled retard in a husbandless woman's funeral will disgrace his name by association."

If only Uncle could see that, in merely two years after Mama's funeral, May would pass the National University Entrance Exam and major in English in a prestigious school. Upon graduation, she would pass seemingly endless rounds of governmental exams to become a librarian in her alma mater. This was a motherless girl who grew up in an institution, bullied all her life, and achieved beyond her physical limitations. A crippled retard? No. I don't see how May and her hard-earned accomplishments could possibly disgrace Ah-Gung's good name by association. But I couldn't fight against Uncle's decision. We Chinese girls and women were expected to obey the men, silently waiting for them to tell us what to do.

Blah!

The undertaker, who doubled as the funeral conductor, set up chairs in a conference room in the hospital basement. Unlike a traditional funeral, the makeshift altar here wasn't decorated with a sea of fresh white chrysanthemums or white lilies or white carnations. On the center of a long folding table was an enlarged photograph of Mama in a black frame. On one end of the table was a boom box that perpetually played monotone Buddhist scripture chant.

Uncle stood by the entrance of the conference room, greeting and receiving white envelopes from clan relatives and village guests. Each envelope was stuffed with condolences cash intended to help cover the funeral cost.

Mama's body had been transferred into a wooden casket. The undertaker pulled some dollar bills out of a white envelope and put them into Mama's palm. He made a fist with her hand so it looked as if she clenched the money.

"What—?" I asked.

"Tell you later," he said while handing Dee and me identical white linen hooded robes. "Put them on, Children of the Dead."

It was customary for immediate family members of the deceased to wear scratchy goat-hair linen robes at the funeral, symbolizing mourning. While this aspect of the tradition was observed, Mama wasn't offered a decent funeral service on the street, the same way a Taiwanese Buddhist was honored at death. Her casket wasn't respectfully placed in front of her house under a canopy so large that the entire alley was blocked like a road construction site. Uncle gave Mama a homeless person's burial. The simplest, fastest, and cheapest ceremony performed in the hospital basement where the unclaimed corpses of those who had died in the ER were stored, then straight to the crematorium. I guess this had to do with not losing face by advertising Mama's passing. In the time and place where she passed away a divorcée, she was considered a disgrace to her family. So much so she didn't even have an obituary in the papers.

An awakening thought hit me: if I told my family about my marital status—which I hadn't—and if I died here today, then they probably would treat me the same way, not bothering to remember or celebrate my life. "You're like your mama," people told me.

However, the more I thought about it, the clearer it became: I have absolutely no power over what people do at my death. All I have control over are my choices while I'm still alive. I might've resembled Mama, but I wasn't her. I didn't have to live like her if I chose not to. Mama made choices for herself. I'm one of the consequences of her choice to marry Baba and to have children with him. Always, I'll thank her for having chosen to give me life.

After a brief bathroom break, I was returning to the conference room when a middle-aged woman stopped me at the door. Pointing at my robe, she asked, "Family of the dead?"

I nodded. "It's my ma's funeral."

From the floor she picked up a cardboard box with the Chinese

characters *Incense Fire Money* written on the side. "You want to put
a lot of money in this donation box, so the arch nun will pray
extra hard for your ma. The arch nun is Buddha's right-hand
person, you know? Her prayers will give your ma a pass straight
to paradise. Without a donation, your ma will reincarnate into an
animal and be abused!"

"You're kidding, right?" I didn't bother to hide my rage. "I
hope you yourself don't even believe what you just said!"

Leaving her standing in the empty hall with an empty box,
I entered the conference room only to discover something else
unexpected: Baba stood next to Mama's casket with his hands
cupped behind his back, greeting the guests who filed into the
room. He wore an old, wrinkled dress shirt, dark dress pants, and
a pair of worn leather shoes. From across the room I could smell
his distinct body odor.

Dee also returned from the restroom. As soon as she saw
Baba, she ran over to link elbows with him. The two of them
lowered their heads in a private conversation. They looked like
family; I, like a guest.

I'd never rehearsed for this—dressed in a linen robe at Mama's
funeral. Should I lace my fingers in front of me or should I rest
them behind me? Should I smile at people coming in or should I
keep my eyes on Mama's portrait on the table? Should I ask Baba
why the ex-stepmother was Mama's death announcer? But then,
what was the point? What was I thinking? It was done, and I
loathed having to talk about that person.

The undertaker rounded up Dee and me by the casket. He
then asked the attendees to sit in rows of folding chairs. After
Uncle took the front row center seat, the rest of the relatives sat
down in reverence. Baba sat at the very back, alone and stoic.

Because Mama put Ah-Gung and Ah-Po through the cruelest
tragedy any parent could possibly experience, she needed to sym-
bolically apologize. Dee and I represented her, the unfilial child,

kneeling and kowtowing and apologizing to her acting father–Uncle. *Forgive me, forgive me, forgive me.*

Then the undertaker instructed us sisters to take the cash in Mama's hand. "This is the 'Hand Tail Money,' the money that trails behind your ma's hand like a tail. A symbolic gift she left you. Leaving you when you're still young is sad. Nothing she could do. It was her time to go. But she couldn't leave in peace. She worried about you because you're young, so she left you some money to grow up with. It's a mother's love. Now, take it and grow up."

My heart and mind were full. I tried to process what I just heard, but it was too much. Too much wisdom, too much wisdom, too much wisdom! And I fought with all my might not to cry, remembering Mama had shed blood tears so I wouldn't have to. Why had I been so cruel to her the last time I saw her? Why was I? If her spirit were here, would she forgive me, the unfilial child? The child who ran far away from her mother's life she was afraid might become her own.

I'll never forget the last time I saw her. Of course, there's nothing I can do to change the past, and there's no point in continuing to beat myself up for what transpired. I was conflicted at the time, torn between her and Cameron. In that vulnerable state, with terrible emotional pressure from both sides, I simply didn't have enough strength for the battles I was facing. I did what I thought was the right thing at the time. Understanding that, I've developed compassion for myself and forgiven myself. Given another chance, I still would've chosen to leave Mama. I was a floating flower, roots in air. Tribal nation is where my life began, diaspora is where it ends. Mama's and my life choices would always have us wave at each other. *Hello. Good-bye. Travel safe.*

I took the two Taiwanese hundred-dollar bills from Mama's hand, keeping one and passing the other to Dee. It was about $3

USD, what Mama had posthumously left me. I scrunched up the money and put it in my pocket. *Take it and grow up.*

The undertaker closed the casket and promptly handed me a hammer. He instructed me to seal the casket by pounding down the nails in the four corners, but instead I pounded my chest with my fist. I was suffocating; my chest was so dense I couldn't fully breathe in. My vision was so blurry from welling tears I couldn't see the nails. Dee took the hammer from me and sealed the casket. One clean, crisp pound at each corner, done.

Six of Mama's male cousins carried the casket out. Some of them played with me when I was little, showing me their farm animals and letting me feed them. Each one solemn and red-eyed now. The undertaker instructed us sisters to kowtow to every attendee as they filed out of the room.

After the guests were gone, I carried Mama's portrait, placing it between my neck and torso, and led Dee to the hearse. Because Mama was husbandless and sonless and Uncle was acting as Ah-Gung's substitute and her cousins were pallbearers, there weren't any other male relatives left to carry the clay pot filled with sand in which burning incenses stuck. Baba volunteered.

The casket was loaded onto the bed of a rusty, matted blue Ford truck. The undertaker got in the driver's seat; Baba and us sisters sat on plastic stepstools next to the casket in the truck bed. The hearse took us out of the city, into a lush forest country, and up a narrow, windy gravel mountain road. My eyelids got heavy. All sounds around me mingled into a muffled, humming white noise. The last thing I heard was Dee saying, "Jetlag."

Dee woke me when we arrived at the summit, in front of a concrete building with flat roof, huge windows, and blackened chimneys. The crematorium overlooked the valley of endless rice fields, wild flowers, tiny farm houses, ribbons of country roads, and matchbox-sized cars cruising around. Everyone had a place to go, a home to return. I was home now. To light Mama on fire. To send her home above.

The undertaker went to the office to sign in. Soon, six Buddhist monks in yellow robes followed him out. Their heads were shaved. The ping-pong-ball-sized wooden prayer beads around their necks looked like fashionable necklaces. Their low, unified, monotonous chant shook me up with a mysterious melancholy.

The undertaker led us into a wide-open lobby with a marble floor that looked as if it could be used for a dance hall. Along one wall were six stainless-steel furnaces. Plenty of natural light flooded into the lobby through the huge windows. Six young muscular men in white shirts carried Mama's casket in and rested it on a conveyor belt in front of a furnace. One man took the incense pot from Baba, and another took the framed portrait from me. Both of them thoughtfully positioned those items by the foot of the casket on a concrete table. Everyone was quiet. The only sounds were the monks' throaty chant and the undertaker's instructions:

"Family, kneel!"

Dee and I knelt.

"Family, kowtow!"

We kowtowed.

"Family, second kowtow!"

We kowtowed again.

"Family, third kowtow!"

We repeated. There was a fierce roar of the metal door opening on squeaky hinges and the conveyor belt rolling. Dee and I, we were in the same lobby with Mama's body, repeating the kowtow motion while she burned. Each time our heads touched the cold floor at the undertaker's command, the monks chanted more energetically, louder, faster.

Abruptly the chanting stopped. The monks bowed, then walked away. The undertaker gestured for us to get up from the floor and pointed at a spacious alcove off the lobby. "Go rest."

A sand box was on a rectangular table at the center of the alcove, and a row of chairs was pushed against a wall. We sat for a few minutes in silence before I dozed off again. When Dee elbowed me awake, the undertaker was pushing a metal cart toward us. On the top tier of the cart was a metal box and an urn. With his gloved hands, the undertaker set them up on the table, as if preparing to do a live demonstration. With horror, I watched him do what he did for a living—handling the dead.

He reached into the metal box and picked out a piece of bone and left it on the table. He bent over to fetch a hammer from the bottom tier of the cart. He was gentle. With a soft blow to the bone, it shattered. With a few soft pounds to the shards, they pulverized. He sifted the bone powder slightly in his cupped hands and poured it into the urn. Then he lifted a skull in the air and studied it with interest. "Aw, so beautiful. Your ma was a beauty."

The skull!

I had seen plastic skulls at Walmart during Halloween season in America, but never a real one. Now I was looking at Mama's skull, perfectly intact and pure white. Hollowed eye sockets. Upside-down heart-shaped hole for the nose. High cheek bones. This was her head, where her brain and mind were shielded. Where her lifelong thoughts and memories were stored. It was in a stranger's hand now. He held it like a volleyball. Was he going to hammer Mama's skull? Once, twice, thrice, like me knocking my forehead on the marble floor repeatedly, each time with belated gratitude for each thing Mama had done for me. Changed my diapers, breastfed me, bathed me.

The undertaker hammered away, bashing and smashing. It reminded me of the times when Baba pummeled that same head the same way.

Once, twice, thrice, Baba was drunk and mercilessly out of control.

Once, twice, thrice, Mama stormed out of the house, gone for weeks.

Once, twice, thrice, I tiptoed to look out the bedroom window at Mama's leaving.

Finally, the undertaker scooped out a handful of ash from the metal box to fill the urn and dumped the leftovers into the sand box, dust to dust.

Your ma was a beauty.

The fire devoured Mama whole, ate everything: her compass-drawn round face, her willow-leaf-shaped brows, her double crease eyelids, her heart-shaped smiling lips, her elephant-leg-like arms, her flooded lungs. Gone.

All gone.

She was the ash in the urn, in the tray, in the air, no longer the woman who lived with a packed suitcase, always ready to leave Baba.

No longer the woman who took me to a noodle shop to pry for updates on Baba.

No longer the woman who cough-peed her white cotton slip, leaning against the mossy cinderblock wall of her house, begging me to stay.

What a way to have lived fifty years of a turbulent life, to receive the least dignified burial of all—no obituary, no eulogy, no embalmment! After two years of not being able to lie down to sleep, she could finally, finally rest.

I blinked and caught my reflection in the stainless-steel furnace door.

Motherless!

80

The night of Mama's funeral, Lily called to tell me University of Utah admissions office sent me a letter. I asked her to read it for me.

"Oh, they've accepted you," she said.

Me? Accepted by University of Utah? What much-needed good news! I laughed with delight and thanked Lily.

"I underestimated you," she said. "You got in? Pffft! I was born and grew up here and couldn't get in. I speak better English than you, forgodssake! What you got?"

Although I always appreciated Lily's bluntness, what she said burned me. At this time, I was emotionally exhausted from the seemingly endless challenges before me. I became impatient, easily offended, and had no tolerance for her sour-grape attitude. It sickened me that she would insult me when I finally had a small glimpse of joy amidst tragedy. Why I let her comment dictate my academic future, I can't say. But filled with indignation, I refused to return to Salt Lake City, to her house, to attend the nearby University of Utah. That narrowed my school options down to one—Brigham Young University in Provo, an hour away from Lily. Looking back, I feel that even though I was immature, impulsive, and irrational, making my education decision solely based on Lily's comment, I was, in fact, directed by an unseen hand to the place I was meant to be.

As soon as Lily hung up, I called the BYU admissions office to check on my application status. To my disappointment, I was told to wait for a couple more days to hear from them.

"But U of U already accepted me. I want to know if you will too. I need to make a decision now."

"Yes, I understand," the lady on the phone said. "Your application is currently in the prayer meeting."

The prayer meeting?

I shouldn't have been surprised. After all, BYU is a church-sponsored school. But I was surprised to hear that a prayer meeting was part of the process of consideration for prospective students. Before my mission I attended a Catholic university. But, to get in, all it took was high scores on the entrance exam, which made me think BYU students were blessed to have the admissions committee pray about them individually. I saw it as an entire village kneeling in a circle to pray for one child before the first day of school, and that made me even more anxious to go to BYU. I dreamed about walking on BYU's campus, waving at classmates and greeting professors. I avoided thinking about the fact that I had a fifty percent chance of not being accepted. Soon, all I could think was *The library—what does it look like? Oh, the cafeteria—what do they serve there? And the bookstore—I hope they carry cute journals.*

Two days later I called BYU again from Uncle's guest bedroom. The lady on the phone chirped, "I'd like to take this opportunity to be the first one to say, 'Welcome to BYU!'"

Oh—my—gosh! Her voice was like liquid gold. I could listen to her say it a thousand times over. *Congratulations! Congratulations! Congratulations!*

Outside the window, a line of teenage girls biked down the tree-canopy road to school. It was only six years earlier when I wore the same high school uniform and biked down the same path every day. I could feel the heaviness of their book bags. I could hear them recite English vocabulary in preparation for the morning quiz. I could see the worry in their eyes—*Will I pass the National University Entrance Exam?*

I wanted to shout encouragement to them from the rooftops: "Keep going! Your hard work will pay off. Look at me! I was where you are, and now I'm heading for a great university in the U.S. You can do it too!"

When Brigham Young led members of the Church of Jesus Christ of Latter-day Saints in handcart companies—persecuted and driven out of Missouri for their faith—and arrived in the Salt Lake Valley on July 24, 1847, he announced, "This is the place." Utah was the place, the shelter, the haven, the refuge for the pioneers then. One hundred fifty years later, it was going to be my emotional, spiritual sanctuary too. It was going to be the place where the unseen hand guided me to, the place God circled on a map for me.

81

The day before I flew to Utah, Dee dropped me off at Ah-Gung's.

To broaden the street, the city had torn down Ah-Gung's bamboo forest fence that surrounded his property. His once-secluded orchard was plowed over and now the straight shot to the downtown train station. From his front door, I had an unhampered view of a new, booming city life: high-rise business centers that stood together like a park of glass towers, multistory residential buildings with balconies that looked out to more tall buildings, American restaurants, internet cafes, luxury cars, tour buses, and the never-ending honking noises. But, despite how much the village landscape had changed, how the hustle and bustle of the end-of-twentieth-century modernization engulfed Ah-Gung's living space, he stubbornly kept his traditional wooden farm house the same. I felt this was Ah-Gung's effort to help his descendants— the sojourners, the adventurers, and now, the deceased—to find their way home to him. It was his way of leaving the porch lights on at night for a gone-away child.

I could walk around Ah-Gung's living room with my eyes closed. For decades, everything in this room remained the same: the marble floor, the chiming grandfather clock, the shimmering textured wallpaper, the rattan couch and matching chairs around the glass-top coffee table, the blackboard on the wall with Ah-Gung's neat handwritten quotes from *The Book of Changes*.

Gone were his Japanese guests—his boyhood classmates—who used to visit frequently when I was little. Gone were my cousins who used to live here during the weekdays when their mother worked full-time at the airlines. Gone were the teasing, the laughter, the clanking of chopsticks against rice bowls at the round dining table, where the family gathered for Ah-Po's homemade meals.

I sat in a chair across from Ah-Gung. It had been ten years since I was in his house. Six months prior, when Cameron and I were in Taiwan together, Ah-Gung and Ah-Po went to Uncle's house to visit us.

Ah-Gung hadn't changed much. Five foot ten, tall among the Chinese. Full, straight gray hair, oiled and combed to the right. Deep-set brown eyes. Eagle-beak nose. Mama got her heart-shaped smile from him. But her high cheekbones? Definitely from Ah-Po.

Knowing that Ah-Po hid in the kitchen whenever guests visited, I asked, in Hakkanese, if she was there. But Ah-Gung said, "Well, no. Your uncle took her to the Import Street."

"She's shopping?"

"No, no—not shopping. Your ma owed money there. Ah-Po went to settle her debts."

I reflexively felt the urge to apologize for what Mama put them through. How could she have done this to them? "How . . . much?" I asked, then gulped.

"Don't worry about it. It's not your responsibility."

I was annoyed by the thought that even after Mama's death, Ah-Gung and Ah-Po continued to make sacrifices for her. Was there ever an end? Were these sacrifices good or bad? I thought I could make a sharp, swift judgment on my grandparents' parenting skills, but I had forgotten I didn't know everything that went on in their lives, in their relationships with Mama. I didn't know what it was like to have her for a daughter, or the battles they fought as her parents. I felt bad about the whole thing but didn't know what to say.

After a moment of silence, Ah-Gung said, "You're a beautiful girl."

In a world where people say *thanks* to compliments, the Chinese were taught to be humble and polite by denying the compliments extended to them. *No, no, no. Not at all. I'm not beautiful. Not smart. Not amazing. My kids aren't cute. Aren't talented. Aren't awesome. They eat booger. I'm not good enough. Not–at–all.* How easy is it to just say *thanks* with a smile, as Americans do?

So I told Ah-Gung *thanks* and pulled out a wallet-size picture of myself. When I stayed with Lily, one day her photographer friend, Jeremy, came to hang out and asked if I could model for him. That afternoon he took me to a city park for the shoot. My black hair cascaded down my back and touched my waist. My skin was pale from staying indoors all day, every day in Utah winter. My bright red sweater hung loosely over my eighty-nine-pound skeletal frame. My legs looked like chicken feet. I smiled at the camera, my eyes tired. In my wallet I kept my favorite picture from that shoot. I handed it to Ah-Gung.

He studied it, so focused, so reverent, as if reading an ancient scroll. After a moment, he looked up from the picture, and his lips quivered. "Your ma, you look . . . " When he returned the picture to me, I told him to keep it.

I didn't know then that Ah-Gung would pass away ten years later. After his funeral, Uncle went to clean out his belongings. Under his pillow, my picture was discovered. Water damaged. On the back of it, Ah-Gung's handwriting: *My Daughters.*

I excused myself to use the bathroom. I didn't need to go. I only wanted to stand where Mama last stood, on the kitchen concrete floor. Mama saw the invisible men here. She panicked here. Cried here. Shooed away the men here. Collapsed here. The medics arrived here. In my mind's eye, I saw Mama taken away in her white cotton slip, her hair damp, her face wet, her double eyelids drawn, her lips closed. Words were taken away from her. Life was taken out of her. She entered and left this world right here in the same house, on the same date. The Chinese believe the spirit of the dead lingers in his house for seven days before departing to the underworld. And if the family of the dead spills uncooked rice on the floor on the seventh day, they might catch the dead's departing footprints.

This was the seventh day after Mama's passing. Was she here now? If so, would she ask me to stay again? Or would she want me to ask her to stay instead?

When it was time for me to leave, Ah-Gung walked me out to the courtyard. He produced a thick red envelope from his pocket. "It's not really appropriate to give out a red envelope during this time of mourning"–he handed me the envelope–"but you're going to America tomorrow, to go to school. It's something worth celebrating."

I took the gift with both hands and bowed, the honorific way to show gratitude that Ah-Gung himself had taught me when I was little. My entire body tingled as if covered by a colony of ants. I couldn't distinguish the moving feeling of gratitude from the guilty feeling of unworthiness. Ah-Gung was like this: he sacrificed and gave, protected and provided, loved and cared, quietly and willingly. I was like this: I needed, I lacked, I hurt. I took. I took. I took.

However much it was in the red envelope, I could use the gift money. But the memory of Cameron withdrawing and depositing Ah-Gung's $10,000 into his father's account was still fresh, raw, and painful. I almost wanted to apologize to Ah-Gung for having lost that money, but I didn't have the heart to hurt him with that awful news when he'd just lost his daughter. The only right thing to do was to promise him I would put the money to good use, and keep that promise.

I stood on the sidewalk and waved good-bye to Ah-Gung. Twenty years earlier the land under my feet was dotted with wax apple trees and persimmon trees. Ah-Po had taught me to sing the song "Beautiful Jasmine" here. Village children had run up and down rows of trees here, playing hide-and-seek. Mama had. Uncle had. I had. The orchard was long gone, and we all belonged to different places now. Deep down I knew Ah-Gung's wooden farm house would someday become a memory I told my children, and they wouldn't be able to imagine its old, majestic glory, as it was, the cradle of my heart.

Ah-Gung stood by the front door, waving and watching me going away. The porch lights were on. They always would be—even after the people left, one by one.

82

B YU was where I did everything on my own for the first time in a foreign country: checking in at the international student office, moving into the girl's dorm, talking with an academic counselor, registering for classes, paying tuition, buying health insurance, opening a bank account. With each completed task, I felt more confident in speaking English—not merely for survival but also for advancing myself in life. *What should I major in? What do BYU alumni do with this major? Considering the limitations of my student visa, what can I do with a bachelor's degree in that major?*

After some heavy thinking, I decided to change my major from German to Chinese. I wanted to become a Chinese professor in the U.S. If that didn't work out, I would return to Taiwan and teach English at a cram school.

Almost every month there was a celebration for a dorm girl in the lounge. The guest of honor looked like a kindergarten girl with pink cheeks, pink lips, pink nails, and a pink dress, and was surrounded by pink balloons, banners, confetti, cupcakes, and a mountain of sparkly presents. All the partygoers looked similar: milky-skinned blondes with straight, bleached teeth, clean and chic. I wouldn't have believed it had I not heard it with my own sacred ears, but the monthly festivity wasn't a birthday party; it was a bridal shower!

Yeah, the kind of American social event that gave me anxiety like nothing else.

Behind my anxiety was jealousy. I was jealous of those pretty late-teen girls who seemed to never have had heartbreak for breakfast, betrayal for lunch, destitution for dinner. I was only five years older than they were, but it was as if I grew up in their grandmothers' time: at nineteen, I walked, biked, or rode a bus around town. These girls drove Lexus. I worked as a part-time middle-school tutor to pay bills. These girls lounged at poolside after classes. In retrospect, I understand that back then I only chose to see what I wanted to see. Bitter in my experiences of a disowned daughter and an abandoned immigrant bride, I dwelled in a victim's emotional state and chose to see everyone else as an undeserving chosen one. I exhausted myself with unceasing complaint: *Life is so unfair! Why are those girls so lucky? What didn't I do in the premortal life to deserve it all?* The act of comparing myself with others and becoming jealous of them is the epitome of the saying "Drinking poison and expecting others to die."

Unable to connect with those chosen ones, I looked for someone or something to belong to and identify myself with—a group, a club, an organization. No human was born into solitude. Born to parents, into a family, a community, a society, I somehow broke away from my people, clan, country. Here in Utah, I wanted to find my tribe.

One day at the cafeteria, I saw an Asian girl for the first time since coming to BYU. She sat at a table with five white young men, chatting and laughing. Her presence had a pull on me. Convinced that she was my people, I couldn't resist the urge to approach her. When I stood quietly next to her, she looked up and smiled.

"Yo, sup? Can I help you?" she said. Her English sounded different, but the same. Different from mine; same as everyone else's. She smelled like an American—cucumber-melon-scented body lotion. Dressed like an American—bodysuit tucked in jeans.

"Your English is . . . so good!" I gulped in intimidation.

"Well, I'm ABC," she said.

I stared at her in confusion.

"American Born Chinese. You didn't know?" She chuckled. The young men at the table laughed.

ABC was what she told others to explain why she looked Asian or why she didn't have an accent. She said her parents were my kind, first-generation immigrants from Taiwan. But she was American through and through. When she asked about my major, I told her I wanted to be a Chinese professor someday.

"You should teach ME Chinese!" She rolled her eyes. Then, facing her friends with her nose scrunched, she said, "My mom keeps complaining that I can't even pronounce our last name right. Like, who cares?"

Naturally, I didn't develop the *my people* kind of friendship with her. She was already among her people every day, everywhere. She continued to sit with them at the cafeteria table while I looked to sit elsewhere.

From then on, I waited for other Asians to befriend me. But it rarely happened. Most of the time, judging from clothing, hair, or even hand gestures, I could tell if a girl was straight out of Asia. But our interaction—if there was any at all—turned awkward. It was my problem. In the presence of a fellow Asian student, I spontaneously avoided eye contact. My accent suddenly magnified and went out of control, as if I had taken the very first English lesson of my life that morning. The closest example I could think of to explain this strange phenomenon was the way I played volleyball in junior high. Whenever we played a high-ranking team, the competitiveness in me surged, and it put me in top performance. Inversely, when we played a lower-ranking team, I struggled serving over the net. It might have been a mental thing or a psychological thing; I'm not entirely sure. But when I spoke English with non-native English speakers, I sounded like Jackie Chan, without the charisma. Weird science.

Among those who looked like me, I felt a new kind of

alienation. Most of the ABCs I met on campus displayed disinterest in forming a relationship with me. I knew it wasn't personal. They were the lucky Chinese. The distance between us was created the moment their ancestors left the homeland while mine stayed. All in all, I was reminded of the power, influences, and consequences of human choices. My social, spiritual, financial decisions all carried lasting impacts on my posterity, through generations of time. And when I thought of my future descendants, somehow I felt less alone in this new, strange land. Could this be the price every pioneer pays for those who come after, to give them the best, to make them the lucky ones? If so, then it's not really about me finding my tribe, is it?

It's about me creating it.

83

When I was thirteen, when Elders York and Copinga visited my family for the first time, I asked them where they learned to speak Chinese so well. They said the MTC—Missionary Training Center. Eleven years later, now, outside of my BYU dorm room window was the MTC.

Sharing thirty-nine acres of BYU's campus, the MTC provides intensive training programs to over six hundred thousand missionaries from nearly every country in the world, in fifty-five languages. Believing my Chinese skills could help prepare those missionaries heading to Taiwan, I filled out a student-employment application form to teach Chinese at the MTC, and was assigned to attend a rating session on May 15, 1997.

For the rating session, I put on my favorite outfit: a white, short-sleeve, ankle-length silk qipao—a body-hugging traditional Chinese dress with a side slit at the knee, a Mandarin collar, and white frog buttons running down from the collar, across the chest, and ending at the right armpit. Then I stepped into my white glossy high heels. I arrived at the rating session room and was surprised to see two young men in white shirts, neckties, dark pants, and dress shoes sitting in folding chairs arranged in a horseshoe formation. At the front of the room was a wall-to-wall whiteboard, a platform stage, and a pulpit. Two young men in dark suits stood by the pulpit. As I stepped in the room, one of the standing guys asked, "Sister Hong?"

I nodded.

He came up and extended a hand to me. "Welcome! I'm Brother Wade, supervisor over Asian languages."

I shook his hand. He pointed at the chairs and invited me to sit. The other standing man introduced himself as Brother Olsen. I wanted to know why the rating session wasn't a one-on-one job interview. But something about this moment and space—the atmosphere in the room, the setup of chairs, the young men's serious faces—made me shrink into my awkward self as if in the presence of fellow foreign students, even though I was the only Asian in the room. Speaking English suddenly became arduous.

One of the sitting young men said he'd served his mission in the Philippines, the other Korea, Olsen in Hong Kong, Wade in Japan. As we introduced ourselves, two more young men came in. "Cambodia," one of them said when asked where he'd served his mission. The last one said Singapore.

Wade looked at his wristwatch and clapped. "Thanks for coming. We'll go ahead and start with a prayer."

The guy who had served in Cambodia offered the prayer, pleading on behalf of all the applicants to the Lord to help us do our best. With that, the rating session commenced. Olsen explained the procedure: Each applicant would be assigned a topic. Upon his turn, the applicant would stand on the platform stage and do a five-minute roleplay to demonstrate how well he could teach the specific gospel principle he had been assigned.

During Olsen's instructions, a young man entered the room and asked, "Is this where the rating session is?"

Wade said, "Are you applying to teach an Asian language?"

The young man nodded and smiled. "Yep, Japanese. Just got home from Okinawa two months ago."

Wade pointed at the only chair left in the room, next to me, and said, "This is the place, brother. Have a seat."

The Okinawa guy nodded at me, then sat down. It was all I

could do to not get caught staring at him. He had jet-black hair that looked like Arby's curly fries. Thick, long, curly lashes framed his deep, round blue eyes. Long, chiseled face. Freckles across the tall bridge of his nose and over his cheeks. Dimples at the corners of his lips when he smiled. Big ears. My thoughts strayed off to a guessing game of who this guy could possibly be. Unlike Chinese people, Americans have tons more fun when it comes to lineage; their ancestries cover almost all continents. This guy looked like a combination of Irish, Italian, and Iranian, maybe.

I was the first one to do the roleplay. Standing on the platform stage and looking out to a room full of American young men, I suddenly became extra conscious about my disadvantage.

"I never went to the MTC," I told Olsen and Wade, hoping they would understand how much harder this rating session was for me than for the others. This was the exact location where all of them learned their first word, first sentence, in Japanese, Korean, Tagalog. Surely, they knew how this language-training program worked at the MTC. I wanted the supervisors to be keenly aware of where I came from: the odd one without the same experience as everyone else and who was now competing with them to get a job. Secretly, I hoped I got five hundred bonus points as compensation.

"You'll be fine, Sister Hong," Olsen assured me. Wade nodded.

I thanked them, then smoothed the front of my qipao, cleared my throat, and started the roleplay on my assigned topic: How to Invite People to Attend Sunday Church Meetings. I gave special attention to words that had more than one syllable: baptism, covenants, sacrament. I was extra careful with words that had *L* or *R* in them: doctrine, auxiliary, principles. I made sure to enunciate those words distinctly and slowly so I didn't say them wrong. And I pretended that everyone in the room was a potato.

Olsen and Wade occasionally nodded and jotted down things on their clipboards. The young men in the room were intensely quiet. They leaned forward, elbows on knees, all eyes on me. This didn't make me nervous. Instead, I took it as a confirmation that I captured everyone's unadulterated attention. To me that meant successful teaching. That meant wonderful performance. That meant I would get the job. I couldn't stop a little premature celebratory grin. Then, powered by the newfound confidence, I decided to say "magnify your calling" in a sentence to spice up my roleplay, to show off my vocabulary bank. But no sooner had the word "calling" slipped off my tongue than I heard a loud nasal chuckle from the audience. And no sooner had I heard that chuckle than I stopped in midsentence, unable to continue. I stiffened on the platform stage, slack-jawed and speechless, as a burning rage engulfed me. Self-doubt and embarrassment instantly crept into my mind. I wanted to run out and hide in the ladies' room until someone came to tell me I got the job.

After the light-switch incident, it had taken me tremendous courage and effort to restore my confidence in speaking English. I thought I did well without Cameron's help, getting myself into BYU and communicating with people just fine, until this—a laugh from someone in the audience over something I said in a job interview.

It was sorely disappointing that the Okinawa guy was the one who destroyed my nearly perfect demonstration. I should've ignored him and kept going. But I couldn't. I glanced over at Olsen and Wade, who were scribbling on their clipboards, and I knew it was over. But could this actually be part of the rating session procedure? Was I being tested on how to handle negative feedback? And to pass this test, was I supposed to gracefully—as gracefully as I could possibly fake it—step down and return to my seat next to that horrible Okinawa guy? To act like a Mother-Teresa-type of saint who garnished her thoughts with Christ's teachings, *Forgive him, for he knows not what he did?*

When the rating session was over, the Okinawa guy walked

alongside me out of the building. Seeing that he was pulling his keys out of his pocket and we were about to go our separate ways, I called to him.

"You . . . uh . . ." I pointed at the general direction of the rating session room. "You laughed . . . when I was doing the roleplay."

"Oh, yeah." He laughed again. I didn't understand this guy. He clearly had no idea how harmful his laughter was.

"So—why? You, why . . . you laughed?"

"Oh, I wasn't laughing at you. I was laughing at myself."

What? Why is this guy so weird?

"You used a word. A verb, I think. You said something about calling . . ." He squinted.

"You mean, when I said 'magnify your calling,' it made you laugh . . . at *yourself?*"

"Yes, that's the word! 'Magnify.' Wow!" He clapped and laughed again. He made absolutely no sense.

"What about that word?" I didn't get it. This guy was so special. But instantly an image came to my mind: a child burns an ant under the sun with a magnifying glass. A voice said in my head, "That's how you use the word *magnify* in a sentence."

"Well, that's a big word," the Okinawa guy said. "I was really impressed when you said it. I tried to think how to say it in Japanese, but I couldn't, so I laughed at myself. Hahaha!"

Whaaa—?

Who does that?

Okay, if, miraculously, a messenger from God appeared in front of me—no, actually, the messenger didn't even have to be in front of me; he could just send me brainwaves or electric shock or whatever it was, as long as I could understand the message clearly—telling me that this weirdo's seemingly illogical behavior was just how he was, I most definitely wouldn't be so quick to judge him.

"Uh . . . that's . . . cool. You laughed at my word choice. So, you think maybe you could tell Olsen and Wade this, uh . . . that you were laughing at yourself, not at me? I think your laughing might've cost me the job."

"Oh, no. Don't worry. They knew," he said assuredly, laughing again.

What perfectly captures this exact moment is the Chinese saying, "Playing on a harp to a cow," which depicts a wasted effort. Realizing this conversation had come to an obvious end, I started to walk away without saying "good-bye" or "good luck" or "hope you get the job." I kept walking, not knowing the kind of hellfire and brimstone I was walking into.

PART NINE

Justice

84

A letter from a Texas court summoned me for an appearance in July 1997 to finalize the divorce. I called Ethan to apologize for having left Texas without saying good-bye. Maybe his study and training in psychology helped him develop patience for people like me; he told me not to worry about it, assuring me he understood completely. When I asked if I could crash in his living room when I went to Texas for the court appearance, he said it would be a great pleasure to return the favor I'd offered him when he first arrived in Edinburg. It was interesting how the table turned and how drastically things could change in less than a year.

The same day I received the court letter, I also received an email from Cameron: *Go see a shrink and get your head fixed before the court date, then I might consider taking you back.*

Where did he get the imaginary superiority and the phantom authority to treat me this way? What convinced him I wanted to be taken back? This guy drew strength from my sorrow, making me doubt the true worth of my soul. A spiritual terrorist. A vulture of joy. Why should I satisfy his egoistic demand?

When Ethan picked me up from Edinburg International Airport, I asked him to please drop me off at the courthouse for my appointment. He insisted on accompanying me in court. I wanted him to; I needed his support. But after the divorce I would fly back to Utah, and he would still be there, attending the same school as Cameron. They could possibly bump into each other on campus. We used to be friends, the three of us. What kind of friend would I be to let Ethan face my tormentor for me? This was my battle, and mine alone.

Outside the courthouse, I assured Ethan I would be fine and waved good-bye. As he drove away, he poked his head out of the van window and watched me. He said, "Come home when it's over," like a father or a brother would say to a little girl-David who was heading out to slay Goliath. Ethan thought where he lived was my home, my shelter, my refuge, where everything would be right again. I wanted to believe that too.

I walked the wide concrete steps leading up to the courthouse grand entrance, my stomach in my throat; my knees trembled almost audibly. This was the consequence of my choice to marry Cameron; no one in the world could walk this path for me.

Eight months earlier, the immediate effects of Cameron's abandonment forced me into a survival mode. Taking care of my physical needs, dealing with emotional turmoil, and tackling ongoing schoolwork left me with no brainpower to remember I should work with a divorce lawyer. Then I moved to Utah. Then I went back to Taiwan. Then I moved back to Utah. In those mentally grueling months all I could manage was to keep up with life. When the letter of my court appearance arrived, I was suddenly struck with the reality of needing an attorney. Through a friend I found Mr. Smith in Edinburg, Texas, who offered me pro-bono legal service. I was grateful for that, of course. But there wasn't much he could do for me, really. Except the 1982 Volvo we purchased together, Cameron and I didn't own any community property that required a lawyer's intervention to split. My surname wasn't changed to Chastain because Cameron never filed my immigration papers; I couldn't even give the attorney the tiny job of changing my name back. But I did call Smith on the phone and express my desire to get back the $15,000 Cameron had taken. I had only $2,000 left to live for the next eighteen months till I was scheduled to graduate from BYU, and I was dubious if I would get the job teaching Chinese at the MTC. I needed the $15,000.

However, there was no proof the money was mine. Ah-Gung gave me cash, as personal checks and Visa gift cards were practically unheard of in the 1996 Taiwan, at least in Ah-Gung's farming village. I obeyed Cameron and let him deposit the cash into our joint account.

"It's unlikely you'll get it back," Smith said. "As soon as it went into the joint account, the money became his too."

Well, I knew, I knew. I knew what *joint* meant. The power in that word enabled Cameron to take the money. I'd convinced myself this entire time the money was mine, mine, and mine alone because Ah-Gung gave it to *me* and advised *me* to spend it on *my* education. I convinced myself that if I could somehow get the money back, I wouldn't end up losing everything in this marriage. I wouldn't be left with nothing—absolutely nothing.

Now I was walking to my divorce, utterly alone. I told myself I could do this. I would live through this. No matter how bad things got, at the end of the day I would be home with my true friend, Ethan.

When I met Cameron in 1992, on a rainy night, on a Taipei street, I knew he would someday be my husband. Looking at the same man now—my husband for maybe another hour—I was in disbelief. This would be the last time we physically existed in the same space, standing in court, filled with animosity, cutting the legal tie between us. How did we arrive here?

Unlike me, who had lost twenty pounds since the light-switch incident, Cameron had put on so much weight, he was barely recognizable. Double chin, beefy cheeks, protruding belly, thick back. And receding hairline.

His parents were with him. So were his attorney, his friends Will and Leif and their girlfriends, and some of Dr. Chastain's colleagues. They sprawled comfortably on rows of benches on one side of the room, chatting merrily and laughing loudly, as if waiting for a favorite movie to start. I wondered what Cameron and his parents told these people about the night they moved everything out of apartment 21 within two hours, cutting off all utilities, withdrawing Ah-Gung's gift money, closing the bank account, and giving me a restraining order. Did they say, "Yeah, we blindsided Allison reeeal good. It was so much fun"? What kind of people would willingly and gleefully join Cameron this day to cheer him on?

A middle-aged, dark-haired man approached me and offered me a floppy dead-fish handshake. "Mark Smith," he said, pointing to a chair at a desk and telling me to sit. He came prepared to represent me, to protect my rights, and I wanted to feel that he was a trusted old friend like those Cameron had with him, but I couldn't.

Cameron and his attorney sat together at their desk. It had now become a visual reality that we weren't on the same side. First he was my crush, then my husband, then someone who left my side, never to return.

The judge called me to the witness stand. I reminded myself to choose bravery as I created my own history in this moment. Sitting high up and looking down at Cameron and his people, I burned with a raging fire. The air conditioner blasted cold air out of the vent directly above my head, but it couldn't extinguish or cool off my fighting spirit, even though it was clear there was nothing for me to fight for at this point. I was feisty, nonetheless, desiring dignity to save my own face.

Without looking up from the papers on the desk, Cameron's attorney asked me for my name, age, address, and phone number. I answered the questions as clearly as I could, avoiding mispronunciation or grammatical error. I even forced a smile before letting out each sentence, just for show. I wanted to create the illusion that I was completely relaxed and comfortable to show Cameron the opposite of what he came to see. As soon as I started speaking, I saw astonishment on his face. Which delighted me to no end. Most likely he'd anticipated seeing me voiceless, unable to speak for myself in court. He probably expected to find proof that without him my life was over. I'm sure that's what his supporters were there to see too. He could look at me, but he wouldn't understand what he saw. I knew he knew that I was no longer the same Allison abandoned in Edinburg eight months earlier. His leaving made me tough. His absence gave me my voice back. I hoped he knew, deep in his bones, that the vacancy he left behind in my life allowed transforming power to enter; I had only gotten stronger since.

His people shook their heads and exchanged scornful glares and snort-chuckled at me when I spoke. Laughing at me, these people! What was their problem? Wasn't being Cameron's supporters problematic enough? They looked down on me, but could they do anything I had done since Cameron's abandonment—trying to stay alive in a foreign country; begging for money, food, clothing, and a roof over my head; losing a parent; appearing in court alone to face a legal action, speaking a foreign language? Even though no one sat on my side of the courtroom to support me, I imagined that if our spiritual eyes were open, we would all see an army of horses and chariots of angels rushing down from the clouds to stand by me. What reason did anyone have to laugh at me?

Mr. Smith asked Cameron some questions. In his answers Cameron said, "Irreconcilable differences." The judge then ordered me to pay Dr. Chastain rent for having lived in his house from July 1995 to June 1996, during which I was lawfully married to and living with his son. Cameron was ordered to give me the Volvo that he drove away on the night of the light-switch incident.

The judge promptly announced "case closed" and left the room.

Cameron, his attorney, and his support group followed. Mr. Smith shook my hand and left too. He said *good luck*, but it didn't mean anything to me. He was more like a guy sitting next to me in a theater than my lawyer. Everyone seemed to have a plan, or an idea, of what to do and where to go. I stared at the empty room, dazed.

I'm divorced. Now what?

Aimlessly, I walked up and down the long halls, looking for a payphone to call Ethan. In the main lobby Cameron and his friends were chatting in a circle. When Cameron saw me, he approached me.

"Hey." He pointed his double chin at me. "Trade?"

He put his weight on one leg and then crossed his arms in front of his chest. He said something that sounded like, "Hit home paper mud not have signature to hold Baba. Mud grandpa not have signature open Volvo. Give me car, mud not give signature to hold Baba. Mud's humongous pregnant, huh?"

I wondered if he actually just spoke Chinese. If he did, then he thought he said, "Everyone knows you'll never be able to pay off the rent you owe Dad. You'll never afford keeping the Volvo either. Why don't you just let me keep the car, and Dad will pardon your debt? Call it your lucky day, huh?"

His accent was heavy, his tones wrong, his grammar broken, and yet he had a lasting, victorious smirk. I hadn't lived with him for eight months, and his Chinese had gone from being able to solo-travel Taiwan to placing an order in a Taiwanese restaurant and being served dog food. It was easy to see how completely I and my linguistic influences were out of his life.

In my head I hastily practiced saying the sentence "Get out of my sight, you pig!" with the best English pronunciation I could manage. And I wanted to add "Zai jian!" at the end.

Zai jian—good-bye in Chinese—is translated literally as *again see*.

But what I really wanted were answers: How long did he plot the light-switch incident? Why did he take the money? Did he honestly want me to die of starvation and cold? Did he do this because I refused to take pills, wear makeup, and order porn videos?

Before I had a chance to say anything, his friend Leif came up and slapped him on the shoulder. "Let's go, man." And just like that, Cameron was gone.

I was so caught up by the shame, embarrassment, and the loss of self-esteem from the divorce, I didn't have the energy, nor focus, to comprehend the significance of Cameron's final departure. I didn't need, nor deserve, this negative individual in my life. His absence left a part of me open, vacant, available for good things to come. It would be disrespectful to myself if I mourned his leaving. But it would take a while for me to understand the meaning of it all, to gain more experiences, more maturity, more wisdom to really see how this grievous event was a part of God's grand design for me.

Decades after watching Cameron leave that day, I now remember a fragmented story I once stumbled upon on the car radio while aimlessly changing stations. Because I missed the first part of the story, I imagine my own version of the beginning to go with the rest:

In a lawless village, a heavily armed mobster broke into a home and took everything in sight. When the parents of the victim family tried to stop the robbing, the mobster killed them both in front of their teenage son. Then he threatened to gouge out the young man's eyes for witnessing the cold-blooded murder, to which the young man said, "Take my left eye, for it has seen too much evil. But keep my right eye. I'll need it to see God."

I can never forget those powerful words. Now I can see what my divorce means: let go of the eye that has seen too much evil, so to keep an eye single to the glory of God. By so doing, I invite His guidance to where He wants me to go, what He wants me to do, who He wants me to be, free from Cameron's dictation. God so loved me that He removed this guy out of my eyes, out of my path, so I could start moving freely, confidently toward the blessings He'd prepared for me.

I trailed behind Cameron to the courthouse's grand entrance and stood still on the wide concrete steps, watching him drive away in the Volvo—the settlement of my debt. That image gradually got smaller, smaller, until it became a tiny black dot in the backdrop of Edinburg city. A tiny black dot like a grain of pepper in the palm of my hand that I could blow away. Soundlessly, out of my sight.

I didn't say *zai jian*.

85

Ethan picked me up from the courthouse, dropped me off at his apartment, and went back to the gym where he worked part-time as a fitness trainer. When I closed the door behind him, I glanced over the corridor at apartment 21. In my mind's eye I saw myself open the door on that fateful night, my hand reaching out for the light switch. It had been eight months since that night, but the raw anguish was still there. Now adding the suppressed heartbreak, disappointment, and rage from the day's hearing, my heart simply couldn't contain it all. *I'm a twenty-four-year-old woman,* I thought, *alone in a foreign country, walking out of a courthouse in tears. But––*

Who cares?

Who cares?

Who cares?

I shut the door and broke down into a wailing fit on the floor, gasping, coughing, and salivating, soiling my shirt and the carpet.

Why wasn't justice served? Why did Cameron get everything? Why? There must be a day when any Cameron-related news—positive or negative—wouldn't stir up one iota of feeling in me. It didn't happen fast enough; I wanted it to be now.

I fell asleep on the floor and woke up to the skin irritation from the crusty carpet under my face. My legs fell asleep from the hour-long bent-folded-twisted position. I wobbled to the bathroom. With each of my reluctant steps, sharp pain shot up from my feet. I filled the tub with hot water, stripped naked, hopped in, and wailed some more.

I didn't know that if I soaked in the mixture of steamy water and my own tears, snot, and slobber, I would get thirsty. I didn't know that if I got out of the tub to look for a bath towel to cover my nakedness, there would be none to be found in the bathroom. But I was so thirsty from all the crying I was dying for a glass of ice water, so I headed for the kitchen. In that exact same split second—no mistake—when I stepped out of the bathroom, Ethan stepped into the house. Nothing could've calculated the event in a more precise manner. It was as if Ethan had been stalking me with binoculars, waiting to catch me emerge from the bathroom in my birthday suit. I have no other explanation to this jarring madness.

The steam from the bathwater floated out and enveloped me. I wished there were something I could cover myself with—a wash-cloth, a hand towel, a napkin, a tissue—but there was nothing! How did Ethan live with nothing to cover nakedness? The steam floated to the living room, to him. Now it looked as though he were standing in a mist of fog, a gossamery veil, looking at me, shocked, stunned, and speechless.

Despite the panic, the embarrassment, and the urge to flee, I couldn't move. My feet were glued to the floor. Ethan shut the door behind him. I think he said something to me, but I don't remember verbally responding. We stared at each other for a second, in full astonishment and silence, before I darted back into the bathroom, trembling.

While I picked up the soiled clothes on the bathroom floor and frantically put them back on, Ethan's footsteps approached. My muscles tightened and my heart beat erratically. I thought maybe he would break in. But that was ridiculous . . . ridiculous of me to think he would. But then, I wasn't thinking right. . . . I was wondering . . . about something, although I couldn't remember what

I was wondering about. . . . There was a knock on the bathroom door. I freaked out and jumped.

"NO! I'M NOT HERE!"

"Allison, it's okay. I'm not asking to come in."

"Walk away, Ethan. I've had a bad day."

"Okay, yeah. I know. Do you . . . you need anything?"

"No! Just walk away, Ethan."

"Okay, I'll be in the van until you come tell me I can come back."

That's when I remembered my suitcase was still in the van. I hollered at Ethan and asked him to bring it in for me. I apologized for yelling at him. He said that was okay. Said that he would leave my stuff by the bathroom door. Said that he would be in the parking lot if I needed him.

I took more than an hour to bathe and get dressed. And just when I thought I was ready to go see Ethan, I decided to change into a different outfit. Then I considered taking another bath. Reluctantly I went to Ethan, dreading every step toward him. I still experienced the aftershock, and really, how would I recover from this? How could I look at Ethan in the eye now? What ran through his mind? Would he get PTSD from this?

It was warm outside. A family walked out of Hardee's, their toddler kids in swimsuits and licking ice cream cones. Across the street, a young boy skipped out of the corner gas station with a jar of pickles. The peaceful, carefree summertime was for everybody else to enjoy, not for me. How many people within my peripheral vision just got divorced today? Were they grieving so much they got a migraine headache? Which new divorcée got caught walking naked in a guy friend's apartment—as if getting divorced wasn't traumatic enough—and was now embarrassed and heavy-hearted to face the said guy?

The said guy, Ethan, was reading—was it a psychology textbook?—in his van. If I could have one superpower, I would want to read minds. I wished I knew all of Ethan's thoughts in this moment. Was he judging me? Was he sick of the drama I brought into his life? Was he counting the minutes before I flew back to Utah?

Ethan got out of the van and opened the passenger door for me. There was magic in the gentlemanly way he treated me that made me forget, momentarily, to grieve. Made me forget, temporarily, my heart had been broken by another man only hours earlier. Briefly, I felt special.

We went to a movie, then to a seafood dinner. That night, back in Ethan's apartment, he slept on the couch so I could have his bed. That night, in every insomnious minute, I heard him change TV channels till dawn. I tossed and turned, my face buried in the pillow that carried a faint masculine scent. If this scent spoke his feelings, one of them was probably nightly loneliness.

The next day in the airport, we stood face-to-face at my boarding gate. He wrapped me in a long, silent hug, as though he knew this would be the last time we saw each other. He smelled of the ocean, the wind, the earth—a free spirit that would always choose to roam the world. After this day, there was a great, deep rift between Utah and wherever he rested his head each night, and all I would ever have was the memory of him: an entire universe of tender compassion.

It has been twenty-four years since that airport farewell. Ethan might be living in a ger on the Mongolian rolling plateaus, or bathing in the Ganges in India, or climbing Mount Everest. He might be a professor in Singapore, a gym owner in Prague, or a sports medicine consultant in Paris. Wherever he chooses to be, whatever he chooses to do, to me, he'll always be that thirty-six-year-old Canadian guy who woke up on a Mexican beach one morning and decided to drive north and enroll in the first university he saw in the U.S. He will always be the guy who had a Freudian slip at our first meeting: "Hello, my name is Ethan Leroy. Me and my wife just got here. . . ."

I pray.

I pray that God sends him a woman who loves him, who stays by his side and never leaves, who gives him children to grace his life.

I pray that he lives in a home filled with laughter and love.

And I pray that his heart is always full, his bed is never cold.

86

One day, at BYU, I was talking with some girls in a classroom hall when a young man walked toward us, nodding at the girls and turning to me.

"Hi, I'm Charles," he said with an outstretched hand. I shook it. His skin was so flawlessly smooth and taut he could pass for a tall fifth-grader. "I write songs and sing them to unique girls," he said.

I looked to my friends with raised eyebrows.

That evening Charles and I hung out at my dorm lounge. He said I gave him a song idea that he wanted to write and sing to me the next time we met up. I said I looked forward to it. Then we took a ride up to Provo Canyon, listening to U2 and talking about our favorite 80s bands. When we returned to my dorm parking lot, before I got out of his car, he asked for my number. I wrote it down on a receipt I found in my wallet. "By the way"—I handed him my number—"I'm divorced."

Charles fell silent for a few moments, biting his bottom lip and staring straight ahead into the dark night. "Well, Allison," he finally said slowly. "I don't—"

It suddenly felt as though I were back in Tyler Tanner's room a few months back, trying to tell him the very same thing.

"I understand." I walked out of his car into the lovely desert night and waved at him, knowing he would never dial my number. It stung a little, the rejection, but Charles taught me a great lesson that night: not everyone would be willing to love the crows on my roof. I needed to learn to be at peace with that.

87

Went on a blind double date and became more impressed by the other guy than by my own date? Yep, I did that.

It wasn't because Gavin stood six feet tall and had straight blond hair, a strong jaw, and narrow, puffy blue eyes. Or the fact that his skin was so translucent that his veins on the forehead and cheeks were visible. And it definitely had nothing to do with how skinny he was—a literal stick figure. The power of Gavin was in his brain. The most intelligent twenty-one-year-old I'd ever met, Gavin could talk about anything—politics, history, poetry, music, science, language, math, chess, anything—and sound like a professor in that specific field.

Yeah, I was mighty impressed. But Gavin's girlfriend, Liz, stuck her nose in a romance novel the entire time, ignoring him. So maybe he wasn't an expert in everything, after all.

Brother Wade left me a message while I was in Texas: I would be teaching Chinese at the MTC! Instead of jumping up and down and shouting for joy, I wondered if that meant I would be working with the Okinawa guy. Then I remembered how much he laughed, as if every insignificant thing—even ants—made him happy, which made me smile.

The first day of work I reported to the prayer meeting in the Asian language teachers' lounge, and the person who came up to offer me a handshake was none other than Gavin himself.

"Remember me? Gavin Hansen. I teach Chinese here," he said.

Do I ever? I don't forget a genius.

I shook his boney hand. "How's Liz?"

"Oh . . . Liz, right. Well, we broke up. But, uh . . . see that Chinese girl over there?" He dipped his chin at a group of other teachers. "My girlfriend, Angie. She teaches Cantonese."

Gavin might've said something, then laughed at his own joke, but I wasn't listening. I scanned the room for the Okinawa guy and was disappointed to not see him.

A couple weeks later Gavin asked me out. He had apparently broken up with Angie too. Maybe I felt sorry for him for his seeming struggle to keep a girlfriend. Maybe I felt sorry for myself for being rejected because of my divorcée status. Whatever it was, I said *yes.*

Based on my observation of the 1990s BYU courting culture, I felt, at twenty-four, like an old hag among young single female students, hence less desirable. Nothing I could do about it, though. I couldn't change my age. But because the church places such tremendous emphasis on family, most of the female students I knew back then got married and had babies before they turned twenty-four. Some of these young mothers pushed baby strollers on campus as if going to a playdate in a park. It was common to see a bouncy ball or a baby bottle roll from the back of the classroom toward the whiteboard wall. None of the fussy babies or rattling toys bothered me. It was, instead, the crippling shame of being a stigmatized divorcée while the church teaches *Families Are Forever* and *No Other Success Can Compensate for Failure in a Home.* It was the humiliation when a dorm girl suggested that I request a tuition refund if I couldn't find a husband before graduation. It was the phantom pressure from comparing and competing with young bachelorettes on campus. *Other girls my age are now expecting their second child. What's my problem failing a marriage and being childless?*

Even though the church's doctrines are perfect, I interpreted them imperfectly. I imagined that other BYU girls lived a perfect life. That they had arrived in a place where I had been crawling to get to, only to keep being bitten by a gale and pushed back, unable to reach the ultimate life goal of starting a family of my own. Why did I ever allow myself to believe anyone's life was perfect? We all have our own cross to carry; I know that now. Had I learned to accept myself back then, to love myself, to be patient with myself, I would've been much happier being myself. Nonetheless, the damaging social pressure got to me, and I vowed to take advantage of absolutely every opportunity to go on a date, to get married, to have children.

I gladly hopped in Gavin's Camry, sitting where Liz used to sit, but instantly knew it was a mistake.

This sounds shallow and horrible, but it's true: before Gavin, I had never gone out with anyone I wasn't physically attracted to. To take a friendship to a higher level, I needed to first be in love with the guy's looks. Although, to be fair, in a romantic relation-ship a person integrates her mind and emotions to interact with the body and spirit. I just happened to be a bit more critical in the looks department. Couldn't help it.

Gavin didn't have it: the face or the physique. Nope, nothing. He had the build of a scrawny ten-year-old boy, with perpetual bad breath. His brilliant mind, high intelligence, and great talents just couldn't cut it. I was so sure I wouldn't go on a second date with him that I didn't bother telling him about my recent divorce.

But then, he wrote me a poem.

A poem!

For me!

Nobody had ever done that!

And he promised to write a book for me.

So the next night we went out again. Then the next. For two weeks straight we were inseparable. For two weeks straight he wrote me new poems and brought me red roses and showed me what it was like to know everything: aero science, literature, history, cultures—I mean, this guy and his intellect! I was flattered to befriend a genius, but that was the highest degree of my admiration for him. Nothing more.

On the Friday of the second week, close to midnight, Gavin took me to the Provo Temple grounds. We sat by the wrought-iron gate on the lawn under the autumn starry night, looking out at Utah Lake's shimmering reflection of the bright silver moon. In that exact moment when he said he had a question for me, a sharp, dark feeling coursed through my veins. I knew I was about to face a distressing predicament; I feared I'd run out of chances to tell him about my divorce. Well, of course I still had a chance to tell him. I just needed to tell him before he asked the question. It was only fair—he needed to know what he was getting himself into. But he beat me to it by whispering in my ear, "Will you marry me?"

If this were a slow-motion movie scene, it would show that immediately after Gavin proposed, I looked away from him, my internal conflicts in captions:

What was he thinking? We've only gone out for two weeks, for heaven's sake!

I can't marry him! I'm not attracted to him.

But if I don't say yes, who else in the world will ever want to marry me? This might be the only shot I've got at getting hitched. . . .

Still facing away from him, still debating within myself whether or not I should accept his proposal, my traitor mouth said *yes*, and immediately my heart started drumming up a guilt song.

Guilty me!

That *yes* was the wrong answer, as wrong as Gavin's question. Moreover, besides deliberately betraying my own conscience, I lied to Gavin by withholding my past from him. I had a good reason for it, though: I was marginalized and stigmatized in the past because I told. Those guys responded differently, but, really, it was all the same:

Guy #1: Got up from the couch and walked out of the dorm lounge wordlessly, never to be heard from again.

Guy #2: Tightened jaw, mean stare. Smacked his lips and said darkly, "Have a nice life."

Guy #3: Chuckled, snorted, shook his head, eyed me up and down. "Your ex walked out after only sixteen months? What did *you* do?"

What did *I* do? "I married the devil himself, that's what!" Is that what he wanted me to say?

Speaking of the devil, here was Cameron who, after the divorce, emailed me to brag about his drop-dead-sexy girlfriends and the most important reminder he wouldn't want me to ever forget: *BYU kids don't recycle used goods. Why would guys want Allison when they could easily marry eighteen-year-old fresh white meat?*

Thorn in my side, rock in my shoe, sand in my eye. Cameron, born in July with Cancer for his astrological sign, was the cancer in my life. I used to be jealous of his ex-girlfriends, whom he wouldn't stop talking about. Now I pitied his drop-dead-sexy girlfriends, whom he wouldn't stop bragging about. They not only recycled used goods, but they also recycled cancer. But I would say that, wouldn't I?

I'd learned to be quiet about my past and just enjoyed meeting and hanging out with BYU guys, until this night of doom. Sure, silencing my voice got me opportunities to go out and have fun. And look what happened now; I even got myself engaged! But this moment felt completely opposite of when Cameron slid a ring on my finger in the airport. With Gavin, there was no ecstatic hugging, no celebratory squealing, no enthusiastic jumping. I sat there, on the temple lawn, regretting my choice to be untruthful to him and to myself.

Gavin clapped at my answer and rubbed his hands together

vigorously. "Great! Now, we've got to keep the engagement a secret."

I wondered if this was only a test, or a joke, or maybe he was just a weirdo.

"We can't tell anyone yet. I still need to figure out a way to tell my parents you're Chinese."

Oh my gosh, are his parents racists?

PERFECT!

Surely this was a golden opportunity to tell Gavin about my divorce and call off the engagement. But instead, I clung to the victory of finally getting a fiancé, no matter how loveless that felt. I intentionally ignored the guilt of hiding my past and forced myself to imagine what it would be like to live with a genius for the rest of my life: going on family vacations, seeing the world, having dinner conversations with a walking library. I told myself that if Gavin wanted to keep the engagement a secret, then it meant no one should ever know I'd just said *yes*. Which meant this whole thing didn't even happen. And if it didn't happen, then I didn't actually lie. I was okay. I did nothing wrong.

Of course, the wrong thing was just that–my denial of wrongdoing.

The lie.

The excuse to justify the lie.

The untruth I fed myself to continue living in my own deception.

Wrong, wrong, wrong. All of those were wrong.

At this moment, in this space, my choice of not honoring the truth caused me to lose the courage to do the right thing. That's all it takes for me to quickly become spiritually blind, losing the ability to discern between truth and error.

88

In third grade I learned that China lost the First Opium War (1839–1842 AD) and ceded Hong Kong to Britain. In 1898, Britain pledged to return Hong Kong to China when the ninety-nine-year lease ended. According to my history teacher, that pledge was a complicated agreement. The implication was in the number ninety-nine.

In the Chinese language, *nine* and *a long time* are homophones. Ninety-nine sounds like double the long time, which means never-ending. Britain believed they would keep Hong Kong forever. A ninety-nine-year lease really meant eternal colonization. However, in 1984 the British prime minister, Margaret Thatcher, agreed to honor the lease.

Two months after I arrived at BYU, the handover of Hong Kong to China took place on July 1, 1997. It was a hot topic of discussion in the Chinese community on campus. There were speculations and predictions concerning Hong Kong's political future. Some zealous students flew to Hong Kong to witness this historical event. Among them was Osmond. It almost felt as if we weren't meant to meet, that Osmond left for Asia from Utah the same time I came to Utah from Asia.

After Gavin and I entered the secretive agreement to wed in an unknown future (so stupid!), one morning I went to work and found a group of Chinese teachers circling a desk in the center of the teachers' lounge, enthusiastically chatting and passing around photos. I was pulling out the daily log from a file cabinet in the corner of the room when a guy approached me with an extended hand.

"Hi, I'm Osmond," he said in Chinese with a Beijing accent. He stood about six feet. Blond wavy bangs. Robust and fit. Through his fitted white dress shirt, the outline of his compelling chest and thin-cut waist was visible. Being a daughter of an honorably released Taiwanese Frogman—the equivalent of a U.S. Navy SEAL—I recognized an elite swimmer's body when I saw one. Osmond might be into water sports.

I shook his hand and told him my name. As if a furnace had just been turned on inside me, my cheeks were fevered. I was instantly attracted to the guy, and it made me so shy that I promptly excused myself.

"Oh, wait," Osmond called. "Do you want to do something together?"

The married girls in the circle behind him smiled and nodded with great enthusiasm, waving their thumbs up in the air as a sign of approval. My conscience—my right-shoulder angel—instantly appeared and warned me of being a cheater. But no sooner did the right-shoulder angel show up than the left-shoulder angel popped into the scene. "Technically, this isn't cheating," he said. "It's a fair game for everyone before the wedding."

So wise, the left-shoulder angel!

Essentially, I was choosing the father of my future children. This was an important decision for myself and my descendants. I didn't want to end up with the wrong person, again. Since I already knew Gavin wasn't the right one, I had a right to know if Osmond was. So I said *yes* to his invite, almost guiltlessly.

The circle of girls invited me to join them at the desk to hear about Osmond's experience in Hong Kong. The person who held a photo album turned it back to the first page and explained to me what she knew about each picture. For a brief moment Gavin was completely out of my mind, until he walked in the room. The distasteful look he threw at me annoyed me to no end. It made me feel as if it was sinful to have a social life. He tilted his head and signaled me to go out to the hall.

"What?" I stood in front of him, arms crossed.

"What do you mean what? What were you doing in there?"

"What do you mean what was I doing in there? I was listening to—"

"But you can't do that!" Gavin shook his head and furrowed his eyebrows. "You're engaged. To me!"

"So? I can't listen to someone talk about Hong Kong?"

Gavin's narrowed eyes were twitching. Blue veins bulged on his forehead, and I was worried they would pop any second.

"You can't be all sweet on other guys. You're mine."

"But no one is supposed to know that, remember? *You* didn't want anyone to know that. So what was I supposed to do when someone asked me out?"

"What? Who asked you out?" Gavin's face contorted into a grotesque rage.

"Osmond did. And I said *yes*, because I couldn't tell him *your* secret."

"Oh my gosh! What have you done? You're cheating on me!" A forceful gush of foul breath rushed out of Gavin's mouth and hovered over my nose. He slapped his forehead, and I supposed I should feel bad. But on the contrary, I wanted to challenge him, to upset him, the way an impossibly rebellious teenage girl tormented her parents.

"You know what, Gavin? I should be allowed to go out with whoever I want. The so-called engagement is practically nonexistent."

"You can't do that, Allison!" Gavin barked. His eyes were suddenly red and misty.

"Yes, I can," I said firmly.

"No, you—" Gavin looked defeated now. His voice broke. "What—just tell me what you want me to do . . . please. Don't leave me. I'll make you happy."

That's how I manipulated Gavin. How I made him stay away while Osmond and I went out. How I turned disloyal and stony-hearted. I am ashamed of and loathe myself for having acted that way.

For two weeks, as agreed, I was free to go out with Osmond, under the condition that by the end of the second week I made a public announcement that I was no longer available. I was obviously young, immature, and dramatic, living a petty, twisted, shallow life, creating chaos for me and others by deceiving, cheating, and betraying. My dilemma was that even though I didn't have the slightest desire to be with Gavin, he was the only sure candidate for a future husband. And I couldn't, in my right mind, let him go. At this point, my romantic life was like trying to balance on a lake with each foot in a different leaky kayak that represented my broken relationship with Gavin and Osmond. Every time I told one of them personalized lies to convince him I wanted to be with him, more water leaked into the kayak. Through time, I forgot to whom I lied about what. It became confusing and shaky, and I eventually lost my footing and the kayaks.

At the beginning of the two weeks with Osmond, I told him about my secret engagement to Gavin. He laughed at the silliness of the whole thing, then we commenced an expanded version of speed-dating, cramming what felt like a year's worth of fun activities into those two weeks: driving up to a mountaintop at night to see Utah valley soak in a glowing sea of lights. Going to plays, movies, concerts. Playing racquetball. Doing homework in the library. Talking about hometown, family, and childhood.

On Thursday night of the second week, after work, he brought me a rose. Blood red, in full bloom, a pink-and-white polka-dotted bow tied to the long stem. He invited me to drive home with him the next day to spend the weekend with his family. "It'll change my life forever if you say *yes.*"

Osmond's family lived in a vast desert in southern Utah, 220 miles away from BYU. I know I was overthinking at this moment, but I was under an unusual circumstance: on the following Monday I would return to my engagement to Gavin. Like Hong Kong returning to China, it would be permanent. I had to make a decision about my relationship with Osmond now. I had to think deep and hard about us, about his family, about his hometown. Yes, hometown. Hometown was important. What would it be like to be a Taiwanese immigrant bride in a Western-movie type of small town, in the middle of nowhere? Would I be happy?

But I'd just met Osmond; I didn't even know his middle name! What he asked me to do was the same thing Gavin did. Perhaps driven by raging testosterone, these two young men felt the urge to secure a bride after barely telling her, "Hello, my name is. . ." Which wasn't really much different than how Cameron and I got together. The common phenomenon of young adults around me rushing into marriage affected me in a way that blinded me from rational judgment.

I had a powerful hunger to fit in, to be accepted, to be loved. I was a foreigner who didn't get cultural jokes, didn't have blonde hair and milky skin, didn't have parents or relatives in church leadership positions, or pioneer ancestors who pushed handcarts across the plain to come to Utah. But I could at least get married while still an undergrad, like everybody else.

I realize now that by having entertained those thoughts, I was dangerously close to emotional suicide. Comparison is poison. It begets dissatisfaction, which begets jealousy and envy, which begets resentment and hatred, which robs people of peace and joy. I'd unwittingly let myself fall into the trap of actively competing with no one in particular, leaving no time to appreciate what made me unique. What I needed to know then was that when God created me, He said, "Ta-da." I needed to know that God saw the great worth of my soul, and I had to do the same, to be at peace with the way I was: from humble beginnings, dark-skinned, spoke English with an accent. Although flawed and imperfect, I had His love. I didn't need to chase those young men's love to elevate my self-worth.

For once, I chose to be honest and brave and tell Osmond about my divorce, so he could decide if he still wanted me to go meet his family. Osmond looked equal parts shocked and disappointed. After a long pause for deep thinking, he did change his mind about me meeting his family, saying that his decision was purely out of his respect for Gavin. "Wish I'd met you before he did. A small margin; a huge loss. Like in a swim meet."

If that was a lie, I totally deserved it, didn't I?

89

When I was in seventh grade, the school volleyball coach approached me one day and said she had seen me play volleyball before and wanted me to join the school team. The intense training started the next day after school.

I wasn't a natural athlete. It would require tremendous amount of hard work for me to be any good in a sport. But I'd always loved playing volleyball and didn't mind the strenuous practice and conditioning. I was only on the team for a few weeks before my homeroom teacher ordered me to stop.

Ever since fifth grade I had been the class president every year—the kind of student leader who was expected to rank within top three in every schoolwide exam. Naturally, in the 1980s academically competitive Chinese culture, where scholars were praised and athletes were despised, where P.E. class was replaced by supplemental math and science classes, my involvement in a sport was deemed a sign of rebellion—almost a type of revolution against school authority and insurgency against the traditional education system. My teacher convinced me that wasting time playing sports instead of studying would rob me of academic excellence and a bright future, so I stopped playing volleyball. Although, I never had the audacity to ask why we even had a school volleyball team.

Gavin wanted us to take Marriage Preparation 101 together (Yes, it was a legitimate undergraduate class at BYU). One of the homework assignments was a survey with the question: *What qualities do you seek in your future spouse?* I wrote, among other things, *I hope he plays volleyball.* When Gavin saw it, he turned ballistic. Near tears, he screamed, "You know I don't play volleyball! What are you trying to say?"

I resisted the urge to tell him I meant what I wrote, that I wanted to marry a volleyball player, that I wanted volleyball to be a family sport in my future life. But mostly, I wanted a future life without cultural or personal expectations to dictate what I do.

Gavin's rage left as abruptly as it came. We never talked about volleyball ever again. But I never forgot what my subconscious mind truly wanted either.

90

Upon entering the secret engagement, I moved out of the dorm and into an off-campus one-bedroom apartment. No roommates. Gavin asked for a copy of my apartment key. I didn't want to comply, but at this point I wanted more than anything to redeem myself for having acted like a jerk around him.

Whenever I was in class or at work, Gavin went in my apartment and checked my answering machine. He yelled at me when he found old messages from Ethan that I didn't delete. Maybe my speed-dating Osmond caused his insecurity and paranoia; he demanded that I avoid looking at, talking to, or smiling at other guys. Once, he crouched behind a hedge outside of my apartment laundry room window, watching me wash my dirty clothes. When a guy who was waiting for his clothes to dry flirted with me, I stared at the tile floor and kept silent. I feared Gavin would make me wear a cone of shame on my head if I responded to that guy.

I did what Gavin wanted, even though I secretly wanted to throw him over my shoulder, then karate chop him in half. But I was convinced that I deserved to be treated badly as a punishment for having kept my divorce a secret, for having gone out with Osmond. I was afraid to offend Gavin in any way lest he call off the engagement. My mind was functionally kaput, obviously. How did I ever end up being afraid that he would call it off? Pffft! Only weeks earlier I was the one dying to call it off!

The week before Thanksgiving 1997, Gavin's mother flew to Utah from D.C. We met in his apartment living room. She was a middle-aged Amazon: about six feet tall, big fluffy blonde hair, blue eyes with huge bags—a high-class woman who quoted classic literature, frequented Broadway, and dined with well-established, prominent people. I imagined she had a staff of uniformed house servants at home who all dressed better than I did. Yeah, she was the kind of lady I had only seen in films, and I didn't know how to break through the movie screen to enter her reality.

After a handshake, she asked me job-interview-like questions of hometown, family members, work experiences, GPA, life goals. As soon as she was done with me, she called her husband. Within earshot, I heard the first thing she said: "Well, she's shorter than I thought." She clicked her tongue, then added, "A lot shorter, actually."

I wanted to laugh. I judged her son by his looks when we first met; now she was giving me a taste of my own medicine. Bitter, but I totally deserved it. I left the room to avoid further eavesdropping on what she might say about my ethnicity or my practically orphan status.

After the phone call, she announced that she would take Gavin and me to a studio for engagement photographs the next day. She was visually horrified when I showed up for the shoot fresh-faced, in a wrinkled white button-down shirt that I'd bought at a thrift store, and a pair of baggy jeans. But it was too late to go shopping for new clothes. Gavin and I posed in front of a roll of brown paper background that draped from a ceiling rod. While the images were processed, we sat down with the studio manager in his office to discuss invitation design. It was when Gavin's mother dictated to the manager the text for the announcement that I learned the wedding would be in the Washington D.C. Temple. Gavin's father was a successful business owner with a large network of wealthy partners and clients. They would all be invited to the event. I became increasingly uneasy as more wedding details were unfolded: Gavin's parents had rented a horse-drawn carriage and hired a driver. Immediately after our ceremony, Gavin and I would ride in the carriage to a luxurious reception in a fancy hotel. Dozens of noble guests would celebrate with us. For our honeymoon, Gavin's parents would fly us to an exotic destination. This sounded like my girlhood fantasy of a dream wedding, and I got to be a fairytale princess! But I felt gross.

My guilt deepened as more money, time, and energy were invested in the wedding preparation. I wanted to stop Gavin's mother from doing more. I wanted to tell Gavin and her my past that I'd somehow turned into a national-security-level secret. By marrying into their family, I would pollute their prestigious name and highly respected reputation. I feared Gavin and his folks wouldn't be able to withstand judgment and criticism from the upper class they belonged to. I couldn't imagine the consequences of them finding out about my lies after the wedding. The time to tell them was now. But I did nothing. I'd lost my courage. I said nothing. I'd lost my voice once more.

Two weeks before the wedding, one night I got home from work and found Gavin sprawled on my couch like a deflated balloon, his eyes bloodshot, his lips swollen, his head shaking mildly. I instantly knew this was the end of my secret keeping.

While I was at work, Gavin got into my apartment, digging through my calendar, journal, and files. He checked my answering machine and heard a recent message from my bishop, concerning the cancellation of Cameron's and my marriage record in the church. Gavin also found my notes on the calendar, on those summer days when I traveled to Texas for my court appearance.

Wordlessly and repeatedly, he played my bishop's message, my bishop's voice the only sound in the room. Every time Cameron's name was spoken, I cringed with guilt. Before this moment I'd rehearsed in my head several different ways to tell Gavin what he was now demanding to know. I never thought this was how it would actually play out.

I sat on the couch, listening to the message that had now become white noise. After gathering what little courage I had, I said the only four words that night—the only four words I ever said to Gavin about my past. "Cameron is my ex-husband."

I'd never in my life felt so rotten. Little by little, I had fallen farther and farther away from God's Light. Deception and destruction travel together. Lies eventually develop into cancer to the soul. The consequences of my choice to lie clung to me like ankle weights, anchoring me firmly at the bottom of a hole of villainy and misery. I loathed myself so much; I didn't care if Gavin strangled me to death. I let the couch swallow me, my face hidden behind a throw pillow, my feet tucked under the cushion. I refused to communicate with Gavin. Emotionally I'd shut down. I wished Gavin would get out of my apartment, out of my life. But he wouldn't stop interrogating me. *Why did you lie? What else haven't you told me? How could you do this to me and my family?*

I gave him the silent treatment because I lacked the integrity to take responsibility for my wrongdoing. I reasoned that being quiet was the best thing to do in this moment. If I tried to explain myself, I might come up with more lies. But I wasn't decent enough to at least apologize, to say, "Sorry, please forgive me. I wanted to tell you earlier. . . ." Instead, that entire night I ignored him. As Gavin went on asking the same questions in vain, he eventually broke down crying. It killed me to hear him sob for the emotional injury I inflicted on him. I'd destroyed an innocent soul. Darkness has an eye for its own. Had I been truly penitent, I would've repeatedly apologized for all the weeks, days, hours, and seconds I hid the truth from him, and my repentant voice would've turned into a never-ending elegy. But I remained quiet.

Gavin's body trembled from bitter sobbing, his eyes and lips swollen; his veins on his forehead bulged in vibrant blue, a stark contrast with his sweaty red face. Slowly, he became exhausted, so much so that he started apologizing for making both of us feel bad! Now it was all his fault for making me mad, for making himself sad. I couldn't make sense of it. "I'msorryI'msorryI'msorry," he cried. "Please don't leave me!" For a brief moment, I actually believed he was the one who brought all this mess upon us. But as the adage goes, "When one person drinks wine, does someone else get the headache?" Of course not. Gavin shouldn't be responsible or be punished for my deception.

The next day when he called his parents, they redirected his train of thoughts to the truth of my wrongdoing. Consequently, he informed me of the cancellation of all wedding preparation. He was going to start seeing someone else, he said. That day he got back together with Angie, his ex-girlfriend who taught Cantonese at the MTC.

I should've felt relieved to be off the hook and celebrated this newfound freedom. But, instead, I felt terrible. If there's a word stronger than *remorse*, I'll use it here. But my English vocabulary is limited. All I can say is I felt like crap.

In retrospect, I wish I hadn't let the unique BYU dating culture get to me. Millions of girls elsewhere graduated from college without finding a husband in class. I was just fine. But I was like a horse wearing a visor and seeing only tunnel vision. The path before me had me unceasingly focused on getting hitched. I fought other bachelorettes on campus in an imaginary dating war so hard that I became arbitrary, confused, and disoriented. I forgot why I even came to BYU. Now, I started thinking about going home to Taiwan for good after the semester was over. I could try getting a job teaching English at a small cram school in Taipei, or working on an assembly line at a computer hardware factory in the Science Park. The more I thought about it, the more I was convinced that was the plan.

I had run in a huge circle and met myself again at the starting line. I took a detour in life to come to America, only to go back to where I was in the beginning, accomplishing nothing. Nothing at all. Disowned, divorced, dropped out. What good was I, a shameless liar?

I skipped classes and locked myself in my apartment all day, kneeling next to my bed, elbows on mattress, and sob-begging in hour-long prayers. I asked God for forgiveness and promised Him that from now on I would choose the right. I asked Him to help Gavin and his family to forgive me. I went to my bishop's office and told him what I had done and asked him to help me set goals to be a better person.

Sometime after I approached God in prayers with a broken heart and contrite spirit, He did forgive me. I imagined He tore off the page of my life story with Gavin and shredded it. Pointing at a blank page of my Book of Life, He smiled and said, "Get up, my child. Go, write a new story. And never forget that I love you."

PART TEN

Righteousness

91

There was a prayer meeting for all MTC teachers before every shift started. Those who taught Asian languages gathered in the lounge and grouped themselves with those who spoke the same language. Chinese teachers in one corner, Japanese in another, Korean in the back of the room, Cantonese in the middle, like so. After a hymn, a prayer, agendas, and spiritual thoughts, we were dismissed to our own classroom.

Eight months after the rating session, one night I spotted the Okinawa guy at the prayer meeting. The electrifying, sheer bliss of seeing him was like seeing a childhood best friend after being apart for a lifetime. My heart suddenly came to life, as if it hadn't truly lived before. Deep down, I had been yearning for his friendship all this time. I watched him from the Chinese corner and was mesmerized by the entirety of him: his resemblance to the actor Hugh Grant, his athletic build, his almost regal demeanor.

I was raised in a conservative culture deeply rooted in the crippling ancient belief that women had their place in the society, and that place was invisible. They should always wait for men's commands. They were expected to be fiercely obedient to their father, to their husband, and, when they became widows, to their son. Women had no voice. Women had no choice. They lived for men only, to serve them, to please them, to satisfy them. I was supposed to be that kind of Chinese woman, quietly waiting for men to notice me and grant me permission to speak. Except

I believed that good things happen to those who wait, but better things happen to those who go out and get them.

It pained me to be in the same room with the Okinawa guy every night at the prayer meeting and feel a world away from him. My heart desired him, but I didn't even know his name! The intense crush I had on him instilled in me courage to break the cultural expectation of waiting for a guy to initiate a relationship. During breaks and after work I pretended to look for my class log in the teachers' lounge, but I was secretly trying to scan the Japanese teachers' directory on the bulletin board for his name and phone number. I don't know why I thought this would work. There were about thirty male Japanese teachers in all shifts combined, including substitutes. But I couldn't be easily defeated in this task. I had a strategy.

Always, I struggled with math. But this is when math actually helped me in real life. I used the elimination method . . . or so I thought that was math. . . . Anyhow, to more effectively find the Okinawa guy's name on the directory, I ignored Japanese names: Okimuro, Nagayama, Inori, Nakamura, Saito. Now I only had to guess which one of the twenty-five remaining names belonged to him!

Of course I was unsuccessful. But the harder it was to get him, the harder I tried to get him. I just had to eliminate the option of using math.

Two weeks later, one night I found the Okinawa guy walking down the empty hall after work, and I was prompted by some impulsiveness I didn't know was in me to jump out in front of him. My heart danced erratically. I didn't know what to do next.

No one was around us, but I wonder if my progenitors' spirits had rushed all the way from the silk road of China to crowd the hall at the MTC, stacking on top of one another in a mound—the heap of Hongs—waggling their fingers at me. "Don't don't don't don't don't! Don't you dare! You're a GIRL!"

Well, if that's really what happened, I simply didn't see or hear them.

"Hi, hello . . . hi, hey!" I waved down the Okinawa guy with a close-lipped smile.

He was startled. Looking up from the class log in his hands, he smiled with a dimple on each side of his lower lip. "Oh heyyy, it's you! I remember you"—he looked at my name tag—"Sister Hong."

I don't know how I remained standing after hearing him say my name. His voice sounded so deep, strong, and yet dreamy. But clear-headed as I was, I immediately snapped into the realization that all the while I had been dying to get to know him, he hadn't even noticed me until now. That . . . hurt, just a little.

Following suit, I read his name tag.

Brother Merrill.

Why must there be double L *and double* R *in the surname? @#$%^&*!*

Merrill Merrill Merrill. Mmm . . . is there a Merrill on the directory?

Oh, why does that matter now? I won't have to torture myself with the stupid elimination method to guess his name anymore. Sweeeeet!

"Brother Merrill." I couldn't keep my facial muscles from stretching into an ear-to-ear grin.

"Oh, call me Drake."

"Ah, Drake." Only one *R* in the name. No big deal.

I wanted to ask why his name wasn't on the directory, but it would make me sound too desperate. Also, if my ancestors were still hanging out in the hall, they might chuck their shoes at me for venturing this far into the forbidden territory.

"So . . . tomorrow. We have tomorrow off," I said. This was a totally impromptu idea. I had never done it before, and no one had taught me how to do it either. What should I say next? Drake was looking at me expectantly. Gosh! The way he looked at me set my entire being on fire. I must not mess up and lose his attention. I needed to come up with something.

"Want to see a movie together?" I asked. "Like . . . *Titanic?*"

"Um . . . what should I call you?"

"Oh, right, you don't know my name, hahaha! I'm Allison."

Wait, did I say Ayhreesong? Did I—

It suddenly felt so warm I started hand-fanning myself.

"Yeah, that'd be fun, Allison. Let's do it."

I believed that when I was determined, a floodgate of opportunity was unbarred. I believed this tiny moment of interaction between Drake and me would morph into something hugely impactful, because the universe acknowledged the fact that I was finally ready to use the gift of agency to create my own destiny.

Oh, but—

Asking Drake to go to a movie on a first date was the worst idea ever!

During the showing I couldn't talk to him, which was a wasted opportunity to build a relationship, to explore his personality, and to examine his compatibility. But of course I didn't know that. I'd never asked a guy out and was simply overwhelmed by the pure joy of being with him. We went to see *Titanic*, starring Leonardo DiCaprio and Kate Winslet, then we said good-bye. We might as well have gone to a testing center and taken a GRE test for two, three hours and called that a date. Worse, being so inexperienced, I didn't think to follow up with a second date. Worst, I didn't even think to ask him for his number. So basically, it was a train wreck of a date, yeah. Drake must've thought so too, because for the ensuing weeks we remained a world apart in prayer meetings— he in the Japanese corner, I in the Chinese corner. Every time I saw him talking with his group, I regretted not having picked up Japanese from Ah-Gung and Ah-Po when I was little. I would do anything to be with Drake again, but I wasn't sure if I should approach him as I did the last time. Should I be the one always asking him out on a date? Once an initiator, always an initiator?

This unbearable silence lasted for almost two months. Two months! I didn't know our date was so horrible that it was worth two months of quiescence. Such a test of my patience! Although it reminded me of the saying "The moon needs time to become full." This period of silence provided me plenty of time to reflect on my life path.

It seemed I had become a full-time love pursuer. By spending my entire focus and energy on finding my true love, I'd neglected my studies. Instead of being on the Dean's List, I was now in jeopardy of being on academic probation with a GPA below 2.0.

But I don't believe I completely messed up.

I was twenty-five then, marriageable age, and lived by the motto: "There's love, then there's everything else." If I were to live a hundred years, and my lifetime was divided evenly on a clock, then I would be standing at quarter past the hour on my mortality clock right now, my mind and my soul nudging me to pair up and form a union with a mate, just as the Creator intended. Once I did that—once I got married—I would enter the next quarter of my mortality clock, a different stage of life, and focus on other things. *To everything there is a season, and a time to every purpose under the heaven.*

What I did with guys during my BYU days only represented a phase I went through. Sure, I made mistakes. I created messes. I caused chaos. A villain in Gavin's book; I couldn't believe it myself! But I'm a human with weaknesses and shortcomings. My intention was pure; all I wanted was love. Love, not hate. From the beginning to the end of our mortal experience, we either walk toward love or away from it. Despite being bruised and scarred along the way, I kept pressing forward. If I ended up not finding love, it wouldn't be because I never tried. I got credit for trying. So, really, I didn't lose, because the ultimate victory that echoes for generations of time and throughout all eternity is the desire, willingness, and choice to love and be loved.

Under the heavens, love is what makes a human life worth living.

92

One evening Drake came in while I was in the teachers' lounge. Energetic and calm at the same time, he was magic.

"Hi, Allison. My family's having a birthday party for my sister this Sunday. Do you want to come?"

I couldn't say *no* to him. I had been waiting all this time to say *yes* to anything he asked.

I wanted him to like me, but in his presence I didn't feel the need to, as the Chinese say, "Slap my face long and hard to make it swell, thus creating a false image of a well-fed wealthy person." My lived-and-learned experience had taught me that I shouldn't lie about myself, or act like someone I wasn't, or conform to fit in, or desperately try to impress. Without that emotional burden, all I felt when I was in Drake's presence could be summed up with the ancient Chinese philosopher Mencius's words: "The time is right. The geographic and social conditions are favorable. The people are harmoniously matched."

Harmoniously matched, yes, we were.

Drake's parents lived in a 1970s multilevel single-family home on a half-acre lot, the last house on a dead-end street, next to an orchard. I gasped at the sight of an international-standard-size sand volleyball court in the side yard. Pointing at it, I asked, "Is that part of the house?"

"Yeah, my brother and I play volleyball."

I didn't ask God for a sign to know if Drake was the right person for me. God didn't give me a thunderous confirmation that he would be a significant person in my life. The volleyball connection, though . . . Drake started playing volleyball long before I met him. Volleyball was his family sport. The only question I had while gaping at the court was: *Where had he been all this time before I asked him out?*

Speaking of question, I wanted to know where he had been during the two-month silence. He explained that he'd ended a brief relationship with another girl before I asked him out, but she wanted to get back together. It took him that long to convince her they wouldn't have a future together. "I wanted to make sure that relationship was completely over before I came to you."

I was stunned! Why didn't I think that my asking him out might break another girl's heart? Was she crying in bed now as I was going to meet his family? I felt terrible, though my guilt was short-lived. No, I wasn't cold-blooded. I just knew that some relationships weren't meant to be. Cameron? Osmond? Gavin? Nah, no, nope. None of them was a harmonious match for me. As the Chinese say, "A couple is like double doors; they need to be rightfully matched." That girl might be crying in bed right now for her mismatch with Drake, but in time she might meet someone who was perfectly suitable for her, and all would be right again.

Since Drake confessed, so to speak, I decided to tell him I had recently broken up with Gavin. Calm and empathetic, he nodded and said, "I'm sorry."

I'm not, though. Not anymore.

This would seem the logical time to tell him about my divorce, but my confession ended here. The time didn't feel right to talk about Cameron yet, which made me anxious. When the perfect occasion arose, would I have the courage and strength to be honest with him? How would he take it?

Drake's parents' house was filled with party guests: grandparents, cousins, nieces, nephews, and friends. I learned that Drake was the youngest of four siblings. The guest of honor, Raylynn, the firstborn child who turned thirty, was there with her husband and their four children. Drake's brother was there with his girlfriend. The only absent family member was Drake's second sister who was attending school in Texas.

Drake's father, Dr. Merrill, a white-headed BYU professor, stood about six foot one. Lean and fit. Reserved and quiet. So quiet, in fact, he could easily pass as a wax figure. He reminded me of a Chinese saying "A bottle filled with water doesn't jingle. A half-filled bottle jingles loudly." It means that a well-educated person—full of knowledge, wisdom, and humility—knows to be quiet in public, to listen and learn. On the contrary, a petty person with limited knowledge brags loudly, dying to show off what little he knows.

After the party Drake drove me back to my apartment. On the way, I was prompted to ask him what he thought about divorced women.

"Well, Raylynn was divorced once. My other sister is in the middle of a divorce. My brother is dating a divorced single mom. There're lots of good girls who've been married before. Sometimes things just don't work out."

There're lots of good girls who've been married before. He said that! I hadn't expected those words. Everyone I'd told about my divorce seemed to have forgotten this simple truth: bad things happen to good people. This is horrible to say, but I was ecstatic that Drake's siblings' experiences with divorce opened his mind, so he not only accepted those who had experienced a failed marriage but also chose to see the good in them.

Instantly I knew this was the moment I should tell him about Cameron.

Drake pulled into my apartment parking lot and turned off the car. We sat quietly in the dark night. I was pumped, yet nervous. I only had to do it once with him; I could be brave. Afterward, our relationship had a fifty percent chance of growing, or not. I was ready to find out what direction it would go.

"So . . ." I cleared my throat. "When I was a college freshman in Taiwan, I met this missionary—a Texan. He finished his mission and went home. Then I went on my mission."

"Okay." Drake nodded.

Here goes here goes here goes. I can do this!

"Anyway—" I swallowed hard. "He wrote to me every week during my mission. He—uh, wanted me to marry him."

The street light shone through the windshield and reflected off Drake's face. He looked deep in thought. Then he asked, "Did you?"

I exhaled slowly. "Yes."

The tiny moment before he responded was unbearably long. I wished I hadn't had to do this. I wished the feelings of shame, guilt, and embarrassment weren't so ready to pounce on me. But there they were, making me doubt if telling the truth was the right thing to do.

"How long . . . uh . . . you and him?" His voice was small.

"Sixteen months. No kids. He walked out on me." My voice was small too. "I thought I'd tell you."

There was a fifty percent chance he could say, "Nice meeting you," or "Have a nice life," or "He walked out on you after only sixteen months? What did *you* do?" And I would return to the emotional wreck that had become a pattern of my social life lately. I waited for it to come. But it didn't. Instead, a strong force came, pulling me on my waist to the left, and now I was suddenly hip-to-hip with Drake in the front bench seat of the car. No sooner did I figure out what was happening than he leaned in to kiss me, tongue-twisting and fever-inducing and goosebumps-creating. One of his hands gently held the back of my head while the other firmly supported my spine. He was on fire. And I was so swept up in this passionate gesture, I was convinced this couldn't possibly be a good-bye kiss. *Nice meeting you. Have a nice life. Bye.* Nah!

Drake pulled away from me and said, "You should never think it's your fault. You're a good girl stuck with a guy who didn't know to cherish you."

I was speechless. No one had told me that before because no one had seen me that way before. All this time, since the light-switch incident, I had been burdened by a divorcée's shame, until now. Guilt, embarrassment, and self-doubt all died this day, and I was reborn.

"I'm glad that Texan let you go, Allison. I'm glad he did—so I can be here."

Oh—my—gosh! This guy!

I wished Cameron could've heard this. If I hadn't heard these words myself, I wouldn't have believed anyone could be so kind. How did I deserve this gift?

It seemed that God had lifted a corner of the veil that separated time and eternity and allowed me to peek into His grand design of my life. Among all the people I'd met in my twenty-five years, I knew there was a reason why I met Drake. There was a high purpose.

It's been said that there're two things a woman needs to know about her birth: *when* and *why*. I didn't know who Drake really was when I first met him at the rating session. After taking a punishing, miserable detour, I finally found my way back to him. When I did, I was delighted to know that he had been standing here, ready to welcome me, embrace me, respect me as who I was. This was a man who chose to love the crows on my roof because he saw the glowing crown on my head.

I finally finally finally understood that he was the *why* of my birth.

In the car with Drake, watching early March snowflakes gently falling on the windshield, I felt as though we were on our own tiny island of tremendous joy. Even if Armageddon was raging outside—the sky raining fireballs, mountains crumpling, the ground breaking, cars falling into lava rivers—Drake and I would be in the front bench seat, talking, laughing, and saying *I love you* to each other over and over until the end of time. But time had no stings on us. There wouldn't be the end of time. There would only be the end of my journey.

As Shakespeare wrote, *Journeys end in lovers meeting*; Drake marked the end of my searching.

93

In April 1998, Drake's childhood friend Eric returned to Utah from Texas for spring break. Drake invited me, Eric, some MTC Japanese teachers, and his high school buddies to a game night at his family's mountain cabin.

Meeting Eric confirmed the truthfulness of the Six Degrees of Separation theory. There was no other rational explanation for the spiderweb-like relationships among me, Drake, Eric, Cameron, and his brother Christopher Chastain.

Eric was a law student at Texas A&M University and was, coincidentally, in the same class with Christopher Chastain. They were good friends. It only took Eric and me about a minute of self-introduction to figure out who we knew. Even though I knew Drake didn't care about my past, I was still a little worried about the conversations Eric might have with Drake and Christopher. I was sure guys gossiped as much as girls. I believed everyone with a tongue did. And I feared the spoken words traveling among those guys might affect my relationship with Drake in a negative way.

After spring break Eric went back to Texas, and as day follows night, he called Drake one day when we were watching ESPN in his parents' basement. Drake left the room to answer it. When he returned, he said that Eric had tried to pass on warnings against me from Christopher.

Christopher sent out warnings against me, did he now?

Christopher had served his mission in Taiwan, two years before Cameron did. During my short marriage to Cameron, I'd only talked to Christopher three times. Each time he spoke Chinese with me, trying to practice the basic greetings and simple phrases he remembered. Our conversation never lasted more than a minute. How could he possibly give Eric any warnings against me to pass on to Drake? Did he not like the way I asked if he had eaten? What?

In reality I knew perfectly well where the warnings were really from. It seemed that Cameron had created a new life calling: annihilating me.

I'd barely started my emotional healing process to develop my confidence, self-worth, and healthy relationships with new eyes, but I wasn't quite there yet. Naturally, faced with gossip, I acted like a typical twenty-five-year-old woman that day. I wanted revenge.

"You know Christopher is training to be a lawyer," I told Drake. I didn't hesitate to add, "He's a glib liar." But as soon as I said those words, I realized I, myself, was gossiping. I didn't even know Christopher; how could I say that about him behind his back, when he wasn't there to defend himself? But what else was I supposed to do, if not defend myself? I thought "an eye for an eye" was how it should be done.

There was a lesson I needed to learn—the right way to treat others—and none other than Drake would be my best teacher. He wrapped his arm around my shoulder and said, "I know. I know. I figured that much. Eric tried to tell me what your ex's brother said, but I told him no."

"You what?" I looked up and saw his face split with a grin.

"I told him I didn't want to hear anything from what's-his-bucket. I already knew what he'd say. I'm with you, I know you, and I believe you. That's enough."

Mic drop!

As the adage goes, "A tongue has one customer, the ear." Cameron's tongue couldn't have Drake's ear for a customer after all.

I felt I'd cheated the universe, because how could I possibly deserve Drake after the terrible thing I did to Gavin? And yet, Drake showed me love really was all I needed. His choice to be kind to me helped me forget to revisit the thought of revenge. Being with Drake was more than a sweet revenge. It was a true blessing.

94

The winter semester was coming to an end and, with it, the expiration of my immigration form I-94. At the beginning of the semester, before I asked Drake out, I'd contemplated going home. So instead of renewing my I-94, I purchased a ticket to Taiwan, leaving on the last day of school. Even though we had only been dating for two months, at this point in our courtship, I was confident that Drake shared my desire to get married. He hadn't said anything about it, of course, because I heard that men are from Mars and women are from Venus, hence different reasoning, rationales, and approaches to the same task. But I was sure—one-hundred-percent positive—that he had been thinking about and secretly planning for the proposal. I knew I was right when, on my departure day, he showed up at my apartment to take me to the airport, looking dazzling in a gray slim-fit blazer and matching tapered dress pants. And the long-stem blood-red rose in a shiny glass case he gave me before the kiss? Yep, enough hints. Instantly my heart thumped wildly, and my knees turned weak at the excitement. But the proposal could happen any minute; I couldn't faint just yet.

We loaded my suitcase in the trunk of his car and hopped in the front bench seat. He said there was enough time for dinner before my flight, and he'd made a reservation at a special place. I thought, *Classic! Propose in a fancy restaurant, of course.*

Of course.

We arrived at Joseph Smith Memorial Building in downtown Salt Lake City, a majestic structure featuring a shiny travertine floor, grand staircases, thick Persian rugs, marble pillars, and an ivory balcony. Classical music played softly in the background. We stepped in an elevator and landed on the top floor of the building, in a high-end restaurant named The Roof. This place was no joke. A plate here cost three hours' worth of my pay at the MTC. There were wall-to-wall floor-to-ceiling glass windows that showcased a panoramic night view of the city. Amidst a pool of warm glowing city lights stood the Salt Lake Temple. Its six spires jutted heavenward with the gold statue of Angel Moroni on top, facing east and blowing a trumpet.

I was blown away by Drake's delicate planning of the proposal. This restaurant, with its sophisticated setting and grandiose ambience, certainly presented itself as an elegant choice for bringing a romantic relationship to its highest form. I felt spoiled and flattered and truly, truly loved.

In the dimmed light, listening to the live piano performance, we enjoyed a world-class gourmet buffet: Kobe strip steak, slow-roasted prime ribs, grilled shrimp, salmon, steamed vegetables, mashed potatoes, chowder, salad, pasta, fruit, and countless dessert selections. This was a different life than the one I had always known. Certainly with my humble background I would never have a chance to set foot in a luxurious place such as this, to sit at a white-clothed table with a flickering candle, freshly cut roses in a glass vase, delicate china, and heavy sterling silverware. I wanted to live in this moment, to take it all in, to savor it. But I could only half-heartedly enjoy it. With each bite I anticipated not heavenly taste but increasing anxiety over the forthcoming proposal.

Drake sure was taking his time. He was probably working up the courage, which was understandable. This was one of the most special life moments; he wanted to do it right. I totally got it. I wanted the entire process to be perfect too, so I didn't fuss or press him or make the situation more stressful than it already was. I could wait. I'd waited my whole life to arrive here, to be with him, I could wait for another few minutes. I kept telling myself that when he finally did propose, it would be epic. For sure.

For sure.

But as the night went on and nothing happened, I grew increasingly uneasy. My patience slowly waned. All the while I was fretting about the proposal, Drake was, of course, being his usual self: humorous, charismatic, adorable. It boggled my mind just how deeply he could hide his angst and remain casual. Was he waiting for the perfect moment, as I did when I tried to figure out when to tell him about Cameron? This waiting was killing me. When we left the restaurant and drove to the airport, I was certain he was going to ask me anytime. He had to. We were running out of time!

We left the car at the airport parking garage. Drake walked me to the check-in counter and dropped off my suitcase, then we sat at the gate waiting for my flight. I started to see that the airport terminal was actually a better setting than The Roof for the proposal. Here, we were free to squeal, laugh, cry, and we would have an audience—instant witnesses—for the collective celebratory effect. Brilliant!

Brilliant!

But Drake was still taking his time working up his courage. This must be so terrifying for him, asking a question with a significant, lasting impact that would change his life, mine, and generations after us. I couldn't even imagine! He had every reason to be overwhelmed. Possibly that was why he chose to tell me, instead, his summer plan of doing an internship at Disney World in Florida. I paid intense attention to every word coming out of his mouth, not wanting to miss any clue of his elaborately planned big question. Maybe he was going to ask me to marry him with a question like "How would it be to get married in the happiest place on earth?" or "What's your opinion about a Disney cruise for a honeymoon?" How could I not pass out from the excitement now? Only deep breaths, yes.

Deep breath.

Calm down.

Deep breath.

Calm down.

Deep breath . . . and ohmygosh—what's going on here? What's he thinking? Doesn't he know the clock is ticking away his chance? Is it really that hard to ask me the obvious question? He already knows I'll say yes a million times over. What's he waiting for?

Maybe I got it all wrong. Because I asked him out first, did it mean I had to ask his mother for his hand in marriage? Was that why he hadn't made the move? Could that even be true?

The final boarding call was announced. Drake and I exchanged a long bear hug. "Don't forget to write," he said. "I need to know where to find you when I get there."

"Where? Taiwan?"

He smirked, and I sensed something hopeful happening—something different from what I expected or imagined all along. And even though I wasn't sure what exactly he had in mind, I was confident that he had a solid plan somehow. I was secretly giddy about his mind game.

He's going to chase me across the globe to propose! I mean, how romantic is that? I mean, how many girls get to tell a story like that? I mean, this guy! Awww . . .

We broke from the farewell embrace. I waved good-bye and watched him gradually disappear into the crowd, taking a piece of me with him. Promptly I walked in the jetway, faith in every step, hoping all would work out for our good.

I was leaving the American soil again, back to my motherland, the land of my mother, a year after her passing. This was the third time I traveled back to Taiwan since I came to America, and it felt so much different. The people I'd met and the things I'd experienced at BYU in the past year had shaped me into a new person. I liked where life had taken me. I liked that, for the past two months, I got to speak with Drake and heard his voice every day. Then I heard his voice. Not in my imagination, no. I heard him calling my name. Clearly. Urgently. Panicky. Behind me.

I turned around, and there he was, pushing other passengers out of his way to race back toward the jetway while shouting, "Allison! Allison! Don't go! COME BAAACKKK!"

The moment I had been dying for *finally* arrived! Drake had returned to propose to me in the very last possible second, adding dramatic effect to the heightened tension of me, literally, walking away from his life! If this had been a movie scene, I would drop my carry-on and run, in slow motion, back to Drake, whose out-stretched arms were ready to envelop me and spin me in place. Then he would kneel and ask me that one question while I bit my bottom lip so I wouldn't let my unmanageable excitement take over, and burst out screaming or crying. I would say *yes yes yes* because that was the only thing I had been dying to say to him. We would kiss and laugh and kiss and laugh, and the boarding gate crowd would erupt into collective congratulatory cheers. They would tear their boarding passes into tiny pieces of scraps and throw them into the air like confetti. They would shower us with good wishes, and the scene would end with everyone in the airport kissing.

Awww . . .

I ran back to Drake at the end of the jetway. The sight of his sweaty, handsome face made me go wild all over. He was calling out to me again. "Allison, hurry! Come back!"

Oh oh oh, be still, my heart!

One of the uniformed women by the gate walked toward me with a hand pushing forward, as if trying to stop me with an invis-ible force. But no one could stop me, not in this moment. *Are you kidding me?*

As I got close to the lady, I rolled my eyeballs toward Drake and whispered to her, "He's going to propose to me right now!"

Her face dropped for a quick second but then immediately changed into wild excitement. She smiled, clasped her hands under her chin, ran back to the check-in counter, and whispered into another uniformed lady's ear. More uniformed employees—men and women—at the gate whispered and giggled and gave me the thumbs-up. I got the audience. I got the witnesses. This was so *epic*! Yes!

Standing in front of Drake, I didn't bother smiling behind my hand to hide my crooked, gapped teeth and garlicky breath. I knew what was coming; there shouldn't be anything between his lips and mine.

I was ready.

I stared into his eyes. And he stared into mine.

"Allison." He picked up both of my sweaty hands. He was trembling slightly.

"Yes?" I bounced on the balls of my feet.

"I was wondering . . ."

"Yes?"

He swallowed. And I thought, *Oh boy, it's really happening—right now!*

"Do you, uh—"

"YES?"

"Do you have, like" —he coughed, then gulped—"two bucks?"

"HUH?"

"I need—do you have, like . . . two bucks?"

"What? Why?"

He squirmed a little and sheepishly said, "I gotta pay for the parking fee."

Whaaa—?

I was speechless.

This entire evening while I thought about only one thing—one romantic thing–Drake's mind was on something else. I guess men indeed are from Mars, while women are from Venus.

When I pulled out my wallet, the circle of uniformed men and women laughed by the gate. I wanted their supervisor to know these employees were unprofessional. But then it struck me that Martians and Venusians weren't always different; they could laugh at the same thing, after all.

95

During my mission in Taiwan, one of my American companions counted down days until her release from the service. She chirped about her family's elaborate plan for her homecoming party. Like her, I now traveled between America and Taiwan, but couldn't relate to her joy. None of her homecoming celebration would be my experience. Coming home this time, I learned that one thing remained unchanged: Baba didn't want to have anything to do with me. Which meant I didn't have a family to go home to, so I stayed with a friend.

I wrote to Drake with my updates. He wrote back with the news that he'd turned down the internship opportunity at Disney World and, instead, purchased a ticket to Taiwan. I would've jumped up and down and shouted for joy, but the two-buck incident had made me wiser. I didn't want to let my one-sided affection make a big fool out of me, so I calmly wrote back, *Cool. I'll be here.*

Drake would fly to Taiwan after he finished his finals, two weeks after I arrived home. I knew that when he got here, a marriage proposal was imminent. I knew this because he didn't speak the language and didn't know anyone in Taiwan but me. Why would he want to come if he didn't intend to marry me? But, again, I was completely level-headed now. No jumping or shouting.

I picked him up from the airport. There must've been things, feelings, questions he didn't tell me. I wished I could read his mind when I told him we would be staying at my friend's place instead of at my baba's house. He knew I was disowned. But he was born and raised in a loving, supportive family environment; what did he know about being disowned? Nothing, of course. Not until he saw what it was like in my case: moving from one friend's house to another; eating dinner at street vendors with different strangers every night; no baby pictures on the living room wall to show him. What did he come all the way from the other side of the world to see? Who to meet?

He wanted to meet Baba. He wanted to do the right thing, he said. He believed it was mandatory courtesy that he ask Baba in person for my hand in marriage. I didn't know how to explain to him that me being disowned meant I didn't have a father anymore. But he insisted. He'd spent all this time and money to come for this meaningful ritual; who was I to deny him this special experience?

I reluctantly used the phone in my friend's living room to call Baba during his lunch break at work. Drake sat next to me on the couch, stroking my back and waiting quietly. I assumed he wanted to calm me, or to show affection, but it intensified my anxiety. When I heard Baba's voice, I almost choked.

"Ba, it's me"—I took a deep breath—"I'm . . . uh . . . I'm back. In Hualien."

"So?"

"So, I have a friend here. A guy. From America . . ." I didn't know how to continue.

"What?"

"Ba, I . . . No. My friend, he wants to meet you." My heart was racing. I swallowed audibly.

"Why?"

"He, uh . . . he wants to ask you something."

"I hate you! I hate everything related to you! I hate your

friends, I hate America, I hate English, everything! Why would I talk to your friend? Quit wasting my life!"

"Ba! My friend wants to ask you to let him marry me. But whatever I ask—or my friend, actually—whatever he asks, you're going to say *no* anyway. You think it's your only job to say *no* to everything I ask." I was in tears now. Drake started to scratch my back fast and hard, and I wanted to slap his hand.

"You're a disgrace! You dropped out of college to serve your white god, and—oh yeah, you were too good for Taiwan, weren't you? Too good that you just had to run to America to marry a white devil, huh? See what that got you? You got dumped! And now you've got guts to tell me you're marrying another white devil? Have you any idea what everyone's saying behind my back? You make me lose face! Don't ever call me again! I HATE YOU!" There was an abrupt clicking sound, followed by the white buzzing noise of disconnection, and it was done. Over. Finished.

At twenty-one, soon after being disowned, I started to talk about the misery of my childhood as if telling someone else's story, because it was the first time I wasn't living in it. This day, I unwisely ventured back into the territory of domestic calamity. This phone call shook me awake to the reality that Baba was merely playing the role of an ex-father, who stayed true to his feelings of hating daughters.

96

Numerous people declare their love and respect for their father. "I have the best dad in the world!" "My dad is my hero!" "When I grow up, I want to be like my dad!" I could never relate to any of those lucky children. I wished I had someone else for a father. Maybe Baba had the exact same wish. Maybe since my birth he'd wished I had been a boy, or skinnier, or prettier, or smarter, or just better. In the end, I didn't give him a reason to keep his head up high in front of his drinking buddies when they asked about me. Those drinking buddies . . . I guess the reason why I didn't like Baba's friends was the same reason why he didn't want to meet Drake. I disagreed with his choice of friends; he did mine. Today, I've arrived at the understanding that there will be times when I disagree with others' choices, but I can choose to be agreeable.

And, above all else, not being able to connect with my baba doesn't define me. It refines me.

PART ELEVEN

Love

97

Ah-Gung spoke Hokkien, Hakkanese, Chinese, and Japanese with a native speaker's proficiency, but not as much in English. When I took Drake to his home, Ah-Gung bowed deeply to us by the door, sweeping his long arm in the direction of the living room and saying, in Chinese, "Thanks for gracing my humble abode with your presence. Please enter."

I introduced them. Instantly they struck up a seemingly pleasant conversation in Japanese, laughing and slapping their knees like two long-lost best friends. I don't know why I thought I would be their interpreter.

While Ah-Gung and Drake visited over Japanese snacks that Ah-Po had always made sure to keep a full stock of in her pantry, I went into the kitchen to find her.

Ah-Po never aged. She looked the same now as she did when I was a preschooler. For twenty years, every time I asked her for her secret, she told me the same answer, so she must've told the truth. "Two things: always be a vegetarian, never wear makeup."

Another thing that never changed about Ah-Po was her habit of staying in the kitchen when guests visited. "It's not a woman's place to interfere with men's business. Our place is in the kitchen," she taught.

I liked adding "to eat meat" to her sentence and watching her nose scrunch up and her tongue stick out. That day in Ah-Po's kitchen we ate noodles together and eavesdropped on the conversation between Ah-Gung and Drake. Well, Ah-Po was the eavesdropper and interpreter. She sat in a chair against the book-shelf-wall that divided the living room and the kitchen and said, "Sounds like a family reunion out there."

Before I finished my bowl of noodles, Ah-Gung summoned me. I went in the living room and sat next to Drake, whose face beamed with a heightened delightful glow.

"Wow, your grandpa," Drake said in English. He shook his head with a smile. "He's—so incredible!"

I looked to Ah-Gung, who was getting up from a rattan chair and moving to his corner desk. I wondered what they talked about.

Drake raised an eyebrow. "Are you sure he's not Japanese? How does he speak Japanese like a native?"

I shrugged. "Gift of tongue?"

"Actually, he's more like a Japanese-speaking Chinese Yoda. Confucius or something. He taught me Chinese philosophy—all the things I've never even thought of before. Blew my mind!"

I chuckled and turned to tell Ah-Gung, in Hakkanese, that Drake admired him. Ah-Gung broke into a grin and bowed to Drake. Slowly he said, "San Q (thank you). It's Ana (honor) weezit (visit) you."

Drake stood up and returned a curtsy bow. "The honor is mine."

It dawned on me then that the choice I made concerning marrying Drake would have the power to bring these two men into the same family. Years later, Drake and I would have children together. All of them would be added to a pedigree chart on FamilySearch.org, connecting them to their blood relatives: Ah-Gung, Ah-Po, Baba, Mama, Dee, May, Dr. Merrill, Drake, Raylynn, and me. The entire human race is one giant family after all. Ethnicity is irrelevant. Nationality is inconsequential. Language is an insignificant detail. What holds us all together—what links generations of these men and women—is love. And it began with my choice to be with Drake.

Ah-Gung walked Drake to the kitchen for noodles but asked me to wait for him at his desk. When he returned, he asked me if I knew what the greatest number in the universe was.

This was so random. We were here to talk about Drake; why would he ask me math? But now that he mentioned it, I was shocked that I didn't seem to ever learn about this in school. I only remembered my math teacher using a symbol—a sideways 8—to represent the concept of unlimited. But was it a number? What was its proper name?

"Remember, the greatest number in the universe is not a number at all. It's a state of mind," Ah-Gung said as he pulled out a pen and a writing pad from the desk drawer.

This sounded vastly profound. I listened intently.

He wrote four Chinese characters on the pad, then pointed at them with his pen. "See these words?"

At first glance I understood what he meant. The literal translation of the characters was *eternal, river, sand, number*. Together, they referred to the Abrahamic Covenant in the Old Testament: Abraham's posterity would be as numerous as the sand on the seashore.

Ah-Gung was a scholar of philosophy, literature, history, politics, medicine. Even though he didn't belong to a Christian sect, I wasn't surprised he used a biblical account to teach me math, although I had a feeling he wasn't about to teach me just math.

"They make the name of the greatest number in the universe: The Infinite Number of Sand in the Waters of Eternity. Remember, it's not a number. It's a state of mind. Think of it as a spiritual concept. God's creations can't be numbered. They're like sand by waters. Rivers. Oceans. Sand on a beach."

Math has a spiritual side! This new knowledge mesmerized me.

"There're billions of people in the world, and you choose

341

him," Ah-Gung said. "Only you know if he's the right sand on the beach to pick. Your choice becomes your fate. Your destiny."

My eyes stung a little; they got misty.

"He wants to marry you. He asks for blessings. I feel the positive energy around us, in the house. I feel it's right." Ah-Gung nodded. "The right sand. You've picked him, then you stay with him on his beach, by his waters, for eternity. May your tribe increase. That's my greatest blessing for you."

98

Drake and I bought a travelers' map, picked the cheapest car at a rental place, and went on a week-long camping trip. We drove six hours along the east coastline of Taiwan to the southern tip of the island, Kenting National Park.

Kenting had abundant sunshine, with white-sand beaches, coral reefs, lush mountains, and pristine Pacific blue as a backdrop. During the hot, lazy, relaxing day, we explored cool caves and toured the air-conditioned marine biology museum. After stunning sunsets, the town came alive with bustling nightlife: endless live music, smoked salmon aroma wafting in the sea air, local kids dancing in alleyways. Every corner we turned, there were tourists in straw hats, Bermuda shorts, flip-flops, and a camera strapped around their necks, going in and out of seafood restaurants. The streets were lined with souvenir vendors, selling seashell wind chimes, bracelets, earrings, scarves, tie-dye halter dresses.

U.S. dollars stretched far here. Two bucks could buy a bowl of steamy seafood wonton noodle soup and a mound of shave ice, topped with fresh tropical fruit and sweetened condensed milk. Drake and I lived on two-buck meals with water. I binged on seafood wonton noodle soup, as if I had been transported back to all those years earlier when my only daily meal was school lunch. Back in those days when I was a growing, starving teenager, pacing up and down the hall outside of Baba's and the ex-stepmother's room every night and inhaling the aroma of their dinner, all I wanted was to feed my body and spirit and fill the holes in my world where happiness was missing.

We live in the narrative of gravity; life has a way of bringing us down to our knees, to the level of dust. People age. People fall ill. People become weak. People divorce. All my childhood heartaches, desperate cries, and seemingly endless trials and tribulations felt like God's test to try my faith, resilience, and tenacity. It was as though He'd asked me to jump through ninety-nine fire hoops to receive the promised reward, gift, and blessing. Now that I'd passed the test and arrived here, I was astounded. *That's it? That's all it takes to earn the sheer joy of Drake's companionship?*

At night I lay next to Drake on the Kenting beach, listening to the rhythm of crashing waves while gazing at twinkling stars, enveloped in the star-furnace of a divine love.

Drake, my one and only sand on the beach. My one and only star in the sky.

99

On the evening of April 30, 1998, Drake and I walked down the beach, hand-in-hand, talking about his future, mine, and ours together. If someone had taken a snapshot of us in this moment, he would have captured the image of me when I had all that I wanted in the world. I would scrapbook this photo and frame it in a shadowbox and hang it on the living room wall.

Drake and I walked past crowds of camera-happy tourists and found a quiet spot behind a grove of tall scrubs and palm trees. He suddenly let go of my hand and ran toward the waves. I thought he went to retrieve something washed ashore. But he stayed there, half squatting and half sitting on the beach, his chin lowered to the chest, his hands busy at work. Soon, he came back with a huge, gummy smile that brought out his lower-lip dimples. The tropical breeze tousled his curly hair and turned it into a small afro. I loved the way he looked in humidity.

He lifted my left hand, then produced a greenish-black ring made of seaweed. He measured it against my finger. "Oh, good, it should fit."

He knelt down.

Cleared his throat.

In a slightly trembling voice he asked, "Allison, will you marry me?"

There're billions of people in the world, and you choose him. Only you know if he's the right sand on the beach to pick.

Tears welled up in my eyes. I fanned my face with the speed of a hummingbird's flapping wings. "I thought you'd never ask. You're so unpredictable." I cry-laughed. "Of course I will marry you. Of course!"

Your choice becomes your fate. Your destiny.

He carefully slid the wet seaweed ring onto my finger. Perfect fit. "I saw a soda can tab on the beach too, but I thought you'd like this better."

I broke out laughing with running snot. "Yeah, I like this. I love you!"

You've picked him, then you stay with him on his beach, by his waters, for eternity.

Eternity.

Never-ending.

Double the long time.

Ninety-nine.

Drake was mine.

Just then, a group of college-aged kids gathered next to us on a beach volleyball court, singing, joking, and laughing. Someone turned on a light switch, and immediately the floodlights on the court rained down blinding illumination. All I could see was the gleaming, striking outline of Drake's face—the man I would choose a million times over, till the end of time.

Acknowledgments

If Allison Hong Merrill gets two hours of free time at night, after tucking her three little sons in bed, she'll rearrange furniture around the house.

If Allison rearranges furniture around the house, she'll ask her husband to help her move a couch from the basement to the second floor.

If Allison asks her husband to help her move the couch—yet again—he'll sigh and say, "With all this free time, why don't you start a blog instead?"

If Allison's husband complains, he'll accidentally inspire her.

If Allison is inspired to write, she'll quickly realize she doesn't know the first thing about writing, not to mention writing in English as a foreign language.

If Allison realizes she doesn't know how to write, she'll go to the MFA in Writing program at Vermont College of Fine Arts.

If Allison attends Vermont College of Fine Arts, she'll meet people—Sue William Silverman, Harrison Candelaria Fletcher, Bret Lott, Cynthia Huntington, Camilla Sanderson, Linda Murphy Marshall, Jennifer Friedman Lang, Amy Mindell, and Joan Shanti Cousins—who will become influential in her writing career.

If Allison learns anything in school, she'll know that learning continues outside of school.

If Allison knows that learning continues outside of school, she'll seek out opportunities to learn from other writers: Allison

K. Williams, Angie Fenimore, Michael Sheen, and all her friends in the Calliope Writing group.

If Allison learns from other writers, she'll know to find readers for her early drafts.

If Allison knows to find readers for her early drafts, she'll have the honor of working with Jeanne Burgon, Annette Cooper Hullinger, Jodi Orgill Brown, Daisie Jan Dance, Brandy Sutton, Chrissy Cornwell, Laird Session, Laurel Bates, Nancy West, Andrea Hughes, and Tammy Holdeman.

If Allison works with readers for her early drafts, she'll have a polished manuscript for submission.

If Allison has a polished manuscript for submission, she'll get a book deal from Brooke Warner.

If Allison gets a book deal from Brooke Warner, she'll get the privilege of working with Shannon Green and the SWP editorial team.

If Allison gets to work with the SWP editorial team, they'll take exceptional care of her publication process, and she'll get two hours of free time at night to sink into the couch that's no longer in the basement. Her husband will be by her side. Together, they will watch *Sherlock*, while their son tucks his son into bed downstairs.

About the Author

Allison Hong Merrill was born and raised in Taiwan and arrived in the US at twenty-two as a university student. That's when she realized her school English wasn't much help when asking for directions on the street or opening a bank account. By recording each of the classes she took—including physical education—and reviewing the tape every night for a year, she eventually learned English well enough to earn an MFA in Writing from Vermont College of Fine Arts. But please excuse her if she misuses verb tenses or mixes up the genders in third-person pronouns when she speaks. It's no secret; English is a hard language to learn.

Allison writes in both Chinese and English, both fiction and creative nonfiction, which means she spends a lot of time looking up words on Dictionary.com. Her work has won both national and international awards. Visit her at www.allisonhongmerrill.com, where you can sign up for her extremely short monthly email.

SELECTED TITLES FROM SHE WRITES PRESS

She Writes Press is an independent publishing company
founded to serve women writers everywhere.
Visit us at www.shewritespress.com.

At the Narrow Waist of the World: A Memoir by Marlena Maduro Baraf. $16.95, 978-1-63152-588-9. In this lush and vivid coming-of-age memoir about a mother's mental illness and the healing power of a loving Jewish and Hispanic extended family, young Marlena must pull away from her mother, leave her Panama home, and navigate the transition to an American world.

How Sweet the Bitter Soup: A Memoir by Lori Qian. $16.95, 978-1-63152-614-5. After accepting an exciting job offer—teaching at a prestigious school in China—Lori found herself in Guangzhou, China, where she fell in love with the culture and with a man from a tiny town in Hubei province. What followed was a transformative adventure—one that will inspire readers to use the bitter to make life even sweeter.

Her Name Is Kaur: Sikh American Women Write About Love, Courage, and Faith edited by Meeta Kaur. $17.95, 978-1-93831-470-4. An eye-opening, multifaceted collection of essays by Sikh American women exploring the concept of love in the context of the modern landscape and influences that shape their lives.

Notes from the Bottom of the World by Suzanne Adam. $16.95, 978-1-63152-415-8. In this heartfelt collection of sixty-three personal essays, Adam considers how her American past and move to Chile have shaped her life and enriched her worldview, and explores with insight questions on aging, women's roles, spiritual life, friendship, love, and writers who inspire.

Rethinking Possible: A Memoir of Resilience by Rebecca Faye Smith Galli. $16.95, 978-1-63152-220-8. After her brother's devastatingly young death tears her world apart, Becky Galli embarks upon a quest to recreate the sense of family she's lost—and learns about healing and the transformational power of love over loss along the way.